T0323461

Praise for *The Kind Librarian*

'Libraries are places of wonder, with resources and collections that spark our imaginations and allow us to seek information. However, they are also spaces that give us time to step aside from the outside world and lose ourselves in thought, reflection and contemplation – a refuge from some of the challenges of 21st century life. Kindness isn't a word often associated with buildings or institutions, but the act of taking time to read, or write, or listen, can be an act of kindness to oneself in a busy world, and a much needed boost to our wellbeing and mental health. This wonderful volume looks at how we can bring that sense of kindness into the working lives and practices of library staff for the benefit of all, with well researched case studies, excellent guidance and advice about the small things we can do differently that make a big impact on others.'
Nick Barratt, Executive Director, Student Journey, Royal Holloway, University of London

'*The Kind Librarian* is a transformative guide for creating flourishing and nurturing library environments. Drawing on extensive research into the psychology of kindness and wellbeing at work, this inspiring book offers profound insights into how to apply evidence-based knowledge to benefit library staff and users. It's an indispensable resource for anyone passionate about cultivating an empowering and resilient library culture, and a must-read for revolutionising the way we view and experience libraries!'
Dr Rona Hart, Senior Lecturer in Applied Positive Psychology, course leader for The Psychology of Kindness and Wellbeing at Work, School of Psychology, University of Sussex

'The essential topic of workplace kindness is skilfully covered in this invaluable text. Helen and her co-authors present contemporary and classic research that explains the roots of kindness in a practical and relatable way. The narrative is supplemented with fabulous reflective questions, and individual and group exercises to ensure that the knowledge you're gaining isn't just theoretical: it's pragmatic and implementable. A welcome guide for everyone who seeks happiness and kindness as a career librarian!'
Nicky McCrudden, University of Chichester Business School

'*The Kind Librarian* paints an inspiring vision of a kinder future and offers concrete, research-backed steps to help us get there. The case studies provide food for thought and a reminder that there is already so much kindness on display in libraries. Helen Rimmer has thought deeply about what makes a library kind (or unkind) and covers an impressively comprehensive set of topics – including how to be kinder to ourselves. She includes reflective questions and exercises throughout, to prompt us to think deeply too and consider the unique circumstances of our own organisations. This book is itself an act of kindness.'

Dr Gillian Sandstrom, Senior Lecturer in Psychology, University of Sussex

The Kind Librarian

Every purchase of a Facet book helps to fund CILIP's advocacy,
awareness and accreditation programmes for
information professionals.

The Kind Librarian

Cultivating a Culture of Kindness and Wellbeing in Libraries

Helen Rimmer

facet
publishing

Published by Facet Publishing
c/o British Library, 96 Euston Road, London NW1 2DB
www.facetpublishing.co.uk

Facet Publishing is wholly owned by CILIP: the Library and Information
Association.

British Library Cataloguing in Publication Data
A catalogue record for this book is available from the British Library.

ISBN 978-1-78330-712-8 (paperback)
ISBN 978-1-78330-713-5 (hardback)
ISBN 978-1-78330-714-2 (PDF)
ISBN 978-1-78330-715-9 (EPUB)

First published 2024

Typeset from author's files by Flagholme Publishing Services in
10/13 pt Palatino Linotype and Open Sans.
Printed and made in Great Britain by CPI Group (UK) Ltd, Croydon, CR0 4YY.

To Alan,
Thank you for your love, support and belief in me. You've been a rock for our family and I'm so grateful for you every day.

To Evan and Zeb,
I'm doing this for you. I hope your work lives will be kinder and full of good things. You both mean the world to me.

Contents

Case Studies and Feature Boxes

Case studies

Feature boxes

About the Authors

Helen Rimmer

Helen Rimmer is a Kindness and Wellbeing Coach, whose journey has been as enriching as it is inspiring. With over 20 years of leadership experience in libraries and higher education, Helen has a deep understanding of the transformative power of kindness in professional settings. This experience laid the foundation for a meaningful transition into the world of coaching and consulting.

Helen holds a Strengthscope Master certification, a Certificate in Systemic Team Coaching and a Certificate in Business and Personal Coaching. However, it is the Postgraduate Certificate in the Psychology of Kindness and Wellbeing at Work that truly encapsulates the essence of Helen's approach. This unique blend of qualifications underpins a professional ethos centred around the promotion of wellbeing and kindness in the workplace.

In Helen's personal life, a love for film, reading, swimming and yoga not only provides a well-rounded lifestyle but also infuses her work with a diverse range of insights and perspectives.

As a coach and consultant, Helen is driven by a vision to transform the world of work into a place where wellbeing and kindness are not just valued but are the norm.

Kirsten Elliott

Kirsten Elliott works within the Research Support team of University of Nottingham Libraries as a Research Intelligence Librarian. She has previously worked for Imperial College London, primarily providing library services for affiliated NHS staff, with a year on secondment as Academic Liaison Librarian and Library Manager at a medical campus. She is co-founder of the organisation Fair Library Jobs which campaigns for equitable recruitment in the library sector.

Her professional interests include equality, diversity, and inclusion in libraries, research metrics (especially their responsible use), and systematic review searching.

Darren Flynn

Darren Flynn works as the Academic Liaison Manager in Library and Learning Services at the University of Northampton. He has previously worked in HE libraries as a specialist health librarian and a teaching and learning librarian and in the past has worked as a teacher-librarian in the school sector. Outside of his main work he is a PhD student in the Department of Information Studies at UCL, researching social class and the UK academic library workforce. He is a founding member of the organisation Fair Library Jobs. He is also co-chair of the Critical Approaches to Libraries Conference (CALC).

His professional interests include social class in library services and professional cultures, critical library practice and information literacy research.

Amy Stubbing

Amy Stubbing has had a varied career across different sectors, and has held roles in areas including collection management, customer services, and library management. She is currently the University Librarian at Solent University. Previous roles include Academic Engagement Lead at University of Westminster, Campus Library Manager at University of East London, and the Library Customer Care Collections Coordinator at Royal Holloway University.

Amy's interest in data and using it to inform service decisions and developments to improve user experience has been a core part of her career. She has a particular passion for developing data literacy and embedding data practices into all decision making, which led to her writing her first book: *Data Driven Decisions: A Practical Toolkit for Library and Information Professionals*. She has worked with numerous university libraries to begin working towards embedding a culture of data-driven decisions, and has used her varied experience of teaching data literacy.

Preface

Welcome to *The Kind Librarian*. This will be a journey through the transformative power of kindness and wellbeing in the world of work. As a kindness and wellbeing coach, facilitator and trainer who has a wealth of experience in library and higher education leadership, I have dedicated my life to nurturing environments where kindness isn't just a fleeting gesture, but a fundamental aspect of our professional lives.

This book is an amalgamation of my expertise in positive psychology, my academic background in the Psychology of Kindness and Wellbeing at Work and my hands-on experience in senior leadership roles. I have woven theoretical knowledge with practical insights to offer a unique perspective on kindness in the workplace, something I myself developed through my PGCert in the Psychology of Kindness and Wellbeing at Work.

Each chapter of *The Kind Librarian* is crafted to guide you, whether you're a leader, a team member or self-employed, towards creating a more compassionate, supportive and kind work environment. My purpose is to change the world of work into somewhere people thrive and my approach is rooted in the belief that kindness and wellbeing are not just moral choices but strategic imperatives that can lead to greater success and fulfilment in our professional lives.

As you turn these pages, I invite you to join me in reimagining the world of work. Together, let's embark on a transformative journey where kindness and wellbeing are not mere ideals, but the very foundations upon which we build our careers and nurture our professional communities.

Take care and stay kind.

Acknowledgements

I want to say a big thank you to some very special people who have helped me on my journey to write this book about kindness and wellbeing.

First off, a huge thanks to my friend and former colleague Amy Stubbing. Amy, you're an inspiration and the kindest, bravest leader I know. Your influence has been a guiding light for me and you will transform the world. Thank you for your contribution to this book.

Thank you to the Fair Library Jobs campaign team, especially Kirsten Elliot and Darren Flynn for their time and contribution to this book. Your mission to change recruitment has been inspiring.

Thank you to the team at Facet Publishing, who have been a great support and guidance in the process of getting my ideas into a book.

I'm incredibly grateful to my parents, family and friends – your unwavering belief and trust in me have been the pillars upon which my strength and perseverance rest. You have been my support system, my cheerleaders and my comfort during this journey.

I'd also like to thank everyone who took the time to send me their vignettes and case studies – Helen Allen, Michelle Brown, Holly Case Wyatt, Victoria Harrison and the Library and Knowledge Services Team at Royal Berkshire Foundation Trust , Sarah Ekey, Lesley English, Ann-Marie James, Reba Khatun, Tim Leonard, Caterina Reed, Fiona Rhodes, Sarah Sporko, Fiona Tarn, Andrew Walsh, Heather Wheeler and Hannah.

To everyone I worked with in libraries at Royal Holloway, City University, INTO and the University of Brighton, thank you. You started as colleagues and became friends. Your support has been invaluable.

A shout-out to my former colleagues at Westminster – Eleri Kyffin, Daniela da Silva, Amy Tank, Rosey Murdie, Katherine Marshall, Jade Gilmore, Sarah Maule, Dr Elaine Penn, Jenny Evans, Ann Munn, Caroline Lloyd and Gunter Saunders. Your kindness and support remind me there can be light in darkness.

A special thank-you to the course team at Sussex – Dr Rona Hart, Prof. Robin Banerjee, Dr Gillian Sandstrom, Joh Foster and Dr Kirsty Gardiner.

Your guidance and support have been amazing and have really helped me grow. You very definitely changed my life.

And to my classmates on my PGCert, sharing this journey with you has been fantastic. Your friendship and insights have added so much to my experience and it is wonderful to see the kindness we are all spreading. You are special people.

This book is all about making kindness and wellbeing a normal part of work. I hope it helps others to make their workplaces kinder and more supportive.

Introduction

Welcome to a transformative journey that redefines our approach to work in libraries and workplaces in general, reshaping our professional practices and how we think and interact with each other. This book isn't merely a collection of theories; it's a call to action, urging us to revolutionise our workplaces into spaces where kindness and wellbeing are deeply embedded into every aspect of our daily lives.

My fascination with kindness and wellbeing began as an exploration of theory. It quickly became a profound realisation: the principles underlying these concepts are deeply intuitive and remarkably simple to implement, provided there is a genuine commitment at the organisational level. This realisation made me commit to improving workplaces for everyone, starting with those I know best: libraries.

Looking back, I realise my understanding of kindness at work and its impact on wellbeing started at the University of Brighton. There, something simple like making tea for each other brought us together. We'd have tea breaks where we'd chat and laugh, which made us feel like a team. These small things showed how much we cared for each other and the camaraderie was something I saw in other library teams who similarly made the effort to connect. There was trust, safety and respect for each other's strengths.

Another significant aspect of my early work life was flexibility in working hours, a cornerstone of my wellbeing philosophy. This freedom, exemplified by always having the desk covered and contented students, reinforced trust and commitment, emphasising that small acts of kindness and trust enrich a workplace.

At Royal Holloway, the tradition of connecting continued differently through a morning 'coffee club'. This ritual, similar to the Swedish concept of FIKA, provided a space for debriefing and building enduring friendships, setting a positive tone for the day. These moments of pause, whether for tea or coffee, unofficial or scheduled, were common threads in the most connected teams I've been part of.

My experiences have taught me the importance of creating a kind and supportive work environment where simple, everyday actions can significantly impact overall wellbeing. This book invites you to transform your workplace into a space where wellbeing and kindness are not just ideals but the norm.

Beyond the world of libraries, I was inspired by case studies, including the case of Coca-Cola in Madrid, which is a prime example of this simplicity and power. In a study at one of their plants, a group of workers was subtly exposed to acts of kindness by their peers. This simple gesture led to a significant surge in prosocial behaviours, with these workers engaging in ten times more acts of kindness than a control group. Those on the receiving end of kindness reported feeling more in control and happier in their daily routines. This kindness initiated a virtuous cycle, encouraging recipients to reciprocate and extend kindness further within the workplace. The initiators of these acts also experienced a boost in happiness and a sense of control, highlighting the reciprocal benefits of fostering kindness within a work environment.

I've seen the stark contrast between supportive and toxic work environments. As well as experiencing community and kindness, I have also encountered workplaces and situations that were the opposite. These environments were often hierarchical, where bullying was common and wellbeing seemed only for show. Sometimes, the library was positive, but the wider organisation was not or the culture worsened as people left. The structural changes needed for genuine kindness and wellbeing were not undertaken in these places.

These challenging environments highlighted what was absent: a genuine sense of community, flexibility and authentic kindness. I saw how performative actions could not replace actual systemic changes. These challenges, including legacy toxicity, were tough, especially in leadership roles. But it made the lessons I learned in my positive workplaces even more valuable.

I began to understand that kindness and wellbeing in the workplace aren't just nice to have; they are essential for a healthy work culture. These experiences taught me that creating a positive environment requires more than just surface-level actions. It needs deep, systemic changes that foster trust, respect and genuine care among colleagues. While the actions are simple, they are hard and need to be constantly worked on; it takes a change in leadership or attitude from the wider organisation to fall apart, but if the culture is embedded, it will succeed.

This realisation became a cornerstone of my approach to leadership and coaching. I aimed to create spaces where people could thrive, not just survive.

Reflecting on these challenges and revelations has strengthened my commitment to transforming workplaces into kinder, more wellbeing-oriented environments.

Kindness and wellbeing significantly impact workplace dynamics, productivity and employee satisfaction. My observations and research show that environments where these values are prioritised lead to more collaborative and positive team dynamics. Employees feel more supported and valued, boosting their engagement and commitment to their work. Productivity sees a notable increase in such settings. When staff members are happy and feel well cared for, they are more motivated and efficient in their tasks. This is not just about reducing stress; it's about creating an environment where people can thrive and bring their best selves to work. Employee satisfaction also rises in kind and wellbeing-focused workplaces. Staff turnover rates tend to be lower, as employees feel more connected to their workplace and see it as more than just a job. They often report higher levels of job satisfaction and personal fulfilment.

In summary, fostering kindness and wellbeing in the workplace leads to a more harmonious work environment, enhanced productivity and greater overall employee satisfaction. These factors contribute significantly to the long-term success and sustainability of any organisation. This is why this book ventures beyond the traditional confines of workplace culture. It's a comprehensive guide, an invitation to transform the core of our professional environments into places where kindness and wellbeing are not mere aspirations but the norm, where every individual thrives.

While a section of this book is dedicated to leadership, everyone must engage with these insights, regardless of their position. Leadership isn't confined to those at the top; it's a quality at all levels. Understanding the team and organisation's vision and each team member's role is pivotal for a cohesive, kind and productive environment.

The four parts of the book collectively present a comprehensive exploration of kindness and wellbeing in library settings, each focusing on different aspects essential to creating a supportive and nurturing work environment:

Part 1: Theoretical Foundations of Kindness in Libraries as Workplaces: This section establishes the groundwork by focusing on the theoretical underpinnings of kindness in library workplaces. It explores the importance of genuine kindness beyond mere niceties in enhancing workplace dynamics, emotional intelligence, individual wellbeing and overall productivity. This part sets the stage for detailed discussions on the transformative power of kindness in professional settings.

The concepts of genuine kindness and emotional intelligence and their impact on workplace dynamics are universal. These ideas can enhance employee wellbeing and productivity in any organisational setting. Understanding the theory behind kindness and its practical implications in the workplace can help create more empathetic and supportive work environments across various sectors.

Part 2: Cultivating Kindness in the Library: A Holistic Approach to Wellbeing and Team Empowerment: This part explores practical strategies and thoughtful practices to create a supportive environment for librarians and library teams. It emphasises the balance between operational demands and staff wellbeing, advocating compassionate communication and flexible working to enhance wellbeing and productivity.

The strategies for creating a supportive and nurturing environment, balancing operational demands with staff wellbeing and advocating compassionate communication and flexible working, are applicable in all workplaces. These practices can help organisations in different fields foster a culture that values employee wellbeing, enhancing engagement and productivity.

Part 3: Leadership Approaches to Enhancing Kindness and Wellbeing in Libraries: This section explores the critical role of library leaders in creating and maintaining a culture of kindness and wellbeing. It highlights leaders' unique challenges and opportunities in this endeavour. It provides them with strategies and practical examples to integrate these ideals effectively into their organisational culture.

The role of leaders in fostering a culture of kindness and wellbeing is critical in any organisational context. The leadership strategies and practical examples provided for library settings can be adapted by leaders in other organisations to integrate kindness and wellbeing into their culture. This can transform their workplaces into more nurturing and positive environments for employees, clients and users.

Part 4: Embracing Kindness and Wellbeing in Library Cultures: navigating change and toxicity: The book's final part looks towards the future, advocating a continued focus on kindness and wellbeing in libraries. It guides library leaders and staff through the complexities of cultural transformation, emphasising the long-term benefits for staff wellbeing and the overall library experience. The forward-looking vision that emphasises the long-term benefits of kindness and wellbeing in the workplace is highly transferable. The focus on transformational leadership, adapting to the needs of a multi-generational workforce and the importance of creating supportive and nurturing work environments, are relevant for any organisation looking to future-proof its culture and operations.

Each part of the book builds upon the others, starting from theoretical foundations, moving through practical applications and leadership strategies and culminating in a forward-looking vision. Together, these parts create a holistic approach to integrating kindness and wellbeing into library cultures. Although the book is specifically tailored to libraries, the underlying principles of kindness, wellbeing and empathetic leadership are broadly applicable across different types of organisations. These concepts can be adapted to suit various workplaces' specific needs and contexts, thereby creating more positive, productive and human-centred work environments.

Each chapter is structured to provide a theoretical framework and practical applications, with exercises and reflective questions that encourage readers to integrate these concepts into their daily professional practices. The book aims to transform library cultures, making them more inclusive, supportive and nurturing environments for staff and the communities they serve.

As you read the chapters of this book, you'll discover each one focuses on a unique aspect of infusing kindness and wellbeing into library contexts. From enhancing positive communication to integrating wellbeing into staff development, confronting the challenges of daily implementation of kindness and evaluating the success of these endeavours, each chapter is thoughtfully designed to inspire, guide and provoke thought.

I am pleased to be able to include contributions by experts in their fields. Chapter 11, 'Fair Library Jobs: kindness, empathy and equity in library recruitment', by Kirsten Elliott and Darren Flynn is a significant contribution. It extends the ideas of kindness and empathy within library recruitment, emphasising the importance of these values in creating fair and inclusive hiring practices. This chapter is a practical guide to operationalising empathy and fairness in recruitment. Amy Stubbing's Chapter 16, 'Kind Use of Data for Wellbeing and Leadership,' contributes by blending the themes of data literacy, compassionate leadership and workplace wellbeing. This chapter emphasises the ethical and kind use of data in leadership. Amy's expertise brings insight and compassion to this sometimes contentious subject.

This book is for everybody, whether a librarian or not, who believes in the transformative power of kindness in reshaping the workplace. It's written for kindness leaders, whatever their role, who aspire to cultivate an environment where staff are understood, valued and empowered to be agents of positive change. The exercises, reflections, and case studies in this book are designed to engage you actively, encourage deep personal insight, and provide practical experience, with the aim of transforming your approach to kindness and wellbeing in both your work and daily life.

Let's embark on this journey together. Let's re-envision work, not just as a profession but as an opportunity to weave kindness and wellbeing into our lives and those around us, making a significant and enduring impact on our communities. This book is your guide to making kindness and wellbeing a normal part of your work life. Are you ready for the kindness revolution?

Reflective questions

- Your experiences with kindness at work: think about how your past jobs have shown you the importance of kindness and wellbeing. Is there a particular moment that really stands out for you?
- What your organisation is doing: what has been done to make kindness and wellbeing a regular part of work in your current or previous job? Are these efforts just for show or are they a genuine part of the workplace culture?
- Good v. bad workplaces: reflect on the different workplaces you've been in – some supportive, some not. How did these environments affect how you felt and worked?
- The role of leaders: how do the leaders in your workplace show they care about kindness and wellbeing? What could they do better?
- Your role in the workplace: consider how your actions at work help create a kind and healthy environment. What have you done and what more could you do?
- Flexible working: how do flexible working hours affect the way your team works together, the amount of work done and the happiness of your employees?
- Small kindnesses: can you remember when small gestures made a difference in your workplace? How did these acts change the atmosphere and how people got along?
- Significant changes needed: what changes are needed at work to make kindness and wellbeing part of the culture? How can these changes be introduced successfully?
- Your emotional intelligence: how does understanding and managing your emotions help make a better workplace? Consider how your emotional skills have influenced your work relationships.
- Leading from any position: no matter what your job title, how do you show leadership in promoting kindness and wellbeing at work? What challenges have you encountered and how have you dealt with them?

PART 1

Theoretical Foundations of Kindness in Libraries as Workplaces

Understanding and embracing authentic kindness becomes crucial as we navigate the ever-changing landscape of libraries and the organisations they often work within. This introductory section will set the stage, focusing on how genuine kindness – beyond just being nice – can significantly enhance workplace dynamics. We will explore why this topic is essential, considering the rapid evolution of workplace norms, the pivotal role of emotional intelligence and the impact these factors have on individual wellbeing and overall productivity. This context will lay the groundwork for the following detailed discussions, highlighting the transformative power of kindness in professional settings.

CHAPTER 1

Understanding the Importance of Kindness in the Workplace: Moving Beyond Surface-Level Niceness

Introduction

Before we go any further, it is important to understand that kindness is not the same as being nice. Kindness originates from a place of authentic care and concern for others, often involving a deeper comprehension of someone else's needs and a proactive willingness to meet those needs. In contrast, niceness may be surface-level courtesy or politeness, carried out without deeper emotional investment. When it comes to long-term impact, acts of kindness often leave a lasting impression and require emotional intelligence and empathy, whereas being nice tends to make the immediate situation more pleasant but is generally forgettable. Kindness may necessitate personal sacrifice or risk, such as defending someone being mistreated, even when it's uncomfortable. Being nice seldom involves any significant risk or personal sacrifice, focusing more on keeping a pleasant atmosphere. Kindness is usually selfless and unconditional, devoid of expectations for something in return, while niceness can be more transactional, performed with the expectation of future reciprocation.

Kindness often has underlying moral and ethical dimensions, urging us to do good even when it's difficult. On the other hand, being nice is more about adhering to social norms and etiquette rather than making a strong moral or ethical stance. So, while it's beneficial to be nice, striving to be genuinely kind offers a deeper and more meaningful way to engage with the world.

In a workplace setting, the distinctions between being 'nice' and being 'kind' manifest in various ways. Being nice typically involves engaging in pleasant small talk with co-workers, sending courtesy 'thank-you' e-mails after meetings as a matter of etiquette or holding the door open for someone right behind you. You might also tidy up the break room to make it pleasant for the next person or offer your seat in a crowded meeting. These immediate, surface-level interactions often operate within social norms and might involve the expectation of returned favours; they are important but not transformative.

On the other hand, being kind goes a step further. It could mean taking time out of a busy day to support a struggling co-worker emotionally. You might volunteer to mentor a less experienced colleague, providing them with valuable insights without expecting anything in return. Standing up against a discriminatory comment, offering constructive feedback to help a co-worker grow and even staying late to help a team meet a tight deadline are all acts that stem from a more thoughtful, long-term approach. These actions involve emotional intelligence and genuine care for others and they are more likely to be selfless and unconditional. According to Curry et al. (2018), 'kindness is characterised as actions with the intention of benefiting others'. While niceness centres on polite, immediate interactions that conform to social norms, kindness delves deeper, requiring more substantial emotional investment and a thoughtful approach to genuinely helping others. Both have a place in the professional environment but operate on different levels of human interaction.

The roots of kind actions are varied. They include kin altruism, where one helps family members who share genetic ties, indirectly benefiting oneself. Mutualism involves a reciprocal exchange of services, where both parties benefit immediately, such as friends exchanging help with household chores. Reciprocal altruism relies on future returns of favours given, similar to social insurance over time. Competitive altruism is similar to a benevolence contest, where individuals or animals engage in altruistic behaviour to gain trust or social standing.

Reflective points

Take a moment to reflect on these points:

- Understanding authentic kindness v. surface-level niceness: reflect on your own behaviours and interactions at work. How often are your actions driven by genuine care and a desire to support others versus simply adhering to social norms or expecting something in return? Consider instances where you might have chosen to be 'nice' for convenience or social etiquette and contrast these with moments where you acted out of deep empathy and kindness, perhaps even when it was uncomfortable or required personal sacrifice.
- The role of emotional intelligence in kindness: evaluate how emotional intelligence plays a role in your ability to be kind in the workplace. Consider situations where you had to understand and empathise with a colleague's feelings or needs. How did you respond? Did your actions involve a more profound emotional investment and a proactive approach to help or were they more about maintaining a pleasant

environment? Consider how developing emotional intelligence could enhance your capacity for genuine kindness.

- ▪ Impact of kindness on workplace dynamics and relationships: contemplate the long-term effect of kindness versus niceness on your professional relationships and workplace atmosphere. Consider how kindness, such as offering meaningful support, mentoring colleagues or standing up against unfair treatment, contributes to a more positive and collaborative work environment. How do these actions compare to the impact of mere politeness or transactional niceties? Reflect on how cultivating a culture of kindness in your workplace could transform professional interactions and relationships.

Case Study 1.1: Understanding kindness and wellbeing at work

Imagine going to work and feeling overworked and overwhelmed. Imagine not having the flexibility to work from home, especially those who are parents, caregivers or chronically ill. Imagine being physically distant from colleagues and over time feelings of isolation begin to increase. For most of us, these scenarios are not hypothetical but situations we face everyday.

When employees are consistently stressed or unwell, it is unlikely that they will have the capacity to come up with creative and innovative ideas that can help move the organisation forward.

Carrying out acts of kindness can be a powerful tool for increasing morale and productivity. I come to work everyday energised because I know that my colleagues and I will continue to be kind to one another. I have witnessed, participated in and benefited from acts of kindness, from greeting colleagues every morning, to celebrating birthdays, to exchanging recipes and sharing work supplies or extra unopened bottles of water. What motivates me day to day is spreading kindness, not for the sake of recognition, but for the continued hope that every kind act I do will inspire a domino effect of kindness. Lastly, I would like to emphasise the importance of self- kindness. For years, I would stay late after work or opt out of my lunch break. I've realised that taking breaks and not jumping from project to project with unreasonable time expectations is how I can take care of myself at work. For those of you who are kind to others, I ask you this: are you kind to yourself?

Caterina Reed, Academic Engagement Librarian

Why do people behave kindly?

Why do individuals exhibit acts of kindness? The question has piqued the interest of scholars and researchers from many areas. One idea comes from evolutionary perspectives on prosocial behaviour, which are further corroborated by contemporary research examining our biological and genetic attributes. Dovidio and Penner (2003) argue that specific biological and genetic traits can significantly explain why humans tend towards prosocial behaviours. Their work suggests we're inherently wired to be compassionate and considerate towards others.

Looking deeper into the neurological mechanisms, research by Carlson (1998) illustrates the vital role played by the brain's limbic system in nurturing human empathy. This deep-seated ability to understand and share the feelings of others has been observed through neuroscientific studies. For instance, Singer and Lamm's (2009) research shows that simply watching someone else endure pain triggers the same areas of the observer's brain that are associated with experiencing pain. This mirroring of emotional states is a potent facilitator of empathy and, consequently, kind behaviours.

Another layer to consider is the vagus nerve's role in prosocial behaviour. Kogan et al. (2014) proposed that an active vagus nerve promotes altruistic actions. Interestingly, their research also indicated a caveat: extremely high levels of vagal nerve activity can, paradoxically, diminish prosocial inclinations.

If we look at genetic aspects, we find compelling evidence that supports the theory of kindness as an inheritable trait. Studies focusing on identical twins, particularly the work by Davis, Luce and Kraus (1994), indicate that empathy isn't just a learned behaviour but has a significant genetic component. Such research suggests that genetic makeup substantially contributes to one's ability to be empathetic.

The research exploring the biological and genetic foundations of prosocial behaviour strongly suggests that our tendencies towards kindness are not just cultural or learned attributes. Instead, they are deeply ingrained in our evolutionary history and physiological constitution. These findings offer valuable insights into how our intrinsic prosocial traits promote a focus on others and foster an environment of mutual kindness and understanding.

Malti's Kindness Model

Malti's Kindness Model (2020) presents a framework for understanding kindness, portraying it as a complex metaconcept deeply rooted in ethical values and a sincere concern for the welfare of others. The model posits that kindness is not merely an isolated trait or a single type of action; instead, it is a convergence of multiple dimensions such as values, behaviours and cognitive-emotional states.

At the heart of this model lies the profound ability to understand and appreciate the unique perspectives of others. It promotes genuine kindness emanating from an acute sensitivity to our shared humanity and mutual interdependence. To be genuinely kind, we must go beyond self-centred interests and engage in actions that contribute to broader social wellbeing.

Malti identifies three core components that make up the construct of kindness:

- Kind cognitions
- Kind emotions
- Kind behaviours.

Kind cognitions

The cognitive aspect of kindness requires a deep understanding and appreciation of other people's perspectives. It calls for an open-minded approach and a respectful acknowledgement of the different viewpoints within our interconnected human tapestry. Kind cognitions go beyond mere tolerance, embracing the richness and complexity of human diversity.

Librarians are tasked with understanding the varied needs of their users, from schoolchildren to researchers to the general public. By adopting kind cognitions, librarians can better curate collections and create programming that reflects and respects their users' diverse interests and backgrounds. This can lead to more effective information literacy instruction, equitable access to resources and policies that consider the needs of all community members.

Kind emotions

This emotional aspect encompasses a range of feelings directed towards others and oneself. On the one hand, other-oriented moral emotions include empathy, compassion, sympathy, tenderness and gratitude. On the other hand, self-oriented moral emotions like guilt, shame or embarrassment can also emerge when individuals reflect on their actions within relational contexts. These other and self-oriented emotions act as the emotional fuel that powers acts of kindness.

In every library setting, fostering an emotionally supportive environment is critical. The empathy and compassion librarians show can be particularly impactful in public libraries, where users from all walks of life seek information, assistance and, sometimes, a place of refuge. School librarians have the unique role of supporting the emotional growth of children and teens, often becoming confidants and guides in addition to educators.

Kind behaviours

This is the most visible component, involving actionable gestures and activities to benefit others. The spectrum of kind behaviours is wide, ranging from simple, everyday actions like listening attentively, smiling and offering comfort to more deliberate and impactful deeds like helping, sharing, giving and lending emotional or practical support.

The behaviours librarians engage in are the most visible manifestation of kindness. This could mean going the extra mile to assist a user with special needs in a public library, encouraging a student in a school library or providing specialised research support in an academic library. It also involves community outreach, such as delivering books to those who are homebound or hosting events that encourage social cohesion and community wellness.

Additionally, Malti's model significantly emphasises the concept of **self-kindness**. This is the practice of directing the same cognitive, emotional and behavioural elements of kindness towards oneself. Self-kindness can include self-care routines, avoiding undue self-criticism and engaging in self-soothing activities. Self-kindness reinforces the notion that kindness towards oneself can facilitate kindness towards others, establishing a symbiotic relationship between individual wellbeing and broader social health. Self-kindness remains essential for library professionals in all settings. The demands of public service can lead to stress and burnout, making self-care practices crucial for librarians. By addressing their wellbeing, librarians are better positioned to serve their users with patience, enthusiasm and sustained dedication.

In summary, Malti's Kindness Model offers an expansive and nuanced lens through which to view kindness. It integrates ethical considerations with cognitive, emotional and behavioural elements, underlining the intricate interconnectedness and mutual dependencies that form the bedrock of positive human relationships. Across all types of libraries, Malti's Kindness Model can serve as a framework for developing a culture that promotes individual wellbeing and collective social good. The model can guide librarians in their interactions with users and each other, inspiring a service ethos that is as compassionate as competent.

Reflective points
- Exploring the roots of kindness: write down a list of kind actions you have observed or participated in over the past week. Next to each action, note whether you think it was driven by innate empathy, a learned response or a mixture of both. This exercise aims to help you identify how much of your kindness is a natural response versus a learned behaviour.

- Understanding kindness in professional settings: reflect on a recent interaction in your professional setting where you needed to employ kindness. Break down the interaction into Malti's three components of kindness: kind cognitions, kind emotions and kind behaviours. Analyse which component was most prominent and consider how you might bring a more balanced approach in future interactions.

Gratitude in the workplace

Gratitude, a powerful emotion integral to kindness and wellbeing, plays a vital role in the workplace. It involves recognising and appreciating the positive elements of our work and interactions with colleagues. This practice aligns with kind emotions in Malti's Kindness Model.

Research by Algoe, Fredrickson and Gable (2013) underscores gratitude's unique role in building high-quality relationships. Their study found that expressing gratitude benefits the person showing gratitude and positively impacts the recipient, enhancing relational bonds. This effect was evidenced in a study with romantic partners, where expressions of gratitude led to improved relationship quality over six months. These findings highlight gratitude's distinct role in fostering strong social bonds.

Similarly, Lyubomirsky, Sheldon and Schkade (2005) emphasise the significance of intentional activities, such as gratitude, in increasing happiness. Deliberately recognising and appreciating life's positive aspects can significantly influence personal happiness and wellbeing. This idea is particularly relevant in the workplace, suggesting that fostering intentional gratitude practices among staff can boost happiness and improve interpersonal relationships.

In practical terms, a gratitude letter or visit (Hart, 2021, 223) offers a tangible method of applying gratitude. This involves writing a letter to express appreciation for someone's impact on your life, potentially extended to a personal visit. Such practices deepen relationships and provide emotionally enriching experiences for both the writer and the recipient. In a workplace setting, this could translate into some of these ideas:

1 Gratitude journalling: encourage staff to maintain a gratitude journal, noting down things they are thankful for during their workday. This practice helps in recognising and appreciating the positive aspects of their job and work environment. By focusing on the good, employees can feel more content and satisfied, leading to improved job performance and overall wellbeing.

2 Gratitude meetings: begin team meetings with a round of gratitude sharing, where each member shares something they are grateful for. This practice can build a positive atmosphere, enhance team cohesion and foster a culture of appreciation. Regular gratitude sharing can also encourage employees to focus on the positive aspects of their work and increase job satisfaction.

3 Appreciation boards: set up a space in the workplace for staff to post notes of thanks or appreciation for their colleagues. This visible recognition can boost morale and create a culture of appreciation. By acknowledging the contributions of others, employees can feel more valued and motivated to perform their best.

4 Recognition programmes: implement formal programmes to recognise and celebrate staff achievements and contributions. Acknowledging individual and team successes can enhance motivation and job satisfaction. When employees feel that their hard work is recognised and appreciated, they are more likely to feel valued and committed to their work.

Integrating these practices into libraries aligns with enhancing kind emotions and relationships, contributing significantly to a positive and supportive workplace culture. By fostering kindness, gratitude and appreciation in the workplace organisations can create a more pleasant and productive work environment. By focusing on the positive aspects of work and relationships, employees can feel more fulfilled and motivated, leading to improved job performance and overall wellbeing.

Gratitude reflection and sharing exercise
Objective: to foster a culture of appreciation and positivity in the workplace.
Duration: 15–20 minutes.
Frequency: weekly or bi-weekly.
Steps:

1 Individual reflection:
   ■ Allocate 5–10 minutes for individual reflection.
   ■ Each staff member writes down three things they are grateful for in their work life. These can range from small events to significant achievements.
2 Group sharing:
   ■ Form a circle with the team.
   ■ Invite each person to share one of the items from their list. Encourage them to elaborate on why they are grateful for this aspect.

3 Acknowledgement: after each share, the group collectively acknowledges the shared gratitude with a simple gesture, like a round of applause or verbal affirmation.
4 Reflection on impact: Conclude the exercise by asking the team to reflect on how hearing others' gratitude impacted their mood or perspective.

Note: This exercise not only allows individuals to focus on positive aspects of their work but also builds a sense of community and shared appreciation within the team.

Prosocial personality traits

Kindness is part of a group of prosocial personality traits. The concept of prosocial personality traits encompasses a range of enduring characteristics that predispose individuals to act in ways that benefit others. Penner et al. (2005), introduced the notion of a 'prosocial personality'. This construct combines several key attributes strongly associated with an individual's inclination to exhibit prosocial or altruistic behaviours.

Attributes of a prosocial personality
Empathy

Empathy involves emotionally resonating with others, capturing both their feelings and perspectives. It entails intellectual comprehension of someone's situation and sharing their emotional experiences, encouraging actions of kindness and consideration. Empathy is central to the prosocial personality, which goes beyond mere understanding.

Social responsibility mindset

Contrasting with a mindset focused on self-sufficiency, a social responsibility mindset underlines the ethical imperative to help those who rely on us. This mindset nurtures a community-oriented perspective, placing collective wellbeing above individualistic concerns.

Locus of control

This refers to an individual's belief system about how much control they have over life events. A person with an internal locus of control believes they can actively influence outcomes, making them more likely to engage in prosocial activities. In contrast, an external locus of control attributes outcomes to factors beyond one's control, which can sometimes impede prosocial action.

Just-world belief

This philosophical stance posits that the world is fair, rewarding good deeds and punishing wrongdoings. People with a strong just-world belief are often compelled to step in when they encounter unfairness or suffering, aiming to restore a sense of justice and equilibrium.

Self-esteem enhancement

While not altruistic in the strictest sense, the desire to enhance one's self-esteem can be a powerful motivator for prosocial behaviour. Engaging in kind acts often boosts an individual's sense of self-worth and contributes positively to their self-image.

Prosocial orientation

Penner and Orom (2010) expanded on these attributes, referring to people who score highly on these traits as having a 'prosocial personality orientation'. This orientation is often correlated with various kind and prosocial behaviours. Furthermore, a subsequent layer of personality development is the trait of 'helpfulness'. Penner and Orom argued that individuals with high levels of helpfulness have a historical pattern of aiding others and hold a robust belief in their efficacy to be helpful. This belief, in turn, positively reinforces their willingness and likelihood to continue being helpful.

These traits and attributes create a nuanced and multi-dimensional understanding of what constitutes a prosocial personality. This comprehensive framework elucidates why some individuals are more predisposed to acts of kindness and altruism, offering a richer insight into the mechanisms driving prosocial behaviours.

The risks of being kind

Although the benefits of kindness in the workplace are apparent, is it all just positive vibes and friendly emojis? Like many things, kindness also has a shadow side.

Bolino, Klotz and Turnley (2018) highlighted that acts of kindness can lead to burnout, work–life conflicts and diminished productivity. Sometimes workers are urged to engage in kind acts that do not align with their personal values. In that case, they might feel annoyed, consuming more cognitive and emotional resources. There is also a need for a balanced approach to workplace kindness, which promotes a satisfied work environment while preventing potential negative consequences (Reizer et al., 2020). Below are some risks of being kind:

Kindness fatigue

Kindness fatigue is an intriguing but concerning phenomenon where the constant emphasis on compassion and empathy can lead to emotional exhaustion or diminished impact. This could happen in service-oriented professions, such as healthcare, social work or any role that requires a high level of emotional investment. Over time, the reservoir of compassion can run low, leading individuals to disconnect or become indifferent. The routine acts of kindness that were once fulfilling may start to feel like obligations, thereby losing their intrinsic value. While the push for promoting kindness is undoubtedly positive, it's crucial to remember that even the most generous among us are not inexhaustible. To combat kindness fatigue, it's vital to establish boundaries and practise self-care, ensuring that in our quest to be good to others we don't overlook the need to be good to ourselves.

Second-hand stress

Connected with kindness fatigue is the impact of second-hand stress on people. Studies show how our brains, equipped with mirror neurons, are naturally designed to pick up emotions from those around us. This process, known as emotional contagion, can make us susceptible to second-hand stress, just as passive smokers are to secondary smoke.

Researchers Friedman and Riggio (1981) found that visible anxiety in others, whether expressed verbally or non-verbally, can trigger similar feelings in us, affecting our brain's performance. This phenomenon isn't limited to people we know; even strangers' stress can impact us. A study showed that 26% of people experienced heightened cortisol levels simply by observing stressed individuals (Engert et al., 2014).

Our interconnected world has made us more prone to second-hand stress. Negative emotions and stress, amplified by social media, news and open office environments, can significantly affect our mental and physical wellbeing. Recognising this organisations such as the Ritz Carlton and Ochsner Health Systems have started creating 'no venting' zones to shield customers and patients from second-hand stress. This could be something for libraries to consider.

Reflective questions and exercises

1 Personal assessment of kindness and burnout:
   - Reflection question: consider your own experiences in the workplace. Have there been moments when your acts of kindness felt more like obligations than genuine expressions of empathy? Reflect on how these moments affected your emotional state and productivity.

- Brief exercise: for a week, journal your acts of kindness at work. Next to each act, note how you felt afterwards – energised, neutral or drained. Review your entries at the end of the week to identify any patterns. Are there specific kinds of acts that consistently lead to feelings of exhaustion or fulfilment?
2 Understanding and managing second-hand stress:
   - Reflection question: consider instances where you have experienced second-hand stress in your workplace. How did it affect your mental and emotional wellbeing? Were you able to recognise it as secondary stress at the time?
   - Brief exercise: identify a quiet space in your workplace where you can take quick 'mental breaks'. Schedule short, regular intervals (e.g. 5–10 minutes every few hours) to retreat to this space and practice mindfulness or relaxation techniques. This practice can help in mitigating the impact of second-hand stress.
3 Balancing kindness with self-care:
   - Reflection question: reflect on how you balance being kind to others with being kind to yourself. Are there instances where you prioritise others' needs at the expense of your wellbeing?
   - Brief exercise: create a 'self-care action plan' with activities focused on your wellbeing. This might consist of setting boundaries at work, engaging in a hobby, exercising or practising mindfulness. Aim to follow this plan for a month and observe any changes in how you experience and express kindness in the workplace.

How do kindness and positive psychology connect with wellbeing?

Positive psychology is a branch of psychology that focuses on the study of positive aspects of human life, such as happiness, wellbeing and flourishing. It deviates from traditional psychology's emphasis on studying problems and disorders and instead aims to understand and cultivate the factors that allow individuals and communities to thrive. This field explores concepts like positive emotions, strengths-based character, resilience and the pursuit of meaningful life goals.

In the context of integrating kindness and positive psychology into library workplaces, the approach is about enhancing the positive aspects of work life, such as job satisfaction, morale and collaborative relationships. By applying principles such as Fredrickson's (2001) Broaden-and-Build Theory, which posits that positive emotions expand our awareness and encourage novel, varied and exploratory thoughts and actions, libraries can become environments that not only support knowledge and community interaction but also foster employee wellbeing and innovative problem-solving. This is achieved through creating a workplace culture that values positive interactions, rooted in emotions like joy and appreciation and encourages staff and users to engage in a mutually supportive and constructive manner.

An important aspect of the idea of Broaden and Build Theory is the concept of the Upward Spiral (Fredrickson, 2013), which posits that the more we experience pfositive emotions, the more we broaden our mindset and build our resources, which in turn leads to more positive emotions. It's a self-sustaining cycle – like an upward spiral.

Over time, this upward spiral helps to build resilience. People who regularly experience positive emotions are more likely to bounce back from difficulties. They don't just return to their baseline level of wellbeing; they often learn and grow from the experience, ending up even more resourceful and resilient than before. There's also evidence that the upward spiral can contribute to better health and overall wellbeing. This isn't just about feeling good in the moment; it's about setting up a positive trajectory for your life.

The upward spiral suggests that fostering positive emotions in the workplace can lead to a cycle of increased positivity and resourcefulness. For instance, when employees feel happy, appreciated or inspired, they're more likely to be creative, collaborative and open to new experiences. This broadened mindset can lead to the development of new skills, stronger relationships and innovative solutions to problems. Over time, as these resources accumulate, they contribute to a more resilient and adaptable workforce. This is particularly relevant in dynamic work environments where adaptability and continuous learning are crucial.

As well as an upward spiral, Fredrickson (2013) has also found an Undoing Effect, which refers to the ability of positive emotions to counteract or 'undo' the physiological effects of negative emotions. When we experience negative emotions, like fear, anger or anxiety, our bodies often respond with a stress reaction. This is sometimes called the 'fight or flight' response. It includes physical changes like increased heart rate, higher blood pressure and the release of stress hormones. These physical changes are part of how our bodies prepare to deal with immediate threats or challenges. However, if these changes persist over time without relief, they can have harmful effects on our health. Fredrickson's undoing effect suggests that positive emotions can act as a balancing force against these physical stress responses. When we experience positive emotions, they can help to quickly return our body to a state of balance and relaxation. For instance, if after a stressful event you experience joy or amusement, these positive emotions can help lower your heart rate, reduce stress hormone levels and bring your body back to a more relaxed state. Besides the immediate physiological benefits, the undoing effect also ties in with Fredrickson's broader theory of positive emotions. By undoing the physical effects of stress, positive emotions can also broaden our mindset, helping us to build resilience and resources for the future.

The undoing effect highlights the powerful role that positive emotions can play in not just improving our mood, but also in promoting physiological recovery and resilience following negative experiences. It's a key part of understanding how positive emotions contribute to overall wellbeing and health.

In a work context, the undoing effect can be a vital tool for managing stress. For example, after a challenging project or a difficult interaction, activities that induce positive emotions (like team celebrations, humour or expressions of gratitude) can help counteract the physical and psychological effects of stress. This not only improves immediate mood and health but also contributes to long-term wellbeing by preventing chronic stress and burnout.

incorporating these concepts into wellbeing programmes can be transformative. Encouraging practices that foster positive emotions, like mindfulness, gratitude exercises or team-building activities, can initiate the upward spiral and the undoing effect in the workplace. These practices can be tailored to individual and team needs, promoting a culture where wellbeing and kindness are prioritised.

In summary, the Broaden and Build Theory, through the upward spiral and the undoing effect, provides a robust framework for enhancing wellbeing at work. It emphasises the importance of positive emotions in building resilience, fostering a growth mindset and managing stress effectively. Integrating these concepts into workplace practices can help transform the work environment into a space where wellbeing and kindness are the norm, aligning closely with your goal as a wellbeing coach and consultant.

Aligned with Broaden and Build Theory, kindness in library management plays a critical role. When library managers practise kindness by acknowledging staff efforts or providing compassionate feedback, it not only enhances the work environment but also fosters a sense of belonging and motivation among staff (Cameron and Caza, 2004). This approach is in harmony with the principles of Self-Determination Theory by Ryan and Deci (2000), which emphasises the need for autonomy, competence and relatedness in the workplace. In a library setting, offering opportunities for leading projects or initiatives can enhance staff autonomy and competence while encouraging team collaboration can foster relatedness and camaraderie.

Furthermore, kindness in libraries is essential for building social cohesion, a concept highlighted by Putnam in his book *Bowling Alone* (2000). A kind and collaborative work environment encourages teamwork over competition, enhancing team performance and innovation. Organisational psychology suggests that teams with strong social cohesion report higher job satisfaction and are more resilient (Cameron and Caza, 2004).

Lastly, the 'norm of reciprocity', as proposed by Gouldner (1960), indicates that kindness in the workplace creates a cycle of mutual favour. In libraries, this translates to a culture where staff members are more inclined to offer assistance and co-operation, enhancing service quality and reducing conflict (Cameron and Caza, 2004).

In conclusion, positive psychology and kindness in library environments benefit the staff through enhanced wellbeing and job satisfaction. They improve the overall service quality provided to the community.

Exploring the concept of kindness in the workplace

We will explore the subject of kindness at work by examining a real-world example. Then, we'll reflect on what might be considered the shadow side of kindness. While kindness is often regarded as a universal good, we will also explore its challenges and complexities and how it relates to our core values and personal resources.

In our journey to understand kindness in the workplace, let's explore a narrative shared by a library user. The story in Case Study 1.2 vividly captures the impact of kindness or its absence, in a library setting.

Case Study 1.2: Home, sweet, home

As an avid book reader and library user I thought my daughter would follow in the same footsteps. However, a thirty-minute struggle with a heavy pram was not worth the unwelcome atmosphere we encountered at the library. Not only were there no soft furnishings in the children's area but the staff were not what you would call friendly, despite us being regular users. The straw that broke the camel's back was the horrid treatment by the cleaner. She always had to clean where we were and her constant scowls and tutting drove me away from the library. Where I once found solace I couldn't take my daughter there anymore.

Fast forward a couple of years, a house move and the birth of another daughter I plucked up the courage and visited our new local library. Although the library was not modern like the last one it was welcoming and homely. The two main librarians were Sarah and Sue and what a breath of fresh air they were! Not only were they friendly and chatty and remembered our names, they invited us to various arts and craft sessions, baby stay and play sessions and other fun activities.

My two daughters absolutely adored the library and librarians. They so looked forward to their visits and sometimes begged to go twice a week. They weren't asked to be silent when they were excited about books. Or told to sit down when they played hide and seek in the adult section while I tried to look for my books. My little one wasn't told off when she ran behind the counter. We still laugh about it now. Thanks to the immense kindness and generosity of these two librarians, my children have another place they can call 'home'.

Reba Khatun, library user

Expanding our view beyond libraries, let's explore kindness in a more high-pressure environment: healthcare. Stone's study (2018), described here, sheds light on how intentional kindness interventions can significantly impact workplace wellbeing.

These examples demonstrate the impact of kindness in professional settings. They challenge us to consider how we can foster such environments in our own workplaces. As we continue exploring this theme, let's keep in mind these stories as reminders of the transformative power of kindness.

A helping hand for healthcare workers: Code Lavender, a quick support initiative

Originating at the Cleveland Clinic in Ohio, USA, Code Lavender (Stone, 2018) was launched in response to the pervasive stress and burnout in healthcare settings. It includes any intense emotional or spiritual support required.

It is a rapid response support mechanism. When a Code Lavender is called, a team of holistic nurses arrives within 30 minutes to provide therapies like massage and Reiki, food and water and emotional reminders. The broader programme also includes counselling, yoga classes and mindfulness training. The result: staff feel recognised, empathised with and supported.

How to incorporate kindness into library work

Incorporating kindness into library environments involves both individual actions and organisational strategies. Here are some practical ways library staff can integrate kindness, including conducting a kindness audit.

Individual actions

- Empathetic communication: engage in active listening and empathetic communication with colleagues and users. This involves being present in conversations, showing genuine interest and responding with understanding and empathy.
- Acknowledging achievements: regularly recognise and appreciate the efforts and achievements of colleagues, no matter how small. This can be

done through verbal compliments, thank-you notes or even public acknowledgements in staff meetings.

- Offering support: be proactive in providing help to colleagues, especially during busy periods or challenging tasks. This creates a supportive work culture and strengthens team bonds.
- Mentoring and sharing knowledge: experienced staff can mentor newer employees, sharing knowledge and offering guidance. This not only aids in professional development but also fosters a sense of belonging and community.

Organisational strategies
Kindness training programmes

Implement training sessions focused on kindness and empathy. These can include workshops on effective communication, conflict resolution and emotional intelligence. Training programmes can be structured around Malti's concepts of empathy and altruism. For instance, exercises in empathy can help employees understand and share the feelings of others, an essential aspect of Malti's model. Altruistic behaviours, where actions are taken for the benefit of others, can be encouraged through role-playing scenarios and group discussions. Implementation ideas:

- Role-playing scenarios: role-playing various workplace situations can effectively enhance empathy and understanding. This helps employees put themselves in others' shoes and respond more kindly.
- Group discussions and reflections: facilitate discussions where employees can share personal experiences and reflections on kindness. This promotes a deeper understanding of how kindness impacts the workplace.

Creating a kindness charter

Develop a kindness charter or policy that outlines expected behaviours and values related to kindness. This can serve as a guiding framework for staff interactions. The kindness charter can incorporate the elements of compassion and empathy from Malti's model. It can outline behaviours that demonstrate these traits, encouraging a culture of valuing and expressing compassion. Implementation ideas:

- Inclusive development process: involve employees in the creation of the kindness charter. This can include surveys, workshops and discussion groups to ensure the charter resonates with everyone.

■ Visible commitment: display the kindness charter prominently in the workplace and include it in onboarding materials for new hires.

Promoting work–life balance

Encourage work–life balance policies, such as flexible working hours or wellness programmes. A healthy work–life balance is crucial for fostering a positive and kind work environment. Malti's emphasis on altruism can be reflected in policies that consider employees' needs and wellbeing. Promoting work–life balance demonstrates organisational altruism – the company's commitment to the wellbeing of its employees. Implementation ideas:

■ Flexible working arrangements: (This is discussed in Chapter 9.) Offer options like remote work, flexible hours and compressed workweeks. These arrangements acknowledge the diverse needs of employees.
■ Wellness programmes: implement programmes focusing on physical, mental and emotional health. This could include yoga classes, mindfulness sessions or access to mental health resources.

Conducting a kindness audit

A kindness audit is a systematic approach to assess and improve the level of kindness in the library. Here's how to conduct one:

1 Survey and feedback: start with a survey or feedback session where employees can share their perceptions of kindness in the workplace. Questions can cover team support, recognition, communication and work–life balance.
2 Observation: conduct observations of day-to-day interactions within the library. This can help identify positive examples of kindness and areas needing improvement.
3 Review of policies and practices: evaluate existing policies and practices to see how they contribute to or hinder a kind work environment. This includes reviewing management practices, communication protocols and staff welfare programmes.
4 Action plan: based on the findings, create an action plan. This should include specific, measurable steps to enhance kindness, such as introducing new policies, changing certain practices or organising regular team-building activities.
5 Follow-up and re-evaluation: conduct follow-up surveys and observations to assess the impact after implementing changes. Kindness should be an ongoing priority, with regular reviews and adjustments as needed.

Incorporating kindness in libraries not only enhances the wellbeing of employees but also positively impacts the service quality provided to users. A kindness audit is an effective tool to systematically assess and improve kindness levels, ensuring the library remains a welcoming and positive space for staff and the community.

Conclusion

Kindness in the workplace is about deep, empathetic engagement, not just politeness. It's essential for creating a supportive, collaborative environment, benefiting everyone. True kindness involves empathy, mentoring and self-care, balancing personal wellbeing with helping others. Implementing kindness requires both personal efforts and organisational strategies, like empathetic communication and kindness training. It's linked to better job satisfaction and overall workplace wellbeing. In essence, fostering kindness is key to a productive, satisfied workforce and a successful organisation.

Exercises and reflective questions

Exercise for teams

Reflective listening exercise

A fundamental skill for any librarian is active listening. To achieve this, it is a good idea to do a 'reflective listening exercise.' This activity can be conducted during staff meetings or training sessions and is designed to enhance library staff's listening skills, empathy and understanding. Here's how to carry it out:

Objective: to develop active listening skills by practising reflective listening, which involves listening to a speaker and then reflecting on what you heard to ensure understanding and empathy.

Materials needed: a list of prompts or topics related to library work (e.g., dealing with demanding users, managing workload, recent changes in library policies); a timer.

Participants: the exercise can be done in pairs.

Duration: approximately 20–30 minutes.

Instructions:

1 Pair up: divide the staff into pairs. If there's an odd number, you can have one group of three where roles rotate.
2 Set roles: designate one person as the Speaker and the other as the Listener in each pair. The roles will be switched halfway through the exercise.

3 Speaker shares: the Speaker selects a prompt from the provided list and shares their thoughts, feelings or experiences related to that topic for about 2–3 minutes. The Listener's role is to listen attentively without interrupting.
4 Reflective listening: after the Speaker finishes, the Listener reflects on what they heard. This involves summarising the Speaker's main points and emotions. For example, 'It sounds like you felt overwhelmed when dealing with multiple users simultaneously.'
5 Feedback: the Speaker then provides feedback on the accuracy and empathy of the Listener's response. They can correct misunderstandings and acknowledge the Listener's empathy.
6 Switch roles: after the first round, the pairs switch roles and repeat the process with a different prompt.
7 Group discussion: once both rounds are complete, reconvene as a group. Discuss what everyone learned from the exercise, focusing on the challenges and benefits of active listening.

Key points to emphasise:

■ The importance of listening without interrupting or planning your response while the other person is speaking.
■ The value of empathy in listening – trying to understand not just the words but the emotions and intentions behind them.
■ The role of reflective listening in preventing misunderstandings and building more robust, more empathetic relationships among colleagues.

This exercise is beneficial for librarians, as it improves their listening skills and enhances their ability to empathise with colleagues and users, a critical aspect of providing excellent service in a library setting.

Exercise for individuals
Comprehensive exploration of kindness in professional settings
Objective: to deepen understanding and awareness of kindness in the workplace, focusing on its roots, manifestations and impacts, both positive and negative. This exercise is designed to enhance empathy, emotional intelligence and prosocial behaviour, while also addressing the challenges and complexities of kindness in professional environments.

Duration: this exercise is intended to be completed over a period of two weeks, with periodic reflections and analyses.

Part 1: Exploring the roots of kindness
- Duration: three days.
- Activity: list recent kind actions you've observed or participated in. Next to each action, note if it was driven by innate empathy, a learned response or a mix of both.

Part 2: Understanding kindness in professional settings
- Duration: two days.
- Activity: reflect on a recent kind interaction at work. Analyse the interaction using Malti's model of kindness (cognitions, emotions, behaviours) and identify the most prominent component.

Part 3: Prosocial personality traits
- Duration: two days.
- Activity: consider how traits like empathy and social responsibility mindset contribute to prosocial behaviours. Reflect on how these traits manifest in your own actions.

Part 4: The complex nature of kindness
- Duration: two days.
- Activity 1: reflect on the potential downsides of kindness, like burnout or kindness fatigue.
- Activity 2: consider how to balance kindness towards others with self-kindness to prevent burnout.

Part 5: Kindness and positive psychology in libraries
- Duration: two days.
- Activity 1: reflect on how incorporating kindness and positive psychology can improve library environments.
- Activity 2: think about how positive interactions can broaden cognitive abilities and encourage innovation in libraries.

Part 6: Exploring kindness in the workplace – case studies
- Duration: two days.
- Activity: reflect on real-world examples of kindness (or its absence) in libraries and healthcare. Consider how kindness can be transformative in professional settings.

Part 7: Incorporating kindness into library work
- Duration: two days.
- Activity 1: reflect on how individual actions and organisational strategies can integrate kindness in libraries.
- Activity 2: consider conducting a kindness audit to assess and improve kindness levels.

Completion: at the end of the two weeks, review your reflections and analyses to gain a comprehensive understanding of the role and impact of kindness in the workplace. This should help you identify areas for personal development and strategies to foster a more empathetic and kind environment in your professional setting.

Reflective questions

Reflecting on the importance and impact of kindness in the workplace

- Self-reflection on authentic kindness v. niceness: when considering your recent interactions at work, can you identify moments where your actions stemmed from genuine kindness rather than just being nice? How did these actions differ in terms of your emotional involvement and the impact they had on others?
- Evaluating emotional intelligence in kind acts: think about instances at work where you needed to demonstrate kindness. Did you employ emotional intelligence, such as empathy and understanding, in these situations? How did this affect both your response and the outcome?
- Long-term impact of kindness v. niceness: reflect on the long-term effects of your kind actions versus mere niceties in your workplace. How have these actions influenced your relationships and the overall work environment? Can you identify any changes or improvements that occurred as a result?
- Understanding the biological and genetic aspects of kindness: considering the scientific research on kindness, how do you see these biological and genetic factors playing out in your own propensity for kindness? Are there instances where you feel these innate traits have guided your actions?
- Applying Malti's Kindness Model in your role: how do you incorporate the three components of Malti's Kindness Model (kind cognitions, kind emotions and kind behaviours) into your everyday interactions at work? Are there areas where you could improve or balance these components more effectively?
- Recognising and managing kindness fatigue: have you experienced kindness fatigue in your role? Reflect on situations where constant acts of kindness might have led to emotional exhaustion and how you managed or could manage these feelings.
- Balancing kindness with self-care: how do you maintain a balance between being kind to others and being kind to yourself? Are there times when you need to prioritise self-care to continue being effectively kind to others?

■ The role of kindness in enhancing workplace wellbeing: how do you see the principles of positive psychology and kindness interplaying to improve wellbeing in your workplace? Can you think of specific examples where this has been evident?

■ Handling the complexities of kindness: reflect on any complex or challenging situations where being kind was not straightforward. How did you navigate these situations and what did you learn from them?

■ Integrating kindness into library work: as a professional in library and higher education, how do you integrate kindness into your daily work? Are there specific strategies or practices you use to ensure kindness is a central part of your interactions with colleagues and library users?

These reflective questions aim to deepen your understanding of kindness in the workplace, encouraging you to evaluate your own actions and their impact, both on others and yourself. They are designed to help you recognise the various facets of kindness, its complexities and its profound role in creating a positive and effective work environment.

CHAPTER 2

Redefining Wellbeing in the Workplace: Insights and Strategies for Libraries

Introduction

The greatest wealth is health.

(Virgil, quoted in Ivanov, Sharman and Rao, 2015)

Historically, workplace wellbeing initiatives have often centred around individual actions. As libraries often sit within a wider organisation, we have all seen these organisations tick the wellbeing box with common examples like bike-to-work schemes or fruit bowls in office kitchens. While commendable, these efforts represent only a superficial touch on actual wellbeing and place the onus entirely on employees, suggesting that individual choices like cycling more or eating healthier are sufficient for overall wellbeing. This perspective overlooks the significant influence of organisational structures and cultures on employee wellbeing.

In the wake of the COVID-19 pandemic, Deloitte examined the changing nature of wellbeing in the corporate world (Lewis et al., 2022). This report significantly reshaped our understanding of wellbeing, urging businesses to re-evaluate its definition and implementation in today's workplace. It raises essential questions about how wellbeing is perceived and addressed in our offices, the methods used to gauge its presence and impact, the necessity for organisations to invest in wellbeing and the best ways to incorporate it into the corporate structure.

The insights are enriched by a comprehensive survey conducted alongside the Institute of Directors (IoD) and International Institute of Risk & Safety Management (IIRSM) (Lewis et al., 2022), which includes responses from over 30,000 directors and risk managers. A notable finding from this survey is that 50% of respondents observed improved business performance when wellbeing was prioritised. The report reveals key points, highlighting that 67% of directors consider mental and emotional health crucial in discussions about wellbeing. It also emphasises the need for a strategic shift from reactive to proactive approaches, fostering work environments that are both empowering and flexible.

Leadership emerges as a crucial element in this context. The survey shows senior leaders are considered guardians of wellbeing strategies, setting an example for implementation throughout the organisation. Despite these insights, the report uncovers a significant discrepancy: only 16% of businesses have substantially increased their investment in wellbeing, underscoring the necessity for clear metrics and targets to measure these initiatives' effectiveness and return on investment.

To truly work on the future of wellbeing in libraries, we all must acknowledge there's a crucial shift from individual responsibility to organisational accountability. This shift involves creating environments that nurture wellbeing at every layer of the organisation. It's not merely about individual actions but systemic changes that foster a thriving workplace. Even in libraries within the largest systems or organisations, there are things within our gift that we can do for our teams. This book will explore the systemic issues and the things that can be achieved despite issues beyond our services.

What is wellbeing?

Wellbeing is a complex and multifaceted concept, central to the human aspiration for a fulfilling life. More than just happiness or fleeting moments of joy, it encompasses a broad spectrum of experiences and capabilities that contribute to our overall sense of contentment and effectiveness. At its most visible, wellbeing is often associated with emotional wellness, characterised by positive emotions like joy, gratitude and contentment. This aspect of wellbeing, akin to the tip of an iceberg, is immediately noticeable and reflects our daily feelings and general life satisfaction. It is 'feeling good'.

Much more beneath the surface contributes to functioning well. As outlined by Ryff (1989), **psychological wellbeing** plays a crucial role, involving elements like self-acceptance, personal growth, purpose in life, environmental mastery, autonomy and positive relationships with others. It represents the depth of our inner functioning and how we perceive and engage with the world. Moreover, as Keyes (1998) described, **social wellbeing** is determined by the strength and quality of our relationships and social networks. It includes elements such as social integration, contribution, coherence, actualisation and acceptance, underscoring the importance of our connections and roles within the community.

Further deepening the concept, wellbeing also involves virtues and moral worth, encompassing character strengths, ethical values and virtues like kindness, empathy, resilience and integrity. This dimension reflects our alignment with moral and ethical values, contributing to a sense of purpose and fulfilment.

Thriving and flourishing go beyond survival, highlighting the importance of growing, developing and realising one's potential, including self-actualisation, personal growth and pursuing meaningful goals. Additionally, **emotional regulation** and **psychological resilience** are vital, emphasising the ability to manage emotions, cope with life's challenges and recover from adversities.

Finally, intellectual and professional development, involving continuous learning, intellectual stimulation and career growth, contribute significantly to our sense of accomplishment and overall wellbeing.

Understanding wellbeing holistically reveals it as much more than just pursuing happiness. It involves an exploration of an individual's internal world, interactions with others and contributions to broader society, highlighting the importance of nurturing all aspects of wellbeing for a truly fulfilled and effective life.

The spectrum of wellbeing

Along with needing an understanding of the elements that make up functioning well, it is also important to understand that wellbeing is a spectrum and can vary from low to high, with several states in between:

- flourishing: a state of optimal wellbeing
- floundering: being mentally unwell
- languishing: not ill, but not flourishing.

These states encompass the feeling good aspect (happiness) and functioning well aspect of wellbeing.

Flourishing refers to a state of optimal wellbeing or thriving. On the other hand, not flourishing could mean floundering (being mentally unwell) or languishing (not sick, but not thriving either).

Feeling good in wellbeing constitutes the happiness component. The functioning well component refers to how effectively we perform, with optimal performance being the ultimate goal. Functioning well implies fulfilling basic needs and extends beyond practising virtues and accomplishing morally significant tasks. Terminologies synonymous with functioning well include eudaimonia, eudaimonic wellbeing, wellness, optimal experience and thriving.

Thus, wellbeing is a comprehensive state of feeling good and functioning well. Another perspective is to divide wellbeing into two components: hedonic and eudaimonic. According to this perspective the two key components of wellbeing are:

- Hedonic wellbeing: associated with pleasure and positive emotions
- Eudaimonic wellbeing: about functioning well, including aspects like eudaimonia, wellness and optimal experience.

Wellbeing is more than fleeting happiness. It's a composite state encompassing pleasure, engagement, relationships, meaning, accomplishments and sometimes physical health. Recognising these interrelated elements helps provide a more nuanced perspective on what it means to lead a 'life well lived.' Understanding and nurturing these aspects may pave the way for individuals and communities to a more fulfilled existence.

Workplace wellbeing

We will explore Job Demands Resources (JD-R) along with PERMA and ASSET models, which will be the primary models for this book

PERMA

Developed by Martin Seligman (2011), a leader in positive psychology, PERMA focuses on Positive emotion, Engagement, Relationships, Meaning and Accomplishment. These elements are critical to individual wellbeing and can directly contribute to a person's happiness and fulfilment in the workplace.

ASSET

An acronym for 'A Short Scale for Evaluating Tendencies', (Robertson and Cooper, 2011), this model is valuable for understanding and measuring wellbeing in terms of organisational structures and the individual experiences of employees, including demands, control, managerial support, peer support, relationships, roles and change.

Job Demands-Resources (JD-R)

This model (Bakker and Demerouti, 2007) is a framework used to understand the interplay between various aspects of job demands and resources. It posits that every occupation has its own specific risk factors associated with job stress. These are classified into two categories: job demands and job resources. Job demands are the physical, psychological, social or organisational aspects of a job that require sustained physical and/or psychological effort and are therefore associated with certain physiological and psychological costs. Job resources, on the other hand, refer to the physical, psychological, social or organisational aspects of the job that are functional in achieving work goals, reducing job demands and the associated physiological and psychological costs or stimulating personal growth and development. The JD-R Model is particularly effective in identifying the dynamics of job stress and the potential for employee burnout and engagement, offering valuable insights into how a balance between demands and resources can lead to higher job satisfaction and improved overall wellbeing.

These three models are critical to this book because they specifically address individual wellbeing from a positive psychology perspective. They can be directly applied to leadership coaching and strategy, which are relevant to enhancing workplace culture and leadership development – areas of growing importance in modern organisational strategy.

Other models of wellbeing

I want to introduce two other workplace-specific models to give you a variety of tools.

The PROWELL (Innovative Workplace Institute, n.d.) and Business in the Community's Workwell (Business in the Community, 2019) Models are two comprehensive frameworks for wellbeing in the workplace, each focusing on various aspects of employee health and culture. These models are pivotal for a few reasons:

- Holistic approach: both models take a comprehensive approach to wellbeing, considering not just the physical health of employees but also their mental, social and financial health. This aligns with contemporary understandings of wellbeing, recognising that various factors contribute to a person's overall wellness.
- Integration into business strategy: they encourage the integration of wellbeing into the core business strategy, which can help organisations to build a more committed and productive workforce, leading to better overall performance.
- Cultural shift: by incorporating these models, businesses can facilitate a cultural shift towards greater empathy, openness and inclusivity, critical components in driving engagement and fostering a positive workplace environment.
- Leadership and management: both models highlight the role of effective leadership and management in promoting wellbeing. This is critical, because the attitudes and behaviours of leaders and managers are influential in setting the tone for the organisation's culture.
- Employee engagement and productivity: engaged employees who feel their wellbeing is supported are more likely to be productive and stay with the company. These models provide frameworks for improving

engagement, including better health initiatives, supportive management and an inclusive culture.

- Stakeholder engagement: the Workwell Model, in particular, emphasises the importance of collaboration with stakeholders, suggesting that a collective effort is more successful in promoting workplace wellbeing.
- Responsiveness and adaptability: both models stress the importance of being responsive to the individual needs of employees, fostering a culture of support that can adapt to diverse needs.

PERMA, ASSET and Job Demands Resources (JD-R) are specifically chosen for the focus of this book.

Why is wellbeing important?

Wellbeing is critical in the workplace, influencing satisfaction and performance and how individuals interact with each other and approach their tasks:

- Job satisfaction and performance: a high level of emotional and psychological wellbeing among staff positively correlates with job satisfaction and performance (Wright and Cropanzano, 2004). Employees are more likely to perform effectively when they are content and feel psychologically supported.
- Employee interaction: social wellbeing is critical in library settings where teamwork and communication are vital. Positive social interactions can lead to more collaborative and supportive work environments.
- Service quality: for librarians, wellbeing directly impacts their ability to serve the public effectively. Emotional resilience helps manage the sometimes challenging interactions with diverse users. At the same time, psychological wellbeing fosters continuous personal development, crucial in the dynamic information sector.
- Innovation and adaptability: libraries are often at the forefront of technological and educational innovation. A workforce with high levels of wellbeing is more likely to engage in creative thinking and adapt to change positively, which is essential for libraries that function in rapidly evolving information landscapes.

In conclusion, fostering emotional, psychological and social wellbeing in libraries is beneficial and essential. It ensures a productive, harmonious and innovative workplace, pivotal in libraries that are not only information centres but also community hubs promoting lifelong learning and social inclusion.

The Model of Social Wellbeing (Keyes, 1998) plays a crucial role in the work of librarians, extending far beyond the physical confines of libraries. This model, focusing on fostering positive relationships, assesses how individuals engage with others and various groups and organisations, such as their workplace, recreational clubs and community associations. It's a measure of how these social interactions impact overall wellbeing.

Keyes (1998, 121–2) emphasised that individuals are constantly interwoven into social frameworks, facing various social responsibilities and challenges. The model includes five essential dimensions:

1 Social integration: this aspect evaluates the depth of an individual's connection with their community, group or society. For librarians, this means acting as community engagement facilitators, organising events and workshops and aiding in creating a sense of belonging and integration among diverse individuals.
2 Social acceptance: this involves possessing positive attitudes towards humanity, fostering trust and accepting others. Librarians demonstrate this through their respectful and impartial service to a diverse clientele, nurturing an inclusive community spirit.
3 Social contribution: engagement in social structures involves responsibilities. Librarians contribute to society by providing equal access to information and resources, supporting research and promoting information literacy. This enhances both their societal worth and that of their users.
4 Social actualisation: this reflects the potential for growth in groups and societies, facilitated by collective efforts. Librarians aid this development by curating collections and resources that respond to societal changes, stimulating thought and discussion.
5 Social coherence: this entails an inclination to acquire knowledge and understand the world. Librarians are key in assisting individuals to navigate vast information resources, helping them understand current events, history and various perspectives. Their skills in information literacy are vital in fostering a coherent understanding of complex issues.

In summary, the work of librarians is deeply intertwined with the principles of social wellbeing. They significantly contribute to the wellbeing of individuals and communities through their expertise, interactions and services. Their role goes beyond library management to include knowledge facilitation, understanding and community connection, embodying the essence of the Model of Social Wellbeing. An example of wellbeing in action is the Royal Berkshire Hospital NHS Foundation Trust Library's Crafty Wednesdays (Case Study 2.1).

Case Study 2.1: Crafty Wednesdays: chat and craft to build community in a busy hospital

Once a month, a member of the Library team makes the trip over to the Trust's Oasis staff wellbeing centre to host our Crafty Wednesday workshop. This hour-long lunchtime drop-in provides a space for staff to meet and share crafting expertise.

There is a monthly suggested craft for beginners, but people are welcome to bring whatever craft they are currently working on. Previous projects have included knitting dementia wristbands for patients on the elderly care wards, sewing lavender hearts, creating corner bookmarks out of recycled materials and crafting folded book art. This Christmas, we will be making Christmas gift tags.

Materials are provided for the projects and the sessions are free, so there is no financial barrier to taking part. We utilise existing staff skills in the library to facilitate these sessions and to support staff wellbeing across the trust. By conducting these sessions, we demonstrate that the library is an approachable and compassionate, friendly place with a diverse skill set.

The staff who attend find the chance to take a break in the relaxing atmosphere of the Oasis centre beneficial. Engaging in a very different activity to their usual healthcare duties allows them time and headspace to decompress and the opportunity to try new skills which they can develop further in their own time or in future sessions. The informal chat whilst engaged in crafting helps to build networks across the trust and helps to build a sense of belonging.

Several staff who could not attend sessions have also engaged with the activities in their own time after contacting us to ask for the instructions. The opportunity to craft has provided these staff with a welcome outlet outside of work.

Victoria Harrison and the Library and Knowledge Services Team, Royal Berkshire Hospital NHS Foundation Trust

---

The PERMA Model and staff wellbeing

The PERMA (Seligman, 2011, 16–25) Model offers a valuable framework for understanding the multiple facets of staff wellbeing:

- Positive emotion: staff members derive joy and fulfilment by serving their community, fulfilling the 'P' in PERMA.

- Engagement: the various roles that staff members play, from academic guides to community organisers, ensure a high level of engagement with their work, contributing to the 'E' in the model.
- Relationships: the social nature of the library as a community hub provides ample opportunity for staff to build meaningful relationships with users and co-workers alike, meeting the 'R' in PERMA.
- Meaning: being at the crossroads of academia and community wellbeing lends a more profound sense of purpose to the work, fulfilling the 'M'.
- Accomplishments: through continuous learning and skill development, staff find a sense of achievement, aligning with the 'A' in the model.

The ASSET Model for managing work-related stress

While PERMA focuses on individual aspects of wellbeing, the ASSET Model (Robertson and Cooper, 2011) addresses organisational dimensions that can impact stress and wellbeing. The ASSET Model looks at Work–life: Demands, Control, Relationships, Change, Role and Support.

- Demands: increased library services require a reassessment of workloads, aligning them with staff capability and wellbeing.
- Control: staff should have the agency to make decisions, especially as their roles diversify.
- Relationships: building strong relationships among staff members and between staff and users can counteract work-related stress.
- Change: as libraries transform, effective communication and staff input can mitigate the stress associated with change.
- Role: staff should clarify their roles and responsibilities to avoid confusion and stress.
- Support: adequate managerial and peer support, including training and resources for their diversified roles, is crucial for staff wellbeing.

By acknowledging and actively supporting staff wellbeing, libraries can genuinely flourish as community hubs that resonate with kindness, engagement and holistic wellbeing.

Job Demands-Resources (JD-R) Model

Along with PERMA and ASSET, the Job Demands-Resources Model (Bakker and Demerouti, 2007) is used in this book, as it demonstrates that demands are the physical or emotional pressures stemming from one's job responsibilities. These can encompass factors like a tense work atmosphere, overwhelming workloads, time constraints, emotional strain, discordant relationships at work or uncertainty about one's role.

In contrast, resources are regarded as supportive elements in the physical, social and organisational domains that alleviate stress and assist employees in achieving their objectives. Resources might involve robust working relationships, self-governance, ongoing learning and development, coaching, mentorship and career advancement opportunities in this context.

Conservation of Resources and Job Demands-Resources

Conservation of Resources (COR)

The Conservation of Resources (COR) Model (Hobfoll, 1989) laid the foundation for the JD-R Model and incorporated a wider variety of resources. Unlike the JD-R Model, which heavily depends on control to counter demands, COR introduces four specific resource categories. These four categories in the workplace include objects (such as necessary tools for the job), personal characteristics (like skills, optimism and self-belief), conditions (tenure and rank) and energies (knowledge and financial means).

There are then associated stressors:

1 threats of losing resources
2 actual loss of resources
3 absence of resource gain.

The Conservation of Resources (COR) Theory is centred on the premise that individuals strive to retain, protect and build resources. In the context of wellbeing, these resources can be anything an individual values, such as personal characteristics, conditions or energies central to sustaining or bolstering their wellbeing. Concerning wellbeing, each of the COR principles can be expanded upon:

Principle 1. The impact of resource loss

This principle posits that the impact of resource loss is disproportionately larger than the benefits of resource gains. This is particularly relevant to wellbeing, in that losing essential resources such as health, positive relationships or stability can lead to significant stress and be detrimental to mental health, more so than the equivalent gains would improve wellbeing. For instance, the loss of a close relationship can have a profound negative impact on one's emotional state, more so than the positive impact of forming a new acquaintance.

Principle 2. The necessity of resource investment

Wellbeing often requires proactive investment; this can mean investing time in relationships, energy in personal growth or effort in professional development. The investment is not simply for accumulating more resources but also for safeguarding against potential future losses. For example, taking time for self-care activities like yoga or swimming can be seen as investing in one's physical and mental health resources.

Principle 3. The upward spiral of resource accumulation

When an individual has a surplus of resources, they are in a better position to gain more, creating an upward spiral. In regard to wellbeing, this could mean that someone with a robust support network, good health and a positive outlook is more likely to experience opportunities for further positive experiences and relationships, enhancing their wellbeing even further.

Principle 4: The downward spiral of resource depletion

Conversely, when resources are lost, individuals may enter a negative cycle where each loss makes them more vulnerable to further losses. In wellbeing terms, this can be seen in scenarios where an initial loss, such as a job, can lead to a cascade of stressors, including financial difficulty, strain on relationships and deteriorating mental health, contributing to a further sense of wellbeing erosion.

Wellbeing initiatives, particularly in the workplace or personal development, often utilise the COR framework to encourage strategies that help individuals and groups build and maintain resources. Interventions include stress management training, resilience-building exercises and creating environments that foster positive social interactions.

COR theory underscores the importance of early intervention and the benefits of a preventive approach to wellbeing. By focusing on resource conservation and accumulation, individuals can enhance their resilience to stressors and improve their overall sense of wellbeing. Hobfoll stated in his 1989 paper on COR theory, 'The conservation of resources is the central motive around which stress and coping revolves' (Hobfoll, 1989, 516), highlighting the theory's centrality to understanding stress and wellbeing.

Job Demands-Resources

The Job Demands-Resources (JD-R) Model is fundamental to understanding wellbeing at work, due to its comprehensive approach in analysing how various job characteristics impact employee wellbeing. Here's why it's particularly relevant:

■ Balancing demands and resources: the JD-R Model emphasises the balance between job demands (aspects of the job that require sustained physical and/or psychological effort) and job resources (aspects of the job that help to achieve work goals, reduce job demands and stimulate personal growth and development). Understanding this balance is crucial for wellbeing, as high demands can lead to strain and burnout, while ample resources can foster engagement and job satisfaction.

■ Customisation to different work environments: the model is applicable across different occupations and sectors, making it a versatile tool for analysing workplace wellbeing. It recognises that what constitutes a 'demand' or a 'resource' can vary significantly across different work contexts.

■ Predicting burnout and engagement: the JD-R Model helps predict outcomes like burnout (when job demands are high and resources are low) and engagement (when resources are high and demands are manageable). This is essential for wellbeing strategies in the workplace.

■ Framework for intervention: it provides a framework for improving employee wellbeing. Organisations can take targeted actions by identifying specific demands that need to be reduced and resources that should be bolstered.

■ Emphasis on personal development: the model acknowledges the role of personal resources, such as resilience and self-efficacy, in coping with job demands. This aligns with positive psychology principles, focusing on strengths and capacities that enable individuals to thrive.

■ Adaptability to changes: in the modern work environment, characterised by rapid changes and high demands, the JD-R Model offers a robust framework for understanding how these changes impact employee wellbeing and what can be done to mitigate adverse effects.

How the JD-R and COR come together

Here's how the JD-R and COR come together to provide an understanding of wellbeing, which will be discussed throughout the book.

Resource preservation and job resources

According to COR theory, individuals strive to protect their resources to prevent stress. In the JD-R Model, job resources are valuable assets employees seek to acquire and conserve. These resources can help buffer the impact of job demands on stress and facilitate personal growth, learning and development (Bakker and Demerouti, 2007).

Resource loss and job demands

COR theory emphasises that resource loss is more impactful than resource gain, which aligns with the JD-R Model's categorisation of job demands. High job demands can lead to a depletion of an individual's resources and are closely associated with the strain component of stress. When demands exceed resources, employees may experience health problems, decreased motivation and burnout (Demerouti et al., 2001).

Resource investment and balanced job design

Investing in resources, as suggested by COR, is akin to the JD-R Model's recommendation for employers to invest in job resources for employees to facilitate the achievement of work goals and foster employee engagement. Organisations may provide training, feedback and social support, which can be considered as investing in job resources to enhance employee wellbeing and productivity.

Spirals of gain and loss

The upward and downward spirals COR theory describes are reflected in the JD-R Model through engagement and burnout. An abundance of job resources can lead to a positive feedback loop, where engaged employees exhibit high levels of energy and resilience, potentially garnering even more resources (Schaufeli and Bakker, 2004). Conversely, when job demands are high and resources are low, employees may enter a negative spiral, leading to exhaustion and cynicism, which are characteristics of burnout.

Integrating COR and JD-R provides a nuanced understanding of workplace wellbeing. Interventions to reduce job demands and enhance job resources can improve employee wellbeing and organisational outcomes. This integrated approach underscores the importance of designing work environments that consider both the preservation of resources and the balance between demands and resources.

Integrating COR and JD-R into the library context, specifically in relation to both individuals (like librarians) and leaders (like library managers), can create a framework for nurturing wellbeing and efficiency within the institution. Here's how interventions and strategies based on these theories can support individuals and leaders in libraries:

For individual librarians

- Resource Management: Librarians could be trained in personal resource management strategies that align with COR principles. This might include time management techniques, stress reduction practices (like mindfulness or relaxation exercises during breaks) and professional development to enhance personal skill sets, which can boost personal resource reservoirs.

■ Job Crafting: Encouraging librarians to tailor their roles to better fit their strengths and interests (a concept associated with JD-R) can help them to feel more engaged and less drained by their work, leading to better job satisfaction and wellbeing.

■ Social Support: Building a supportive community within the library can be a critical resource for individuals. Strong, supportive relationships among staff can help mitigate the effects of job demands and prevent the depletion of personal resources.

For library leaders

■ Demand assessment: leaders should assess job demands and consider how they can be adjusted to prevent staff burnout. This might involve ensuring reasonable workloads, providing clarity of job roles and avoiding excessive bureaucracy.

■ Resource provision: leaders can focus on providing resources that help staff meet their job demands. This may include access to professional development opportunities, adequate staffing levels and the latest technology to make tasks more manageable and efficient.

■ Feedback and autonomy: consistent with JD-R principles, leaders should provide constructive feedback and encourage autonomy, empowering librarians to make decisions about their work. This empowerment can be a valuable resource, increasing job satisfaction and engagement.

For both individuals and leaders

■ Wellbeing initiatives: libraries can implement wellbeing initiatives focusing on both COR and JD-R models, such as offering workshops on resilience, stress management and job crafting. These initiatives can help individuals and leaders understand how to effectively balance demands and resources.

■ Cultural change: fostering a culture that values and promotes wellbeing can reinforce the importance of both personal and professional resources. Leaders can encourage librarians to take proactive steps in managing their resources and demands by cultivating an environment that acknowledges the significance of wellbeing.

■ Strategic planning: leaders can use insights from both theories to inform strategic planning. By considering the resources required for new services or roles and balancing these with potential demands placed on staff, leaders can plan for sustainable service development.

In libraries, where the demands may include multitasking, managing a diverse array of inquiries and keeping up with rapidly changing information technology, applying COR and JD-R models can guide the creation of a supportive work environment. This approach not only benefits individual librarians, by enhancing their personal wellbeing and job satisfaction, but also contributes to the library's overall effectiveness and service quality.

Job crafting in libraries

Job crafting, is explored in detail in Chapter 13 but it is essentially the process of redesigning your own job to better fit your strengths, passions, and values leading to greater job satisfaction and engagement at work. It is a crucial tool for enhancing wellbeing in the library sector, serves as a practical application of the Job Demands-Resources (JD-R) Model and Conservation of Resources (COR) Theory. In a library setting, librarians face unique job demands, such as managing diverse inquiries, keeping pace with evolving information technology and handling multitasking. Job crafting allows librarians to reshape their roles to align with their strengths and interests better. Just as we can tailor our clothes or create our personal coffee order, job crafting allows us to tailor our roles. By doing so, they can transform potential stressors into opportunities for growth and satisfaction.

The JD-R Model and COR theory provide a robust framework for understanding how librarians can proactively manage their job demands and resources. Job crafting in this context might involve librarians taking the initiative to modify their tasks, interactions and work environment. For example, a librarian skilled in technology might craft their job to focus more on digital resource management. Others might use their interpersonal skills to enhance community engagement and programming.

Job crafting in libraries improves individual librarians' wellbeing and boosts overall library performance. When librarians align their roles with their strengths and interests, they tend to be more engaged, efficient and innovative. This alignment leads to better service quality, enhanced user experience and a positive work atmosphere.

Leaders in libraries can play a pivotal role in facilitating job crafting. By offering coaching, support and flexibility, library leaders can encourage librarians to explore and implement changes that make their roles more fulfilling and less stressful. This might include providing professional development opportunities, encouraging collaborative projects that play to individual librarians' strengths or rethinking workflow to distribute tasks more effectively according to individual skills and interests.

In conclusion, job crafting in libraries, guided by the JD-R Model and COR theory, represents a dynamic approach to enhancing workplace wellbeing. It allows librarians to tailor their roles to their strengths, transforming the library into a more adaptive, resilient and user-centred environment. This approach caters to individual wellbeing and ensures that libraries remain relevant and responsive in an ever-changing information landscape.

Reflective questions

- Evaluating job demands in librarianship: reflect on the specific job demands you face as a librarian. How do these demands impact your day-to-day work and overall wellbeing? Consider aspects such as multitasking, managing diverse inquiries and keeping up with technological changes.
- Identifying personal and professional resources: what are the key resources you have or need in your role as a librarian that help you manage these demands? Think about resources like professional development opportunities, supportive colleagues or personal resilience and how they contribute to your effectiveness and wellbeing.
- Applying COR in your role: how do you actively work to retain, protect and build your valuable resources, in line with the Conservation of Resources Theory? Consider examples of personal characteristics, conditions and energies that are important in your role.
- Balancing resources and demands for wellbeing: reflect on a situation where you successfully balanced the high demands of your job with adequate resources. What strategies did you employ and how did this balance affect your job satisfaction and personal wellbeing?
- Implementing JD-R and COR in librarianship: how can you apply the principles of JD-R and COR to create a more positive and supportive work environment for yourself and your colleagues? Think about practical steps that can be taken to reduce job demands and enhance job resources in your library setting.

Tangible benefits of kindness and wellbeing at work

The impact of kindness and wellbeing on job satisfaction, especially in library environments, is profound and multifaceted. This discussion explores how these elements contribute to a positive workplace, benefitting both staff and users.

Rates and indicators of job satisfaction in libraries

Job satisfaction within library environments is influenced by various factors, including the nature of the work, the organisational culture and the interaction with users. In libraries, particularly within academic settings such as universities, satisfaction often correlates with the sense of fulfilment derived from assisting students and researchers, the diversity of the daily workload and the opportunities for professional development. Indicators of high job satisfaction in libraries include low staff turnover, positive employee feedback and high levels of engagement in professional activities and development.

How kindness and wellbeing improve job satisfaction

Introducing kindness and wellbeing initiatives in the library setting can substantially improve job satisfaction. When treated with kindness, staff are more likely to report a sense of being valued and supported, increasing their engagement and satisfaction with their work. Wellbeing programmes focusing on mental and physical health can reduce stress and burnout, improving overall job satisfaction. This could manifest in more flexible work arrangements, recognition programmes or investment in personal and professional growth opportunities.

Mental health: benefits for both staff and users

Kindness and wellbeing are essential for the mental health of both staff and users. For staff, a positive work environment promoting kindness can reduce stress levels, increase resilience and improve job performance. Wellbeing initiatives such as mindfulness sessions, stress management workshops and physical activities like yoga can contribute to a more balanced mental state. Users also benefit from a kind atmosphere, which can make the library a welcoming and inclusive space, encouraging them to utilise library services more frequently and to view the library as a safe haven for learning and exploration.

Collaboration: enhanced teamwork and partnership

Kindness and wellbeing practices encourage a culture of trust and respect, which are the cornerstones of effective collaboration. When library staff feel supported and acknowledged, they are more likely to contribute to team efforts and engage in partnership opportunities. A library prioritising these values can cultivate a strong team ethos, leading to more innovative services and improved user experiences.

Examples of successful collaboration in libraries

Successful collaboration in libraries can be seen in joint ventures like interlibrary loans, shared cataloguing systems and co-operative community events. For instance, libraries that have implemented shared leadership models have found that they promote a more co-operative environment, where teamwork is encouraged and required for the system to function. This can extend beyond internal operations to include collaborations with external partners such as local businesses, educational institutions and cultural organisations, facilitating programmes that benefit the wider community. To further illustrate the impact of kindness and wellbeing in fostering collaboration and community engagement in libraries, consider Case Study 2.2.

In summary, incorporating kindness and wellbeing into the fabric of library operations yields substantial benefits that enhance job satisfaction, improve mental health for staff and users and foster a collaborative environment conducive to personal and professional growth.

Case Study 2.2: Fostering playful communities: the Counterplay event at Dokk1 Library

Playfulness and playful leadership (enabling play to emerge in others) rarely talks about kindness, but it is core to these ideas. One of the clearest examples I've seen of this was from Mathias Poulsen and the Counterplay events he organised in a fabulous Danish public library, Dokk1 in Aarhus. Dokk1 in itself is a playful community-centred space, from the playground equipment encircling the library's entrance floor to the central bell that is rung remotely by new mothers in the local maternity ward.

Mathias used this space as home for the hard-to-define Counterplay event (part play festival, part conference – he once described it as 'An amalgam or hybrid, combining the intellectual rigour of a "serious" play conference with the life-affirming vitality of the play festival.') It's also the only conference I've ever been to where the morning keynote speech was delayed because attendees were enjoying dancing to merengue music!

The event and the community around it was defined by playfulness, that feeling that play could emerge (and be welcomed) at any time. More than that, the playfulness was enabled, supported, grown by a sense of trust, affection, kindness, love. The generosity of love, of kindness and compassion that was created by the playful leadership approach of the organiser transformed the event into a community, a community whose boundaries leaked from the people who signed up as attendees out to members of the public who were welcomed into activities in the public spaces of Dokk1. It created a psychologically safe space for people to learn, to experiment (and fail and try again), to play, to make connections and grow communities.

Andrew Walsh, Playbrarian

Conclusion

This chapter provides a comprehensive guide to understanding and implementing wellbeing strategies in the unique context of libraries. It highlights the shift from individual-focused approaches to more holistic organisation-wide strategies. The discussion of theoretical models, coupled with practical, actionable strategies, offers a blueprint for libraries to create nurturing environments that promote emotional, psychological and social wellbeing. By prioritising wellbeing, libraries can not only enhance the work environment for their staff but also enrich the service quality and community engagement they offer. Ultimately, this approach underscores the importance of wellbeing as a cornerstone for building thriving, resilient and effective library communities.

Exercises and reflective questions

Exercise for teams
Team wellbeing workshop
Objective: to encourage leaders to facilitate team engagement in enhancing collective wellbeing within the library environment.
Materials needed: writing materials for participants; basic knowledge of the PERMA, ASSET, JD-R and COR models.
Instructions:

1 Group introduction (10 mins): start with a discussion on the importance of wellbeing in the workplace, focusing on how it's influenced by organisational culture and structures.
2 Exploring wellbeing models (40 mins):
   ■ Introduce the PERMA, ASSET, JD-R and COR models. Split the team into groups, assigning each a model to discuss.
   ■ Groups should identify how their model can improve wellbeing within the library context.
3 Team discussion (30 mins): reconvene for a group discussion. Have each group share their model's application and discuss integrating these models into daily work and organisational practices.

4 Identifying wellbeing challenges and opportunities (30 mins): facilitate a discussion on specific wellbeing challenges and opportunities in your library, encouraging team input to identify key issues.

5 Creating a collective action plan (40 mins):
   ■ Work together to develop a 'Team Wellbeing Action Plan', incorporating strategies for identified challenges and opportunities.
   ■ Assign roles and deadlines for strategy implementation.

6 Closing commitments (20 mins):
   ■ Have each team member make a personal commitment toward enhancing team wellbeing.
   ■ Summarise the action plan and emphasise the importance of teamwork in promoting wellbeing.

Outcome: leaders and their teams will collaboratively develop a comprehensive plan to enhance wellbeing, fostering a supportive and productive library work environment.

Exercise for individuals
Personal wellbeing reflection
Objective: to foster self-awareness and personal growth by reflecting on individual wellbeing, especially within the library work environment.
Materials needed: writing materials (notebook, pen/pencil or digital device); basic understanding of the PERMA, ASSET, JD-R and COR models.
Instructions:

1 Defining personal wellbeing (10 mins): reflect on what wellbeing means to you, especially in the context of your work in the library. How has your understanding of wellbeing changed over time?

2 Wellbeing self-assessment (15 mins):
   ■ Using the concepts from the PERMA, ASSET, JD-R and COR models, assess your own wellbeing. Rate aspects like emotional, psychological and social wellbeing on a scale of 1–10.
   ■ Identify your strengths and areas for improvement.

3 Work environment impact analysis (20 mins):
   ■ Reflect on how aspects of your work environment (like workload, community interactions and professional development opportunities) impact your wellbeing.
   ■ Identify both positive and negative influences.

4 Developing a personal action plan (15 mins): create a plan to enhance your wellbeing, focusing on areas that need improvement and

maintaining your strengths. Set achievable goals and timelines for your plan.

5 Commitment and reflection (10 mins):

■ Reflect on what you've learned about your wellbeing and commit to follow through with your action plan.

■ Optionally, share this commitment with a colleague or supervisor for support.

Outcome: this exercise will help participants better understand their wellbeing and create a practical approach to enhance it within their work environment.

Reflection points

■ Emotional wellbeing:

— How often do I experience positive emotions such as joy, gratitude or contentment at work?

— Do I have effective strategies to manage negative emotions or stress in my professional life?

— Reflect on a recent challenging situation at work: How did I handle it emotionally and what could I have done differently?

■ Psychological wellbeing:

— Do I feel a sense of accomplishment and personal growth as a librarian?

— How often do I engage in activities that challenge me intellectually and contribute to my professional development?

— Consider my current work–life balance: how can I improve my psychological wellbeing?

■ Social wellbeing:

— How solid and supportive are my relationships with my colleagues and users?

— Do I actively contribute to a positive and inclusive work environment?

— Reflect on a recent collaboration or team project: what did I learn about my role in a team and how can I improve my collaboration skills?

■ Physical wellbeing:

— Am I maintaining a healthy balance of physical activity, rest and nutrition, considering the demands of my job?

— How does my physical health impact my ability to perform my duties effectively?

— What steps can I take to improve my physical wellbeing, such as regular exercise, better ergonomics at my workstation or healthier eating habits?

■ Work environment and culture:

— How does the culture of my library support or hinder my overall wellbeing?

- — Can I improve aspects of my work environment (like noise levels, lighting or ergonomics)?
- — Reflect on the organisational support available for wellbeing: am I aware of and utilising available resources effectively?
- ■ Professional fulfilment:
  - — Do I find meaning and purpose in my role as a librarian?
  - — How does my work align with my personal values and professional aspirations?
  - — Consider my long-term career goals: What steps am I taking to achieve them and how do they contribute to my sense of fulfilment?
- ■ Personal development and growth:
  - — What areas do I wish to grow professionally and what resources or learning opportunities are available?
  - — How do I stay motivated and engaged in continuous learning and development in my field?
  - — Reflect on a recent learning experience: how did it contribute to my personal and professional growth?
- ■ Work–life balance:
  - — How effectively do I manage the demands of my work and personal life?
  - — Are there activities or hobbies outside work that I engage in to recharge and maintain a healthy balance?
  - — Reflect on a typical week: how might I better allocate my time and energy between work and personal commitments?

These reflection points are designed to help librarians gain insights into their own wellbeing, identify areas that need attention and consider steps to enhance their overall wellbeing in their personal and professional lives.

CHAPTER 3

The Library as a Place of Community Support and Wellbeing

Introduction

Case Study 3.1: The library as community hub

I've worked at my library for 22 years. In that time, I have seen lives changed and enhanced by our services. A bulk of my working day is spent within the children's library. I deliver two sessions a week for preschoolers and each of the groups are very well attended by committed children and parents. Some of the children I sang to when they were babies still come into the library each week and are engaging, bright, happy young adults. Recently, during a session, a child took his first steps. His mother and I were both thrilled and it was such a joyous moment to share. I've also been told by parents that their children took their first steps TOWARDS the library because they were so eager to come in. It's a hub for the community, a warm, welcoming, safe and friendly place for so many.

I love working on the registration desk. It's the first port of call for many new visitors and I enjoy welcoming people and signing them up. Whether it's a student new to the area, a long-time resident of Norfolk or just a holidaymaker needing to access the internet, we can help.

I serve people who have been made redundant after many years in the same job who are utterly petrified of applying for a new job. I try my best to put them at ease and give them the confidence to get on to a computer. I gave a library card to a man who had never learned to read or write, but was so determined to try. One lady had been in an abusive relationship, she'd been told she'd never learn to read. This was then being passed down to her children. They all have library cards now and she is with a new, more supportive partner.

I helped a lady who was fleeing domestic violence and needed to access the council house listings somewhere she felt safe.

I assisted a lady who was looking for help for her husband, who has dementia. She was utterly alone and so desperate for help. I sat with her and talked about what we could do. I then found all the leaflets and information I could and passed on her information to our Community Librarian.

During the pandemic, we had to adapt as a service and ensure the community still knew we were able to help, albeit remotely. We contacted borrowers to make sure they were OK and aware of assistance available while everything was closed. When we reopened we applied for more funding for our Tricky Period scheme that provides menstrual products for free and we have also set up the Warm and Well scheme, which provides hot drinks in the library, bags of toiletries and other really handy items to take away free of charge.

We have a loyal group of regular customers from all walks of life. I see them in the street and we say hello and it makes me feel so proud.

Hannah, Norfolk Libraries

Hannah's experiences in Case Study 3.1 reflect a shift in the function of libraries, from traditional book lending to becoming key community centres that cater to a wide array of emotional, educational and social needs. The transformation observed in Hannah's library – from hosting a toddler's first steps to supporting individuals facing life's more challenging moments, such as unemployment, illiteracy or domestic violence – indicates the broader role libraries are now playing globally. This shift highlights the importance of incorporating principles of kindness and wellbeing into library services. Hannah's narrative shows that libraries are not just about books but about people, community and the support they offer in various aspects of life.

This chapter aims to explore how libraries, like the one where Hannah works, have become integral to community wellbeing. We will explore the responsibilities of modern librarians, who are increasingly finding themselves at the intersection of knowledge guardianship and community support. This change requires a new understanding of librarianship, including crisis management, emotional support and active community engagement.

We will employ the frameworks of PERMA (Seligman, 2011, 16–25) and ASSET (Robertson and Cooper, 2011) to understand and improve the wellbeing of library staff navigating these expanded roles. These models were introduced in Chapter 2 and will provide insights into how staff can manage their wellbeing while effectively serving their communities. The story of Hannah and her library serves as a lens through which we can examine the positive impact of kindness and wellbeing initiatives in these vital community institutions.

As we progress through this chapter, we will discuss the theoretical aspects of this transformation and provide practical exercises and reflections. These tools are designed to support library staff and their teams in fostering environments where wellbeing and kindness are aspirational goals and everyday realities. Hannah's case study sets the stage for this exploration, highlighting the real-life impact of these changes in the library sector.

The evolving role of libraries

Modern libraries have evolved into spaces where community members can learn, request help, interact and grow. Libraries today often triage for other services in their organisation and offer digital resources, workshops and events. The physical space can extend to spaces for relaxation and meditation. More than that, they've become platforms for people from diverse backgrounds to come together, share stories and foster understanding. Still, they are also spaces where people come when stressed, in crisis or having wellbeing challenges. This impacts library teams in ways never seen before.

Public libraries have taken up the mantle of bridging generational gaps. With programmes for the young and the elderly, they serve as a communal ground where wisdom is imparted and absorbed. Similarly, university libraries have become essential centres for holistic student development, fostering academic growth and personal and emotional wellbeing.

Library staff now wear many hats – from being custodians of knowledge to becoming wellbeing facilitators. In university settings, librarians often find themselves at the crossroads where academic assistance meets guidance towards a plethora of resources that aim at nurturing the individual's mental, emotional and social needs. This, therefore, requires a multifaceted skill set, a deep understanding of community needs and a dedication that goes beyond traditional job descriptions.

The shift in the role of a librarian to encompass first-line crisis management while reducing the focus on traditional library tasks can profoundly impact people's sense of identity and wellbeing, both for the librarians and the users.

For librarians

- Professional identity: librarians might experience an identity shift as they incorporate new skills and responsibilities. They could grapple with the tension between traditional library science values and the more inter-personal and immediate nature of crisis management and social work.
- Increased stress: the additional responsibilities of handling crises and social issues could increase stress levels for librarians, potentially impacting their wellbeing.
- Skill mismatch: not all librarians will have the skills or training to handle crises effectively, leading to a feeling of inadequacy or discomfort.
- Job satisfaction: on the positive side, some librarians may find a greater sense of purpose and fulfilment in assisting people at a deeper level.
- Career path: this change opens up new avenues for career progression, although it could deter those who wish to focus on traditional librarianship.

For users

■ Resource availability: if librarians are busy handling crises, users needing traditional library services may feel they need to be more valued.

■ Confidentiality and comfort: users may feel uncomfortable discussing personal or sensitive issues in a library setting, affecting their wellbeing.

■ Community impact: the library can become an integral part of the community, serving as a hub for various services contributing to overall community wellbeing.

■ Accessibility: for those in need, having immediate access to crisis management and social work resources can significantly impact their lives.

Overall, while the role change might offer new ways to serve the community, it could also have a range of implications for the wellbeing and identity of librarians and users. Appropriate training, support and resources are necessary for this transition to be successful.

Importance of kindness and wellbeing in community hubs

Why is there an increasing emphasis on kindness and wellbeing in libraries? The reason lies in the inherent nature of these establishments. Libraries are community hubs where individuals search for knowledge, solace and community, irrespective of their backgrounds.

■ Promotion of kindness: kindness isn't just about being nice. It's about understanding, empathy and support. Libraries promote these values in their quest to serve all community members; through various programmes and workshops, libraries teach individuals to be more compassionate, understanding and, in turn, kinder to one another.

■ Fostering wellbeing: today's world is fraught with mental and physical challenges. People are increasingly seeking places of refuge and rejuvenation. Libraries have responded to this need by becoming sanctuaries for wellbeing. With sections dedicated to positive psychology, spaces for yoga and meditation and events centred around mental health, libraries have become pivotal in promoting holistic wellbeing.

■ Community connection: libraries serve as social equalisers where people from all walks of life can come together. This brings a unique opportunity to sow seeds of kindness and mutual respect. By fostering a culture of understanding and compassion, libraries become more than just a place to borrow books; they become community hubs for positive interactions.

- Access to resources: given their role as centres of learning, libraries often house a range of materials on personal development, including resources on positive psychology, stress management and mindfulness. These resources offer practical tools for improving mental health and overall wellbeing.
- Programme diversity: libraries often host programmes like talks, workshops and community events that focus on the whole person. For example, sessions on healthy eating, stress management or even financial literacy contribute to the wellbeing of individuals and, by extension, to the community.
- Digital and virtual platforms: with the advent of technology, many libraries offer digital resources on mental health, conduct virtual meditation sessions and have forums discussing wellbeing. This broadens the reach of libraries and makes them accessible to those who might not be able to visit in person.
- Inclusivity: last but not least, the principle of 'kindness' extends to creating an inclusive environment. Libraries have become more adaptive to meet the community's diverse needs, such as providing materials in multiple languages, creating accessible spaces for people with disabilities and offering services for the elderly and other vulnerable populations.

The focus on kindness and wellbeing is not just a trend but a necessity in our increasingly complex and challenging world. Libraries, as community hubs, are well positioned to take a leadership role in this area.

Balancing act: services and wellbeing

Library staff continually balance the delicate act of offering diverse services while maintaining their wellbeing. The diversity in services means adapting to new technologies, managing different community programmes and often going the extra mile to offer personalised assistance. The increased workload and the emotional labour involved can lead to burnout. Integrating the PERMA and ASSET models can provide invaluable insights into creating a work environment that fosters excellent service and staff wellbeing. Below I have mapped how different wellbeing areas connect with PERMA and ASSET.

Wellbeing areas connected to PERMA and ASSET

Mental health support and positive emotion (PERMA)

Offering robust mental health support is not just a strategy but a necessity. Regular workshops centred around mindfulness, yoga and positive psychology can contribute to the 'Positive emotion' aspect of the PERMA model. When staff members feel emotionally supported, they are better equipped to manage stress and offer outstanding service.

Skills development and engagement (PERMA)

Skill development is another area that needs attention. By encouraging staff to expand their skill set, libraries address the 'Engagement' aspect of the PERMA Model. Continuous learning initiatives and upskilling programmes aid personal development and instil a sense of achievement. This makes the staff more adaptable and ready to meet the diversified demands of a modern library.

Recognition and relationships (PERMA and ASSET)

A culture of recognition and appreciation can significantly impact staff wellbeing, connecting with the 'Relationships' dimension of the PERMA model and the 'Support' element of the ASSET model. A rewarding and positive work environment where efforts are acknowledged encourages better teamwork and interpersonal relationships. This sense of community among staff can be a strong buffer against work-related stress and emotional labour.

Adaptation, control and role clarity (ASSET)

The ASSET model's focus on 'Control' and 'Role' is particularly relevant here. As libraries diversify their services, it's crucial that staff have clear role definitions and the agency to make decisions. Ambiguity can lead to stress, whereas clarity and control empower staff to execute their roles and adapt to changes effectively and confidently.

Organisational support (ASSET)

Using the 'Support' aspect of the ASSET model, libraries should ensure that human and material resources are adequately available. Staff should feel they have the tools and managerial backing to cope with their extended responsibilities, helping to mitigate the 'Demands' and the potential for burnout.

Community engagement and meaning (PERMA)

Interestingly, serving a diverse community can contribute to staff wellbeing by fulfilling the 'Meaning' aspect of the PERMA model. Making a tangible difference in users' lives provides a depth of purpose that can be emotionally and psychologically rewarding.

In balancing diverse services with staff wellbeing, libraries would do well to adopt frameworks like PERMA and ASSET. These models offer a structured approach to tackle the complexities involved, ensuring that kindness and wellbeing aren't just external services but are intrinsic to the library's culture. When staff wellbeing is prioritised, libraries can truly evolve into the community hubs of learning, kindness and holistic wellbeing they aim to be.

Impact on non-frontline library staff: evolving roles, responsibilities and the culture of kindness

The landscape of library services is continuously transforming, significantly impacting the roles and responsibilities of non-frontline staff. As libraries evolve into community hubs, these staff members find themselves navigating a myriad of new challenges and opportunities.

In this evolving landscape, non-frontline library staff are increasingly responsible for a variety of administrative and back-end tasks. Their roles have expanded to include administering innovative programmes, managing digital platforms and undertaking duties traditionally performed by frontline staff. This shift necessitates a broader skill set that extends beyond conventional library work, underscoring the need for continuous learning and adaptability.

Though their direct interaction with library users might be limited, non-frontline staff play a pivotal role in cultivating a culture of kindness within the library. The manner in which they communicate with their frontline counterparts and manage internal operations significantly influences the overall atmosphere. It's essential to recognise the impact of these internal dynamics on the library's service quality and staff morale.

The wellbeing of non-frontline staff is equally important. Implementing workplace kindness and self-leadership programmes inclusively is vital to ensure the mental and emotional health of the entire library team. These initiatives should encompass all staff members, acknowledging that wellbeing in the workplace is a collective responsibility.

With the broadening scope of library services, effective succession planning becomes imperative. It is crucial to prepare non-frontline staff with leadership and crisis management skills, equipping them for potential transitions to frontline roles. Conversely, it's also essential to offer opportunities for frontline staff to understand and engage with the functions performed away from the public desk. This approach not only facilitates career progression within librarianship but also ensures that individuals from diverse backgrounds have the chance to explore and excel in various roles across the library sector.

This holistic approach to managing and developing non-frontline library staff is fundamental to the transformation of library services. It ensures that as libraries continue to evolve, they remain centres of knowledge, kindness and wellbeing, effectively serving their communities.

Community engagement, staff wellbeing and the synergy with PERMA and ASSET

Many librarians fear the changes to their roles, but community engagement is more than an outreach effort; it can serve as a source of wellbeing for library staff. This connects intricately with the PERMA and ASSET models, providing a comprehensive framework that explains why community engagement can be so rewarding for staff.

Community engagement areas connected to PERMA and ASSET
Meaning and accomplishment (PERMA)

Community engagement aligns strongly with the 'Meaning' and 'Accomplishment' aspects of the PERMA model. When staff see the tangible impact of their work in the community, whether through educational programmes, mental health initiatives or simple acts of kindness, it provides a sense of purpose. The community's appreciation and acknowledgement of the library's role can serve as validation, instilling a sense of pride and accomplishment among staff.

Support and emotional capital (ASSET)

From the ASSET perspective, the 'Support' element is reinforced through community engagement. When there's a reciprocal relationship between the community and the library staff, it can generate significant emotional capital. This support network acts as a buffer against the emotional and psychological demands of the job, potentially reducing stress and burnout.

Relationships (PERMA)

Community engagement also connects with the 'Relationships' element in the PERMA model. Engaging with a diverse group of individuals offers a rich experience and expands the social support network for staff. These interactions, whether with young learners, professionals or older people, provide a continuous learning opportunity, enriching the library staff's sense of community and belonging.

Adaptability and the changing role (ASSET)

ASSET focuses on 'Role' and 'Control' to complement the evolving nature of library work. As staff adapt to broader community responsibilities, clear role definitions and understanding community needs become crucial. In this regard, community engagement can offer insights that help adjust and shape these roles effectively, fulfilling the ASSET model's criteria for 'Role clarity' and 'Control'.

Community engagement isn't a one-way street; it benefits the library staff as much as it does the user. The example in Case Study 3.2 from Camden Libraries shows how innovative libraries can collaborate with other organisations. Through the PERMA and ASSET models' lenses, it becomes clear how this engagement enriches staff wellbeing. The sense of meaning, the support network, the accomplishment and the opportunity for continuous learning all contribute to making community engagement a pillar of staff wellbeing. As libraries strive to be more than just repositories of books, understanding this synergy can help create genuinely nurturing environments for everyone involved.

Case Study 3.2: Camden Libraries

Libraries have the focus of the Libraries Connected Universal Offers, Health and Wellbeing, Culture and Creativity, Reading and Information and Technology and library teams work with communities to make each library space welcoming and relevant to its locality. In Camden Libraries, we are working with the community and engaging through 'What if' imagination sessions to make connections and activate the library spaces. A couple of examples where Camden Libraries are working with community organisations are the pre-loved clothes rails which were installed during #GreenLibrariesWeek in October 2023 to support people living with poverty. The rails are at our Pancras Square Library, where Contact Camden, the Council's in-person customer service, operates. In the first two weeks of operation, 850 items were taken from the rails. Some of the stories and actions we have heard about are mothers accessing the rails, an asylum seeker, staff taking residents over following a meeting with Contact Camden, a person who said they had lost absolutely everything in a fire, a young person who was studying in the library asked if they could access the rails. Word is spreading that the rails are there and Council teams and security staff are saying it is being well received and they are proactively directing people to the rail. It is helping to soften the area next to Contact Camden, which can seem transactional, and it represents an offer of help. The rail was introduced by a community organisation from Somers Town called Life After Hummus who used pedal power to transport the items required for installation. Life After Hummus asked if the security officers minded people coming up to them and they said 'Not at all'. 'This is a very good thing', one of them said. 'I am really, truly pleased. And everyone is playing their part to keep it tidy.' Volunteers from Life After Hummus visit daily to top up the rails. Some of their volunteers are also Council staff. The plan is to create a donation point for Council staff to donate more items. We hope to develop more initiatives with Life After Hummus including a make and mend offer for the community. We already have a monthly make and mend at Swiss Cottage Library combined with a clothes swap, which is delivered by Friends of Earth Camden. Both these initiatives support libraries to be welcoming spaces.

Fiona Tarn, Head of Libraries, London Borough of Camden

Conclusion

To maintain libraries as thriving hubs of community wellbeing, it is vital to recognise the pivotal role played by the library staff in this transformation. By ensuring their wellbeing and continuously promoting kindness within the workplace, libraries can sustain the momentum towards nurturing spaces for all.

It's a challenging yet rewarding journey, inviting a collaborative spirit where the staff and the community learn and grow together, fostering a space rich with knowledge and resonating with kindness and wellbeing. Wellbeing is a complex concept that goes beyond individual actions and encompasses systemic changes. We will delve deeper into this topic in the upcoming chapters.

The library's role in our society has shifted beautifully and profoundly. No longer just silent repositories of books, they are now vibrant centres of community wellbeing and kindness. As we navigate the complexities of the modern world, it is comforting to know that our libraries are adapting to serve as beacons of hope, knowledge and community spirit.

Exercises and reflection points

Exercise for teams
'The Pillars of Wellbeing' exercise
Purpose: this exercise aims to create a structured dialogue between managers and team members regarding the challenges and needs of their wellbeing, thereby paving the way for actionable solutions.
Duration: approximately 60–90 minutes
Materials needed: flip chart or whiteboard; markers; sticky notes; pens.
Steps:

1 Introduction and setting the tone: begin by discussing the evolving role of libraries and its impact on staff wellbeing. Emphasise the importance of collective wellbeing for effective service delivery.
2 Identify the Pillars:
   - Draw four columns on a flip chart or whiteboard.
   - Label each column as one of the 'Four Pillars' of wellbeing: Physical, Emotional, Mental and Social.
3 Individual reflection: ask each team member to take a few minutes to write down the challenges they face in each pillar on sticky notes (one challenge per note).
4 Group sharing and discussion:
   - Invite team members to stick their notes under the appropriate pillars on the flip chart.
   - Facilitate a discussion around these challenges. Encourage team members to share experiences and possible solutions.
5 Identify trends: as the discussion progresses, mark any challenges that appear to be shared across the team. This helps in understanding systemic issues that might need addressing.
6 Generate action points: after discussing the challenges and trends, move towards solutions. Ask the team to suggest actionable steps that could address the identified challenges.
7 Assign responsibility and set deadlines: now that you have a list of actionable steps, assign responsibility for each action point and set reasonable deadlines.
8 Personal commitment: lastly, ask each team member to commit to improving their wellbeing in one area. It could be something like walking as part of their commute or setting boundaries to prevent work–life imbalance.

Conclusion and next steps: sum up the action points and commitments. Share the next steps, including how the team will follow up on these commitments.

Follow-up: conduct follow-up sessions to track the progress of the action points and personal commitments. This could be part of regular team meetings or designated wellbeing check-ins. Take note of successes and setbacks, adapting strategies as needed.

By making a concerted effort to address the wellbeing of your team, you're not just improving the quality of life for your staff but also contributing to the library's role as a community pillar. Remember, a team well in body and spirit is far more equipped to effectively serve their community's holistic needs.

Exercise for individuals

'Wellbeing Wheel' exercise (adapted from *Wheel of Life* by Paul J. Meyer, cited in Whitworth, Kimsey-House and Sandahl, 2007)

Purpose: this exercise aims to help you identify and balance the different aspects of your work and life, fostering your overall wellbeing.

Duration: approximately 30–45 minutes.

Materials needed: a large sheet of paper; coloured markers; sticky notes.

Steps:

1   Introduction: before you begin, take a moment to reflect on the importance of your wellbeing in the context of your multifaceted role in the library.
2   Draw the Wheel:
   - Draw a large circle on your sheet of paper and divide it into eight segments, much like a pie chart.
   - Label each segment with a different aspect that is relevant to your role and life, such as:
   — academic support
   — community programmes
   — personal development
   — mental health
   — physical health
   — interpersonal relations
   — skill development
   — recreation and leisure.
3   Self-assessment: for each segment, consider how much time and energy you currently dedicate to it. Shade each segment accordingly – the more filled it is, the more attention you give that area.
4   Reflection: take a few minutes to contemplate:
   - Which segments are most filled?
   - Which segments are lacking?
5   Discussion (self-dialogue): write down your reflections next to your wheel. Ask yourself how your professional responsibilities may be impacting your wellbeing. Are there any imbalances?
6   Action points: using sticky notes, jot down at least one action you can take to bring more balance to a segment that feels neglected. Place these notes next to the relevant segments on your wheel.
7   Conclusion: take a moment to consider the insights you've gained from this exercise. How can you integrate them into your daily life?

Follow-up: It might be beneficial to revisit your Wellbeing Wheel monthly to assess your progress on your action points. You may also adapt this exercise by incorporating other relevant segments over time, ensuring that the wheel remains a dynamic tool for your wellbeing.

By regularly practising this exercise, you will be better equipped to manage the complexities of your role in the library. Prioritising your wellbeing enables you to serve your community more effectively, maintaining the library as a sanctuary of knowledge, kindness and holistic wellbeing.

Reflective questions

- Your role in evolving libraries:
  - — How do you personally connect with the evolving role of libraries in society?
  - — What has been your most significant contribution to your library in the context of wellbeing and kindness?
- Staff wellbeing and you:
  - — How has your understanding of staff wellbeing changed after reading this chapter?
  - — What elements of the PERMA (Seligman, 2011, pp 16–25) and ASSET (Robertson and Cooper, 2011) models resonate most with you and how can you apply them in your current role?
- Personal understanding of kindness and wellbeing:
  - — What are your key takeaways about the importance of kindness in a library setting?
  - — Reflect on a time when you experienced or observed kindness in your library. How did it impact the atmosphere and the wellbeing of those present?
- The balancing act:
  - — How do you maintain a balance between providing diverse services and ensuring your own wellbeing?
  - — What strategies or methods have you employed or considered employing to prevent burnout?
- Community engagement:
  - — How have you engaged with your community to enhance your own sense of wellbeing and that of your colleagues?
  - — In what ways does community engagement align with or enhance the principles of the PERMA and ASSET models?
- Future goals:
  - — What immediate actions do you plan to integrate kindness and wellbeing into your library work?
  - — How do the insights from this chapter influence your long-term goals?

Feel free to use these questions as a personal reflection tool or a discussion guide for groups exploring the themes presented in the chapter.

CHAPTER 4

Meaning in Life and Purpose

Introduction

> If life has a meaning at all, there must be significance in suffering.
>
> Viktor Frankl (1946, 76)

Libraries are uniquely positioned to benefit from and contribute to the evolving focus on wellbeing and kindness. Central to this is the concept of finding meaning and purpose in one's work, an idea eloquently explored by Viktor Frankl. Frankl, a renowned psychiatrist and Holocaust survivor, posited that the primary human drive is not pleasure but the pursuit of what we find meaningful (Frankl, 1946). This perspective is especially relevant to library professionals whose roles often transcend mere occupational duties, touching the lives of individuals and communities in profound ways. Frankl's insights suggest that by finding meaning in their work, library professionals can not only enhance their own wellbeing but also significantly contribute to the wellbeing of their users.

The application of Frankl's philosophy in library settings is complex. It encompasses the personal fulfilment that library staff derive from their work, the sense of purpose found in aiding users' quests for knowledge and the broader impact of libraries as community hubs. In essence, libraries offer a unique confluence of personal and professional fulfilment, aligning closely with Frankl's views on the importance of finding meaning and purpose in life.

Thus, the integration of kindness and wellbeing into the fabric of library workplaces is not just a trend but a critical component of ensuring that these institutions remain vibrant, effective and meaningful places of work and community engagement. This chapter aims to explore these concepts further, delving into practical strategies and philosophies that can enhance the experience of both library professionals and their users.

The significance of meaningful work in libraries

The quest to understand life's significance has a rich historical and philosophical background. Philosophers such as Aristotle, Aquinas and Kant have deeply contemplated the meaning of life, each offering unique perspectives (Metz, 2021). Aristotle, for example, advocated that living well and doing good is the essence of life's meaning. In libraries, this philosophical tradition finds a practical application, as library work often aligns with doing good and living well through service and knowledge dissemination.

Shifting from philosophy to psychology, we find that life's meaning is considered a fundamental human driver. This concept is particularly relevant in the context of libraries. The work of key figures such as Jung (1933), Yalom (1980) and Frankl (1985) emphasises that life's significance plays a critical role in human behaviour, affecting everything from personal identity to the ability to endure hardships.

In libraries, this translates into the potential for meaningful interactions and services. The Meaning Maintenance Model (MMM), for instance, suggests that humans inherently seek meaning and strive to maintain it (Heine, Proulx and Vohs, 2006). This model can be applied to library environments, where staff members engage in meaningful work that resonates with their values and goals, thereby enhancing their sense of purpose and job satisfaction.

Library professionals play a pivotal role in creating meaningful experiences for themselves and their users. Models of significance in positive psychology, such as Martela and Steger's (2016) model, which breaks down meaning into coherence, purpose and significance, can be utilised in libraries. Library professionals, by aligning their work with these components, not only find personal fulfilment but also contribute significantly to the welfare of their communities.

Furthermore, the concept of Psychological Capital (PsyCap), which includes Hope, Efficacy, Resilience and Optimism (HERO) (Luthans, 2002), is highly relevant in library settings. The cultivation of these elements can lead to improved job satisfaction and performance among library staff, enhancing both personal wellbeing and the quality of services provided to users.

In summary, the significance of meaningful work in libraries is multi-dimensional, blending historical and philosophical insights with contemporary psychological theories. The application of these principles in library environments supports the creation of a workplace that is not only efficient and effective but also deeply fulfilling for both library professionals and their users.

Reflections

■ How do Aristotle's and Kant's philosophies on living well and doing good resonate with your experience as a library professional? Consider how your daily tasks and interactions in the library align with these philosophical views. Reflect on instances where your work has contributed to the wellbeing of others and your sense of living a good life.

▪ In what ways have you experienced the Meaning Maintenance Model (MMM) in your role? Reflect on moments when you have sought to find or maintain meaning in your work. Consider how these experiences have influenced your job satisfaction and your interactions with library users.

▪ How can you further develop and apply Psychological Capital (PsyCap) elements in your library work? Think about the HERO components: Hope, Efficacy, Resilience and Optimism. Reflect on how these elements currently manifest in your professional life and identify areas for growth. Consider specific strategies or actions you can take to strengthen these aspects of PsyCap in your work environment.

Librarianship as an identity and vocational awe

Librarianship, for some, is more than a profession: it is an identity and a calling. This deep sense of purpose and dedication is often described as 'vocational awe', a term that captures the reverence and admiration for the perceived higher purpose of the profession (Ettarh, 2018). Librarians see their roles not just as jobs but as integral parts of their identity, driven by a commitment to service, knowledge and community enrichment. This deep sense of purpose often intersects with personal and cultural identities, including race and ethnicity, and challenges librarians to navigate their professional identity within the context of broader societal structures (Haimé, 2023).

Vocational awe can significantly influence a librarian's sense of meaning in life. This concept ties closely with Frankl's (1946) theory that finding meaning is central to human existence. For librarians, this meaning is often found in the impact of their work – from aiding knowledge discovery to fostering community connections. The role of a librarian transcends conventional job responsibilities, becoming a key source of personal fulfilment and life satisfaction.

While vocational awe can be profoundly rewarding, it also has its challenges. It can lead to unrealistic expectations and pressures, where librarians feel compelled to go above and beyond, often at the expense of their wellbeing (Ettarh, 2018). Recognising and balancing vocational awe is crucial to maintain a healthy work–life harmony and to prevent burnout.

The importance of allyship (Haimé, 2023) can be integrated into the library profession's quest for meaning. Actively engaging in practices that promote diversity, equity and inclusion becomes a pivotal component of both personal and organisational wellbeing and kindness.

Emotional intelligence and empathy are essential skills in library environments, especially when considering diverse user communities (Salovey and Mayer, 1990). Haimé (2023) suggests that understanding and managing one's own emotions and those of others is vital in creating inclusive and supportive spaces. This directly contributes to the quality of service and the overall wellbeing of both staff and users.

The ethos of kindness and wellbeing is deeply embedded in librarianship. The profession's inherent focus on service and community engagement naturally cultivates an environment where kindness is both a tool and a goal. Sustaining this environment requires attention to the wellbeing of librarians themselves. Practising self-kindness and fostering a supportive workplace culture are essential to ensure that the vocational awe remains a source of joy and fulfilment, rather than a burden.

The concepts of compassion and self-compassion are further enriched when viewed through the lens of cultural awareness and allyship (Haimé, 2023; Neff, 2003a). Library professionals, in their quest to alleviate suffering, must recognise and respond empathetically to the diverse needs of users and colleagues, thereby enhancing the quality of service and the work environment.

Understanding librarianship as an identity and the phenomenon of vocational awe offers valuable insights into how this profession contributes to a librarian's sense of meaning in life. It underscores the importance of balancing professional dedication with personal wellbeing, ensuring that the noble pursuit of librarianship continues to be a source of kindness, fulfilment and community benefit.

Reflective questions

- Understanding vocational awe and personal identity:
  - How does the concept of vocational awe resonate with your personal experience in librarianship?
  - In what ways do you find your professional identity as a librarian intersecting with your personal and cultural identities, including aspects such as race and ethnicity?
- Finding meaning and purpose in librarianship:
  - Reflect on instances where you have found deep meaning in your work as a librarian. How have these moments contributed to your life satisfaction and sense of purpose?
  - How does Frankl's theory that finding meaning is central to human existence manifest in your day-to-day activities as a librarian?
- Challenges of vocational awe:
  - Can you identify moments when vocational awe led to unrealistic

expectations or pressures in your work? How did you address these challenges?
— What strategies do you employ to balance the deep sense of purpose in your work with your personal wellbeing and prevent burnout?
- Allyship in librarianship:
    — How do you integrate the principles of allyship in your role as a librarian? Consider specific actions you have taken or could take to promote diversity, equity and inclusion in your library.
    — Reflect on how actively engaging in allyship practices influences both your personal wellbeing and the organisational culture in your library.
- Emotional intelligence and empathy in library services:
    — In what ways do you apply emotional intelligence and empathy in your interactions with library users and colleagues, especially considering diverse communities?
    — How do these skills contribute to the quality of service and overall wellbeing of both staff and users in your library?
- Kindness and wellbeing in librarianship:
    — Reflect on how the ethos of kindness and wellbeing is manifested in your library. How do you contribute to sustaining this environment?
    — Consider the role of self-kindness and a supportive workplace culture in your professional life. How do these elements help in managing vocational awe?
- Compassion and self-compassion in a cultural context:
    — How do you practise compassion and self-compassion in your role, particularly through the lens of cultural awareness and allyship?
    — Reflect on instances where your understanding of compassion has helped you to respond empathetically to the diverse needs of your users and colleagues.

Character strengths and virtues in libraries

The **VIA framework** offers a comprehensive classification of character strengths and virtues (Peterson and Seligman, 2004). The VIA framework identifies 24 character strengths, categorised under six core virtues: wisdom and knowledge, courage, humanity, justice, temperance and transcendence. These strengths are seen as pathways to expressing virtues linked to our values and morals and they are not fixed traits but areas for potential excellence that can be cultivated over time. For library professionals, understanding and leveraging these character strengths is crucial. Recognising one's strengths, such as creativity, love of learning or social intelligence, can significantly impact job performance, satisfaction and social relationships. By focusing on these strengths, library staff can enhance their professional and personal development, contributing to a more positive and productive work environment.

Library professionals are encouraged to take assessments like the VIA Character Strengths assessment to identify their strengths (Peterson and Seligman, 2004). Reflecting on these results can help individuals align their work with their strengths, leading to greater job satisfaction and a more profound sense of purpose. Focusing on strengths, rather than solely on weaknesses, can yield substantial benefits for wellbeing in the library setting. Even perceived weaknesses can be reimagined as strengths that are either underused or overused (Peterson and Seligman, 2004). This strengths-based approach promotes a positive work culture, enhances teamwork and improves interactions with users.

By embracing the VIA framework and focusing on character strengths, library professionals can create a more fulfilling and effective work environment. This strengths-based approach not only benefits individual staff members but also enhances the overall quality of library services, ultimately contributing to the wellbeing of the community they serve.

Exercise for individuals
Strengths discovery and application in libraries
Objective: this exercise is designed to help library professionals identify their personal strengths and apply them in their daily work to enhance job satisfaction, teamwork and service delivery.
Materials needed: pen and paper or a digital device for note-taking; a quiet space for reflection.
Duration: approximately 45 minutes.
Instructions:

1 Personal reflection:
   - Spend 10 minutes quietly reflecting on your past experiences, both in and out of the library. Think about times when you felt most fulfilled, successful or proud of your achievements.
   - Write down these instances and note what skills or qualities you were using. Were you organising, problem-solving, empathising, leading, communicating or something else?
2 Identifying strengths:
   - From your reflections, identify key strengths that you frequently use or that bring you satisfaction. Aim to list at least five strengths.
   - These strengths could be anything from empathy and communication to leadership and creativity.

3 Application in library work:
- For each identified strength, think of ways you can apply it more effectively in your library role. For instance, if one of your strengths is empathy, consider how you can use this in customer service or team interactions.
- Write down specific actions or changes you can implement to leverage these strengths in your daily tasks and long-term projects.

4 Setting goals:
- Set clear, achievable goals for how you will use each strength in your work over the next month. These should be specific and measurable.
- For example, if a strength is creativity, a goal could be to propose and initiate a new programme or display in the library.

5 Review and reflect:
- After a month, take some time to review your progress against the goals you set. Reflect on any changes in your job satisfaction, the effectiveness of your work and the quality of your interactions.
- Adjust your goals and actions as needed based on this reflection.

Outcome: by the end of this exercise, library professionals will have a clearer understanding of their personal strengths and how they can be applied in a library setting. This self-driven approach encourages a deeper engagement with one's work, leading to improved job satisfaction, more effective teamwork and enhanced service delivery.

Psychological Capital (PsyCap) in library teams

The HERO Framework, which stands for Hope, Efficacy, Resilience and Optimism, is a core component of Psychological Capital (PsyCap). PsyCap, as defined within *Positive Organizational Behaviour* (Luthans, 2002), is concerned with leveraging human resource strengths and psychological capacities for performance optimisation in the workplace. This framework suggests that these four elements, when integrated, can significantly enhance job satisfaction and performance.

In library settings, applying the HERO framework can be transformative. Hope in this context means having a positive outlook for the future of the library and setting achievable goals. Efficacy refers to the belief in one's abilities to effect change and successfully execute tasks within the library. Resilience in libraries involves the ability to bounce back from setbacks, whether it's budget cuts or changes in technology. Optimism here is about maintaining a positive outlook towards the future of libraries and their role in society.

PsyCap is crucial for library teams, as it fosters a positive psychological state that evolves over time and is responsive to situations. Enhanced PsyCap in library staff leads to improved subjective wellbeing, job satisfaction and even health outcomes (Luthans, 2002). This is particularly important in libraries, where the nature of work often requires adaptability, continuous learning and dealing with diverse user needs.

Library leaders can incorporate PsyCap elements into their management and team-building strategies in various ways. For example, setting clear and achievable goals can boost hope, while providing training and resources can enhance self-efficacy. Encouraging a supportive environment where failures are viewed as learning opportunities can build resilience. Promoting a positive narrative about the role and future of libraries can foster optimism.

Finally, the HERO framework within Psychological Capital can be transformative in library settings, particularly when fostering a culture supportive of diversity and inclusion (Luthans, 2002; Haimé, 2023). This approach is crucial for library teams, as it fosters a positive psychological state that is responsive to the challenges and dynamics of diverse library environments.

By understanding and implementing the HERO framework of PsyCap, library teams can achieve higher levels of job satisfaction, better teamwork and improved performance. PsyCap offers a practical approach for library leaders to enhance the psychological wellbeing and effectiveness of their teams.

Emotional intelligence and empathy in library services

Emotional intelligence (EI) is a critical skill for library professionals, encompassing the ability to understand and manage one's own emotions and those of others. This skill is essential in library environments, where interactions with a diverse user base are frequent. EI in libraries contributes to improved communication, better understanding of user needs and more effective conflict resolution (Salovey and Mayer, 1990).

Developing EI and empathy involves several strategies that library professionals can employ:

- Self-awareness practices: encourage staff to engage in reflective practices to better understand their emotional responses and triggers.
- Empathy training: implement training sessions that focus on understanding and sharing the feelings of others, a key aspect of providing excellent customer service (Batson, 2006).
- Communication skills development: enhance interpersonal communication skills, which are vital in understanding and responding to users' emotional states.

High EI in library staff can lead to more positive interactions with users. Empathy, a component of EI, enables library professionals to connect with users on a deeper level, fostering a more welcoming and supportive environment. This, in turn, can lead to increased user satisfaction and loyalty.

Emotional intelligence and empathy are vital components in delivering exceptional library services. By developing these skills, library professionals can create a more positive, efficient and user-friendly environment. This not only benefits the users but also contributes to a more fulfilling and less stressful work environment for the staff.

Compassion and self-compassion in libraries

Compassion

Compassion, a fundamental human virtue recognised by philosophers such as Confucius, Buddha and Lao Zi (Schopenhauer, as discussed by Janaway, 1999), is crucial in library settings. It involves recognising suffering in others and feeling motivated to alleviate it. In libraries, this translates to understanding and responding empathetically to the needs of users and colleagues, thereby enhancing the quality of service and the work environment.

Psychological perspectives propose compassion as an emotional state that emerges when individuals witness the suffering of others, motivating them to alleviate that suffering (Goetz, Keltner and Simon-Thomas, 2010). This is particularly relevant in libraries, where staff often encounter users from diverse backgrounds and with varied needs. Exhibiting compassion can lead to more effective and empathetic user interactions.

Self-compassion

Self-compassion involves being kind to oneself in the face of failure or difficulty, an essential practice for library professionals (Neff, 2003a). This includes three main components: self-kindness, recognition of common humanity and mindfulness. These practices help library staff manage stress and maintain a positive outlook, ultimately reflecting in their interactions with users and colleagues. Self-compassion has been linked to numerous psychological benefits, including reduced anxiety and depression, improved emotional coping skills and better interpersonal relationships (Neff, 2003a). For library professionals, this means better job performance, reduced burnout and a more supportive work environment.

Incorporating compassion and self-compassion into library work can significantly enhance the wellbeing of library staff and the quality of service provided to users. By recognising and alleviating suffering, both in themselves and in others, library professionals can create a more empathetic, efficient and supportive library environment.

Conclusion

This chapter reveals that libraries are vital spaces where meaning, purpose and wellbeing converge. Influenced by various philosophical and psychological ideas, including Viktor Frankl's, libraries enrich both staff's and users' lives. They offer a platform for finding purpose and positively impacting communities. Librarians must balance professional dedication with personal wellbeing to avoid burnout. Applying positive psychology, such as character strengths and Psychological Capital, improves staff's professional and personal lives. Emotional intelligence and empathy are crucial for better user services and staff wellbeing. Overall, libraries blend personal fulfilment with meaningful community service, serving as hubs of human connection and growth.

Exercises and reflective questions

Exercise for teams

Reflective workshop on meaning and purpose in libraries

Objective: to facilitate a team discussion and reflection on the themes of meaning, purpose, wellbeing and kindness in library work, as outlined in the chapter.

Materials needed: a copy of this chapter, 'Meaning in Life and Purpose', for each participant; flip chart or whiteboard; markers and notepads.

Duration: 1–2 hours.

Instructions:

1 Pre-Workshop reading: ask each team member to read the chapter in advance and reflect on its key themes.
2 Group discussion: start with a round-table discussion where each member shares their thoughts on the chapter. Focus on how the concepts of meaning, purpose, wellbeing and kindness resonate with their experiences in the library.
3 Identify key themes: on a flip chart or whiteboard, list the key themes identified during the discussion, such as vocational awe, compassion or Psychological Capital.
4 Application in daily work: divide the team into smaller groups and assign each group a theme. Ask them to discuss and note down how this

theme can be applied in your library's daily operations and long-term goals.

5 Sharing Insights: reconvene and have each group present their insights and ideas. Discuss how these can be integrated into your library's culture and practices.

6 Action plan: as a team, develop an action plan based on the discussion. This could include new initiatives, changes in working practices or personal development goals.

Follow-up: schedule follow-up meetings to review the progress of the action plan and make adjustments as necessary.

Outcome: the team will have a deeper understanding of how the concepts from the chapter can be applied in their work, leading to a more meaningful, fulfilling and kind workplace culture.

Exercise for individuals

Personal reflection on meaning and purpose in library work

Objective: to encourage individual reflection on the themes of meaning, purpose, wellbeing and kindness in one's role as a library professional.

Materials needed: a copy of this chapter, 'Meaning in Life and Purpose'; journal or digital document for note-taking.

Duration: 30–60 minutes.

Instructions:

1 Read and reflect: read the chapter carefully, paying particular attention to how the various themes relate to your role in the library.

2 Journalling: use a journal or digital document to reflect on the following questions:
   ■ How do I find meaning and purpose in my library work?
   ■ In what ways do I contribute to the wellbeing and kindness in my workplace?
   ■ How do I experience vocational awe and how does it affect my work–life balance?
   ■ What are my strengths as a library professional and how can I use them more effectively?

3 Goal setting: based on your reflections, set personal goals that align with enhancing meaning, purpose, wellbeing and kindness in your work.

4 Implementation: develop a plan for how you will achieve these goals. This might include specific actions, learning new skills or seeking feedback and support from colleagues.

5 Review: regularly review your progress towards these goals and adjust your plan as needed.

Outcome: through this exercise, you will gain a deeper understanding of how the themes of the chapter apply to your work and life, leading to greater job satisfaction and personal growth.

Reflective questions

- How do you perceive the role of meaning and purpose in your daily work in the library? Reflect on specific instances where you felt your work transcended routine tasks and positively impacted individuals or your community.
- In what ways have you experienced or observed vocational awe in your library career? Consider both the positive aspects and the challenges it presents, such as unrealistic expectations or pressures and how you manage these dynamics.
- How can the concepts of Psychological Capital (Hope, Efficacy, Resilience, Optimism) be more actively integrated into your professional practice? Think about specific actions or strategies you can employ to strengthen these elements in your work environment.
- Reflect on your interactions with library users and colleagues. How do you apply emotional intelligence and empathy in these interactions and what impact does this have? Consider moments where these skills have been particularly beneficial or situations where you see room for improvement.
- Considering the principles of kindness and wellbeing discussed in the chapter, what steps can you take to further cultivate these values in your library setting? Think about both personal practices and team-based approaches that could enhance the overall environment of kindness and wellbeing in your workplace.

PART 2

Cultivating Kindness in the Library: A Holistic Approach to Wellbeing and Team Empowerment

In this section we explore the transformative power of kindness and wellbeing in library settings. Offering a blend of practical strategies and thoughtful practices, aimed at creating a supportive and nurturing environment for both librarians and library teams, each chapter is dedicated to balancing operational demands with the wellbeing of staff. Emphasising the importance of compassionate communication, advocating empathetic and non-violent interactions. Additionally, we highlight the significant benefits of flexible working, demonstrating how it can enhance both wellbeing and productivity. This section embodies the philosophy that a library's greatest strength lies not only in its books but in its commitment to fostering a culture of wellbeing, growth and kindness within its community, especially its staff.

CHAPTER 5

Integrating Kindness and Wellbeing into Library Operations: Practical Strategies and Reflective Practices

Introduction

> I've learned that people will forget what you said, people will forget what you did, but people will never forget how you made them feel.
>
> (Dr Maya Angelou, quoted in Booth and Masayuki, 2004, 14)

Kindness and wellbeing are interlinked and their practical applications in a library workplace setting are critical. Given the high-stress environment often prevalent in libraries, kindness becomes an ethical imperative and a significant contributor to organisational success. Kindness is now viewed as a critical component of leadership and team performance that positively influences wellbeing. A study by *Harvard Business Review* (Seppälä, 2014) suggests that leaders who exhibit kindness are more likely to boost employee engagement and productivity. Libraries are a microcosm for exploring these themes in depth, given their unique blend of organisational and community-serving roles.

This chapter will follow the journey of integrating kindness and wellbeing into library environments. We begin by exploring the crucial step of establishing kindness-centric policies and procedures. Regardless of the library type, be it public, business, corporate, health or university, the principles of promoting ethical conduct, inclusivity and standard operating procedures (SOPs) that prioritise kindness apply universally. This chapter explores the essential elements of creating such policies and procedures for libraries.

Once created, we focus on how these policies are translated into tangible actions and the everyday fabric of library life. From the theoretical foundations, we will seamlessly transition into the practical applications of these policies, providing a comprehensive view that encompasses everything from policy creation to real-life implications. By the end of this chapter, you will have a thorough understanding of how kindness and wellbeing can be effectively cultivated in libraries through thoughtful policy-making and dedicated implementation, ultimately enhancing the staff and user experience.

Theoretical foundations of kindness policies
Broaden-and-Build

The infusion of kindness and wellbeing into library operations is deeply rooted in psychological and organisational theories. The **Broaden-and-Build Theory** (Fredrickson, 2001) of positive emotions plays a crucial role in this context. This theory suggests that positive emotions broaden an individual's awareness and encourage novel, varied and exploratory thoughts and actions. Over time, as discussed in Chapter 1, this broadened behaviour builds skills and resources, contributing to personal and professional growth.

Now, let's apply the Broaden-and-Build Theory to our interactions with library users. As librarians, we aim to provide information and create a positive and supportive environment within the library. Here's how the theory becomes relevant:

- Broadening perspectives: positive interactions with users can broaden their perspectives. Feeling welcomed, heard and valued during their library visits opens their minds to exploring new subjects, resources and possibilities. This is particularly crucial in an educational setting, where intellectual curiosity should be nurtured.
- Building emotional resilience: positive emotions generated through compassionate interactions can contribute to emotional resilience. Users who experience kindness and support in the library will likely navigate challenges positively. They become better equipped to handle academic stress and setbacks, fostering emotional wellbeing.
- Enhancing social connections: the library can be more than just a place for individual study; it can be a hub for community and social connections. Positive interactions between users and library staff can lay the foundation for lasting social connections within the academic community. Users with positive experiences in the library are more likely to engage with their peers and form study groups or collaborative projects.
- Creating a happier community: applying the Broaden-and-Build Theory within the library context can contribute to a happier and more vibrant academic community. When the library is seen as a place where positive emotions and connections thrive, it becomes a resource for educational needs and personal wellbeing.

By recognising the power of positive interactions and applying the principles of the Broaden-and-Build Theory, we can transform our roles as librarians. We create a library environment that goes beyond the traditional resource centre concept and catalyses personal growth, emotional resilience and the development of a happier, more connected community.

Weak ties

Weak ties are our connections with people we don't know very well, like someone we chat with in a café or a person we see often at work but don't work with directly. Research shows that when we talk more to these people, even just a quick chat, we feel happier and more as though we belong. Specifically, in one study, participants who engaged in social interactions with a barista through actions like smiling, making eye contact and having a brief conversation (treating them as a weak social tie) reported higher levels of wellbeing and a sense of belonging compared to those who had a merely efficient, impersonal transaction (Sandstrom and Dunn, 2014; Sandstrom, Boothby and Cooney, 2022).

This means that when library staff are friendly and chat with the people who come in, everyone feels better. It's not just about giving out books or helping find information but also about smiling, looking people in the eye and chatting. This makes the library a better place to be.

Training library staff to recognise and value these interactions can be an effective strategy. This training can encourage staff to integrate these behaviours into their daily interactions with library users. Such an approach would not only improve library users' experience but could also increase job satisfaction among staff. This happens as the work environment becomes more connected and positive, fostering a sense of community and belonging.

Kind interactions workshop

A short exercise for training library staff to recognise and incorporate kindness in their daily interactions with users.

Duration: 30 minutes.

Objective: to help library staff understand the importance of kind interactions and how to integrate them into their daily routines with users.

Materials needed: flip chart or whiteboard; markers; pre-printed scenario cards.

Activity outline:

1 Introduction (5 minutes):
   - Briefly explain the purpose of the workshop.
   - Emphasise the impact of kind interactions on user experience and staff job satisfaction.
2 Group discussion (10 minutes):
   - Divide staff into small groups.
   - Each group discusses what kindness means to them and how it can be shown in a library setting.
   - Groups share their thoughts with the larger group.

3 Scenario role-play (10 minutes):
  - Hand out scenario cards, each depicting a different library user interaction (helping a user find a book, dealing with a frustrated user, etc.).
  - In pairs, staff role-play the scenarios, focusing on demonstrating kindness and positive communication.
  - Encourage creativity and empathy in responses.
4 Reflection and feedback (5 minutes):
  - Groups discuss what they learned from the role-plays.
  - Encourage staff to share how they could apply these kindness practices daily.
5 Closure:
  - Summarise key takeaways.
  - Remind staff that incorporating kindness into daily interactions can significantly enhance the library experience for users and staff.

This exercise aims to create a practical understanding of kindness in everyday interactions and inspire library staff to adopt a more empathetic and optimistic approach in their work environment.

Benefits of kindness policies

The application of kindness in library settings has far-reaching benefits. It creates a positive atmosphere, broadens employees' cognitive resources and contributes to building psychological resilience among employees, which is crucial in managing the stress and challenges inherent in library work. Stronger social connections fostered by kindness enhance teamwork and collaboration, which are vital in a library setting.

A kind and positive work environment for library users leads to kinder, more empathetic service, improving the overall user experience. Libraries prioritising kindness and wellbeing in their policies can become community hubs where everyone feels welcome, benefiting not just the users but also providing employees with a sense of purpose and connection to their community.

Case Study 5.1 is a real-life illustration of the principles discussed in the chapter. It shows how kindness and wellbeing initiatives in library settings (in this case, hospital libraries) can positively impact employees and users, fostering a healthier, more supportive environment.

Case Study 5.1: It's the little things . . .

Health and wellbeing delivered to hospital staff at Surrey and Sussex Hospitals NHS Trust

Our Library and Knowledge Services serve two busy hospital sites in Surrey and Sussex. We provide typical health library services supporting educational activities and underpinning the use of high-quality evidence in the Trust. Alongside the traditional library environment, our hospital libraries have a wellbeing area, boasting a wealth of calming and relaxing activities. These include colouring origami, a selection of public library books, a book swap and information about local activities. We want our space to be an area for relaxation and temporary reprieve from the exceedingly busy and challenging situations that healthcare staff deal with throughout their shift, an area in which to mentally and physically get away from it all as much as possible in the short time they have available. The space is almost always in use, as are the activities we put out. There is one element of the wellbeing area that has particularly taken off in popularity and that is our jigsaws. It doesn't matter what the design is (although the one with Lego people was completed in record time); staff members frequently concentrate on finding 'just one more piece' before the end of their break. It's a pleasure to see because you know that for a short period, nothing more is going through that person's head than the thought of where the next piece is – and whilst working in such highly pressurised circumstances and although it's seemingly such a little thing, isn't that few minutes of 'nothing' one of the most important services we provide?

Helen Allen and Holly Case Wyatt

Reflect on the theory using these prompts

Reflect on how the Broaden-and-Build Theory can be practically applied in day-to-day library operations. Consider specific strategies that can be used to foster positive emotions in users, such as creating welcoming spaces, offering personalised assistance and curating resources that inspire and engage.

Ponder the impact of positive interactions between library staff and users on building a stronger community. How can these interactions enhance the library experience and foster a sense of belonging and connection among users?

Consider the role of leadership in promoting a culture of kindness within the library. Reflect on how leaders can model kindness and wellbeing practices, set policies that reflect these values and encourage staff to engage in kind and empathetic interactions with users.

Contemplate the broader implications of implementing kindness policies in the library setting. How do these policies benefit not only the users but also the staff in terms of job satisfaction, team collaboration and overall wellbeing?

Policy development and strategic planning

The development of library kindness policies begins with a comprehensive approach that includes stakeholder engagement, empathy and inclusivity. It's essential to involve staff, users and other stakeholders in the policy revision process to ensure that the policies resonate with and are relevant to all those affected by them. This collaborative approach helps in creating policies that are not only inclusive but also reflective of the community's diverse needs.

Empathy is a critical factor in policy development. Libraries must understand and address their staff and users' diverse needs and backgrounds. This empathetic approach ensures that kindness policies go beyond mere statements, becoming actionable guidelines that positively impact everyday interactions and operations.

Strategic planning in the context of kindness policies involves setting clear objectives that align with the library's core mission and values. This process includes redefining existing policies to embed ethical considerations, advocating non-discrimination and promoting inclusivity. A crucial aspect of this planning is ensuring that the policies resonate with the library's mission, whether providing equal access to information, supporting patient care or enhancing academic achievement.

Effective strategic planning also involves evaluating existing operations and identifying areas for improvement. Regular policy audits and aligning policies with legal and ethical standards are essential steps in this process. These actions ensure libraries remain dynamic and adaptable to changing needs and technology.

Case Study 5.2, on Royal Holloway's library transition is a testament to the importance of user-centred design and policy development in academic libraries. It highlights the significance of stakeholder engagement, empathy, inclusivity, strategic planning and adaptability. The journey, while challenging, offered valuable insights into managing change and emphasised the dynamic relationship between space design and user interaction. This case study is a model for other institutions aiming to develop effective, relevant policies that reflect their community's needs.

Case Study 5.2: Library zoning and user experience at Royal Holloway University

Whilst I was working there, in 2017, Royal Holloway, University of London, underwent a significant transition, moving its library services to a new building, the Davison Building. This case study encapsulates the essential elements of policy development and strategic planning in the context of fostering kindness and inclusivity in library settings.

Engagement and empathy

Central to the success of the new library's design was the active involvement of students. The university committed to understanding and addressing diverse needs by engaging them in focus groups and advisory committees. This approach aligns with key principles of policy development, where stakeholder engagement and empathy are crucial. The feedback gathered was instrumental in shaping a library space that was not only functional but also resonated with the students' sense of comfort and belonging.

The transition to the new library was marked by efforts to accommodate various study preferences, embodying the inclusivity aspect of kindness policies. The aim was to create a space welcoming all users, including those with disabilities. This approach mirrored the strategic objective of creating a comfortable, spacious and intuitive environment, aligning with the library's core mission of supporting academic achievement and catering to evolving user needs.

The strategic planning for the new library involved setting clear objectives based on user feedback. The real test came post-opening when the library faced unexpected challenges regarding zoning. Despite the intuitive design, some students needed clarification on the zoning, leading to negative feedback. The library's response to this feedback – introducing clear signage for zoning – demonstrated adaptability and a user-centric approach. This response was crucial in refining the library's strategy and enhancing user satisfaction, underscoring the importance of flexibility in policy implementation.

Helen Rimmer

Leadership's role in policy implementation

The role of leadership in embedding kindness and wellbeing in the library culture is pivotal. It is explored in more detail in Part 3. Leaders' behaviour, attitudes and decisions significantly influence how policies are interpreted and implemented at every level. Case Study 5.3, an example from Lancaster University, shows how simple actions can support a culture of kindness and improve wellbeing.

Case Study 5.3: Using Microsoft Teams to build community

Our Library Director posts a weekly Friday update on our Teams site, where they give an overview of their week and share news and upcoming events. They also make a point of recognising colleagues' work and celebrating the team's achievements. There is often a personal element, too, which is important in setting a tone around work–life balance. A frequently used sign-off is 'thank you for all you do'. In terms of culture, this sets a positive tone in terms of openness, transparency and recognising the contributions of the entire library team.

I'm a recent arrival in the team. Still, compared to other places where I have worked, Teams is used very effectively to build community. We have channels for wellbeing and non-work-related discussion and staff at all grades have engaged with this. There are also channels for specific teams and areas of work. The weekly updates from our Director set a clear example. As a result, our Teams community is regularly used to praise colleagues and share successes, which helps to support a kind and collegiate culture.

Tim Leonard, Lancaster University

Leadership in this context goes beyond just endorsing policies; it involves actively modelling the behaviours and attitudes the policies are designed to promote. This includes showing empathy, practising inclusivity and demonstrating ethical standards in all interactions and decisions. Library leaders are crucial in navigating complex situations with a clear moral compass, reducing dilemmas and conflicts and leading by example to create a harmonious work environment.

Leaders are responsible for modelling the behaviours and values outlined in kindness policies. This involves adhering to these policies and actively demonstrating kindness in day-to-day interactions. By doing so, leaders can inspire their staff to embody these values in their interactions with colleagues and users.

Effective leadership also means fostering an environment where kindness is valued and recognised. This can involve acknowledging and rewarding acts of kindness among staff, reinforcing the importance of these behaviours. Leaders can also set the tone by facilitating regular discussions and workshops that help align the understanding and application of kindness values across the library.

Reflective questions
- How do I, as a leader, embody the role of a cultural ambassador in my library?
- How do my decisions, attitudes and behaviour influence the library's culture and the implementation of kindness and wellbeing policies?
- To what extent do I actively model the behaviours and attitudes our kindness policies advocate for?
- How do I demonstrate empathy, inclusivity and ethical standards in my daily interactions and decisions?
- How do I inspire and encourage my staff to practise kindness in their daily interactions?

- How do I acknowledge and reward acts of kindness among staff and how effectively do I facilitate discussions and workshops to align everyone with these values?
- How do I create a harmonious and positive work environment through my leadership?
- How do I handle conflicts and challenges while focusing on kindness and empathy and how does this impact my team and the library environment?

Practical application of kindness policies

The actual test of kindness policies lies in their practical application within the library's daily operations. This involves embedding the principles of kindness and wellbeing into every aspect of library service, from user interactions to staff collaboration. Policies should be more than documents; they must become part of the fabric of the library's culture, influencing how decisions are made and how people are treated daily. I would also recommend that when you have written out a policy and read it back out loud, you need to be comfortable that anything you cover you could say to a user or colleague's face. For example, this is particularly relevant around behaviour or colleague-facing policies such as bereavement or sickness.

One practical approach is the implementation of standard operating procedures (SOPs) that prioritise psychological safety and wellbeing. These SOPs can guide interactions, ensure respectful and empathetic service and create a supportive environment for staff and users.

Staff training and communication

Effective implementation of kindness policies requires comprehensive staff training and effective internal communication. Training sessions should focus on developing skills that align with the core values of kindness, such as empathetic communication, inclusive service and collaborative teamwork. This training helps staff understand and internalise the importance of these values in their daily work.

Internal communication strategies are also crucial in reinforcing the culture of kindness. Regular updates, sharing success stories and open channels for feedback contribute to a supportive and engaged workplace. Continuous education and workshops keep staff aligned with the library's mission and values, fostering a culture of constant improvement.

Case Study 5.4: University of Westminster Library – fines policy

A great example of kindness in action is the University of Westminster Library's approach to fines. Recognising the stress that fines can cause students, especially those facing financial challenges, the library leadership decided to review its fines policy and abolish them, replacing them with borrowing blocks. This created a more equitable approach where everybody had the same experience regardless of whether they could pay the fines.

The impact of this policy change was profound. It decreased stress levels among students, particularly those who were financially disadvantaged. The library saw an increase in the use of its resources and an improvement in the relationship between library staff and students. This case study demonstrates how a policy rooted in kindness can have a tangible positive impact on the wellbeing of library users, fostering a more inclusive and supportive learning environment.

Strategically, abolishing these fines is complex, especially considering they serve as a significant source of income for the universities. For instance, when Canterbury Christ Church University decided to abolish library fines in February 2023, they discovered that 445 library users had accumulated fines totalling £4,899.80 (Canterbury Christ Church University, 2023).

This action, along with the findings from *The Tab*'s (Snepvangers, 2023) investigation into the substantial £7 million fines charged by Russell Group Universities over the past ten years, highlights the amount of revenue potentially lost by abolishing fines. Abolishing fines and instead implementing alternative penalties, such as borrowing blocks, ensures a more equitable system. It places all users on an equal footing, regardless of their financial situation.

This approach aligns with the principles of kindness and fairness in policy-making, ensuring that access to library resources is not hindered by financial constraints. Such policies are vital in transforming library environments into ones where wellbeing and kindness are prioritised, reflecting a commitment to creating a supportive and inclusive academic community.

Helen Rimmer

Exercise for teams

Reflective scenario analysis

Objective: to deepen understanding of how kindness policies translate into daily practices and their impact on staff and users in a library setting.

Duration: 45 minutes.

Materials needed: printed scenarios (provided below), writing materials and a comfortable space for discussion.

Instructions:

1 Divide into small groups: form groups of 3–4 participants. Each group will receive a different scenario relating to the practical application of kindness policies in a library setting.
2 Scenario analysis: each group will read their scenario and discuss the following points:
   ■ How does the scenario reflect the implementation of kindness policies?
   ■ Identify the challenges and benefits presented in the scenario.
   ■ Discuss how staff training and communication strategies could be improved in the given situation.
3 Group reflection: after 20 minutes of discussion, reconvene as a larger group. Each small group will present their scenario and share their insights. Encourage open dialogue and constructive feedback from the whole group.
4 Personal reflection: individually, participants will take 10 minutes to write down their thoughts on applying the insights gained from this exercise to their professional practices.
5 Group commitment: conclude the session by collaboratively developing a set of actionable steps that can be taken to integrate kindness and wellbeing into daily operations further.

Scenarios for discussion:
■ Scenario A – user interactions: a library staff member encounters a user who is visibly upset about being unable to find a specific resource. The staff member applies principles of empathetic communication to assist and comfort the user.
■ Scenario B – staff collaboration: library staff members disagree on organising a community event. They use collaborative teamwork and inclusive service principles to reach a consensus that respects everyone's viewpoints.
■ Scenario C – fines policy change: reflect on the University of Westminster Library's approach to abolishing fines in Case Study 5.4. Discuss how this decision impacts student wellbeing and library operations.
■ Scenario D – Internal communication: a new policy is introduced in the library. Explore strategies for effectively communicating this change to all staff members, ensuring understanding and alignment with the library's values of kindness.

Aligning values with kindness and wellbeing in library operations

Embedding core values such as kindness and wellbeing in daily practices creates a positive and inclusive working culture. This integration extends from policy adaptation to interpersonal interactions and is underpinned by continuous training and development.

Introducing core values into library practices is more than a gesture; it's a shift in operational philosophy. For instance, policies can be restructured to reflect inclusivity and empathy, ensuring these principles permeate even routine procedures (Brown and Treviño, 2006). Regarding the staff and user interactions, every exchange should be conducted with a baseline of respect and understanding, fostering a climate where kindness is not just an abstract value but a lived experience.

Ongoing training sessions are crucial in developing skills and behaviours that align with these core values. Workshops focusing on empathetic communication, inclusive service and collaborative teamwork can significantly enhance the capacity of library staff to embody these values in their daily work (Goleman, 1998).

Empathy, respect, collaboration, inclusivity and balance are not just words but actionable values that can dramatically improve the work environment. Empathy encourages staff to be more understanding and supportive, while respect ensures everyone feels valued and heard (Deci and Ryan, 2000). Collaboration can lead to shared success and a heightened sense of community and inclusivity allows for a diverse and vibrant workplace. Maintaining work and personal life balance is crucial in preventing burnout and ensuring staff wellbeing (Greenhaus and Allen, 2011).

Maintaining these core values is challenging. Resource limitations, resistance to change and varied interpretations of values can pose significant hurdles. Strategies such as prioritising impactful initiatives, involving staff in the change process and ensuring clear benefits. Good communication can mitigate these challenges (Kotter, 1996). Regular discussions and workshops can help align the understanding and application of these values across the library.

Continuous training is essential in reinforcing the importance of these values and developing the necessary skills for their application. Open communication channels where staff can voice concerns, suggest improvements and share successes are also vital. Periodic reviews and realignments through surveys and feedback sessions can ensure that the library's operations and culture continue to evolve in alignment with its core values (Schein, 2010).

Incorporating kindness and wellbeing into the library's operational fabric is a journey that requires dedication and adaptability. By embedding these core values into everyday practices, proactively addressing challenges and continuously striving for alignment, libraries can foster a work environment that supports professional growth and enriches the user experience.

Reflective questions about values

- Reflecting on empathy and respect: consider a recent interaction you had in the library, either with a colleague or a user. How did you apply empathy and respect in this interaction? Were there aspects of the exchange where these values could have been better represented? Reflect on how empathy and respect can transform everyday interactions into positive experiences.
- Challenges in value integration: think about a situation where it was challenging to maintain the core values of empathy, respect, collaboration, inclusivity or balance due to external pressures or internal conflicts. What were the main obstacles and how did you address them? Discuss the importance of maintaining these values even when faced with challenges.
- Continuous improvement and training: reflect on your most recent training session about kindness and wellbeing. How has this training influenced your daily work practices? Are there specific skills or behaviours you learned that you have successfully integrated into your routine? What areas require further development?
- Strategies for overcoming resistance: change often meets resistance. Have you encountered resistance (either within yourself or from others) to the integration of these core values in library operations? How did you address this resistance? What strategies can encourage a more universal acceptance and implementation of these values in the library environment?

Measuring impact and continuous improvement

The evaluation of kindness policies is essential to understand their effectiveness in improving staff wellbeing, enhancing the user experience and positively influencing the library environment. This can be achieved through various surveys, UX observations, feedback sessions and performance metrics. Surveys can be conducted periodically to gauge staff morale and job satisfaction. At the same time, user feedback can provide insights into their experience and the quality of service received.

Monitoring specific performance indicators can also provide valuable data. For instance, measuring changes in user engagement, library attendance and resource utilisation can offer quantitative evidence of the impact of kindness policies. Additionally, observing changes in staff turnover rates and absenteeism can indicate the policies' effects on employee wellbeing.

Continuous improvement is crucial for ensuring the long-term success of kindness policies. This requires regular assessment and the willingness to adapt policies in response to changing needs and feedback. Libraries should establish a feedback loop where staff and users can express their opinions and suggestions for improvements. This could involve regular staff meetings, user forums or anonymous feedback channels. Continuous improvement also involves staying informed about new library developments and integrating these insights into policy refinement. This proactive approach ensures that the library remains a dynamic and responsive environment, capable of adapting to new challenges and opportunities.

The journey of integrating kindness and wellbeing into library environments encompasses several key themes that have emerged as central to our discussion:

- Significance of policy formulation: developing kindness-centric policies is foundational in creating a culture of wellbeing in libraries. These policies, grounded in psychological and organisational theories, set the stage for transformative change, guiding the behaviour and attitudes of both staff and users.
- Leadership's role: effective leadership is crucial in translating policies into practice. Leaders endorse these policies and model the behaviours and values they embody. Their active involvement and commitment to kindness and wellbeing are instrumental in shaping the library's culture.
- Practical application: implementing kindness policies in daily operations reflects their actual effectiveness. This involves embedding kindness in staff interactions, user services and overall operational procedures, making it a lived reality within the library environment.
- Continuous improvement: evaluating these policies and practices is vital for their sustained impact. Regular assessment and adaptation ensure that the policies remain relevant and effective in promoting staff wellbeing and enhancing the user experience.

Conclusion

Implementing kindness and wellbeing policies in libraries is crucial for a positive, productive environment, improving staff and user wellbeing and fostering respect and inclusivity. As library management evolves, future strategies might involve advanced evaluation methods, technological enhancements and deeper psychological insights. Continuously adapting kindness and wellbeing practices is critical to maintaining libraries as informative and supportive community hubs. This ongoing process demands dedication and creativity to ensure libraries are spaces where kindness and wellbeing thrive.

Exercises and reflective questions

Team training exercise
Kindness brainstorming workshop
Objective: to collaboratively identify and develop strategies for embedding kindness and wellbeing into library operations.
Duration: 1½ hours.
Materials needed: whiteboard or large paper sheets, markers, sticky notes and a comfortable meeting space.
Instructions:

1 Introduction (15 minutes):
  ■ Start with a brief discussion on the importance of kindness and wellbeing in the library, using Maya Angelou's quote (p. 77) to inspire the conversation.
  ■ Explain the workshop's purpose: to generate practical ideas for incorporating kindness into daily library operations.
2 Idea generation (30 minutes):
  ■ Divide the team into small groups. Each group focuses on a specific area of library operations (e.g., user services, staff collaboration, policy implementation).
  ■ Groups brainstorm ways to integrate kindness and wellbeing into their assigned area, writing ideas on sticky notes and sticking them on the whiteboard or paper sheets.
3 Gallery walk and idea expansion (20 minutes):
  ■ Participants walk around and review the ideas generated by other groups.
  ■ Please encourage them to add additional thoughts or expand on existing ideas using markers.
4 Group discussion and refinement (20 minutes):
  ■ Reconvene as a whole group. Discuss the ideas, combining similar ones and elaborating on the most promising strategies.
  ■ Focus on practicality and feasibility, considering the unique dynamics of the library environment.
5 Action plan development (15 minutes):
  ■ As a team, select the top ideas to be implemented.

- Develop a basic action plan for each selected idea, assigning responsibilities and setting tentative timelines.
6 Conclusion:
    - Summarise the workshop outcomes, highlighting the commitment to integrating kindness into the library's culture.
    - Schedule a follow-up meeting to review the progress of the action plans.

Workshop focus areas:
- User services: ideas for enhancing user experiences through empathetic service, inclusive practices and proactive engagement.
- Staff collaboration: strategies for fostering a supportive work environment, encouraging teamwork and resolving conflicts with kindness.
- Policy implementation: ways to ensure kindness and wellbeing are reflected in library policies and SOPs.

This workshop aims to harness the collective creativity and insights of the library staff, creating actionable steps to make kindness and wellbeing a tangible part of the library's daily operations.

Individual exercise
Reflective journalling
Objective: to encourage self-reflection on personal values and behaviours related to kindness and wellbeing.
Duration: 30 minutes.
Materials needed: journal or paper; pen.
Instructions:

1 Reflective prompts: participants will spend 30 minutes journalling their thoughts using the provided prompts. The focus should be on personal experiences, feelings and ideas on integrating kindness into their daily library work.
2 Prompts:
    - Describe a recent situation where you could have shown more kindness in the library. How would you handle it differently now?
    - Reflect on when someone's kindness in the library significantly impacted you. How did it influence your perception of the workplace?
    - Think about your interactions with users. How can you apply Dr Maya Angelou's philosophy to make their library experience more memorable?

- Consider your teamwork within the library. How can kindness improve collaboration and communication with your colleagues?
3 Personal action plan: based on the reflections, each participant will create a short action plan on applying these insights to enhance kindness and wellbeing in their daily roles.

Reflective questions

- Contemplate the wider implications of implementing kindness policies in the library setting. How do these policies benefit not only the users but also the staff in terms of job satisfaction, team collaboration and overall wellbeing?
- Reflect on how core values such as empathy, respect, collaboration, inclusivity and balance are integrated into your daily library operations. How do these values influence decision-making, user interactions and the workplace environment?
- Think about any challenges you have faced in embedding kindness and wellbeing in library operations. How did you address these challenges and what lessons did you learn that could be applied in the future?
- Reflect on how you can measure the impact of kindness and wellbeing initiatives in your library. What metrics or feedback mechanisms could you use to assess their effectiveness and make informed improvements?
- Consider your personal role in fostering kindness and wellbeing in the library. How do your actions, interactions and leadership style contribute to creating a positive and supportive environment?

CHAPTER 6

Prioritising Self-Care and Compassion: The Key to Nurturing Library Environments

Introduction

In order to feel compassion for other people, we have to feel compassion for ourselves.

(Pema Chödrön, quoted in Calder, n.d.)

As we continue our exploration of kindness and wellbeing in libraries, this chapter turns its focus to the linchpins of a nurturing library environment: self-care and self-compassion. Within libraries, the wellbeing of our staff is paramount. This chapter shows how prioritising self-care and fostering a compassionate culture can transform our libraries. It's about ensuring those dedicated to serving the community are supported and empowered in their personal and professional growth.

Changing the world of work into one of kindness is not always easy. In some organisations, you will challenge a status quo that has served those in leadership well and given them power. That is why embracing a holistic approach to self-care that includes self-compassion is essential. Dr Kristin Neff's (2003a and 2003b) pioneering work on self-compassion provides a particularly resonant framework for library professionals who strive to be change-makers.

In this context, self-care and compassion emerge as essential tools. Self-care involves taking deliberate actions to care for our mental, emotional and physical health. It's about recognising our own needs and taking steps to meet them. Compassion, especially self-compassion, is about treating ourselves with the same kindness and understanding we would offer a friend in distress.

Why are these concepts crucial in libraries? Because they help staff manage stress, adapt to change and maintain a high level of service. When library staff feel supported and cared for, they are better equipped to serve the community effectively and contribute to a positive, innovative library environment.

The significance of self-care, self-compassion and compassion

The foundations of self-care and compassion in library settings are strong. Central to this is Kristin Neff's ideas around self-compassion, crucial for fostering a positive, caring work atmosphere. Neff (2003b) identifies three main aspects of self-compassion: kindness to oneself, recognising our shared human experience and staying mindfully aware. These are especially relevant for library staff dealing with the pressures of leading change and providing both emotional and intellectual support.

Self-kindness here means accepting the challenges of change and adopting a supportive inner voice, rather than being self-critical. For library workers, this means valuing their efforts and learning from experiences without blaming themselves.

Recognising our shared human experience, the foundations of compassion, is about seeing that difficulties are common, not isolated, fostering a sense of community and mutual support among library professionals. It encourages sharing and learning from each other's resilience tactics.

Being mindfully aware involves being conscious of our thoughts and feelings without getting too caught up in them. Practically, this could involve using mindfulness techniques during the working day to handle the emotional demands of library roles.

Psychological safety

Psychological safety (Edmondson, 1999) is a critical aspect of workplace culture. It refers to an individual's perception of the consequences of taking an interpersonal risk. In a psychologically safe environment, staff members feel comfortable being themselves, expressing their thoughts and opinions without fear of negative consequences to their self-image, status or career. Just as kindness is more than being nice so is psychological safety; in fact in psychologically safe environments discomfort is seen as a catalyst for growth and innovation and welcomed.

In the context of libraries, where adapting to new technologies and evolving community needs is a constant, psychological safety becomes especially important. It allows staff to feel secure enough to take risks, try new approaches and learn from mistakes without the fear of being punished or ridiculed. This fosters an environment of open communication, innovation and continuous learning.

The concept complements self-compassion, as both encourage an atmosphere of understanding and respect for personal limitations and challenges. Self-compassion involves being kind to oneself in the face of failure or difficulty, which aligns with the principles of psychological safety that encourage a non-punitive, supportive response to risks and mistakes. In essence, psychological safety supports a work culture where staff can confidently navigate changes and challenges, knowing they have the support and understanding of their colleagues and leaders. This is essential for libraries to remain relevant and effective in their service to the community.

Emotional Labour Theory

Emotional Labour Theory (Hochschild, 1983) is also relevant. Library staff frequently have to manage their emotions as part of their job, making self-care and compassion important to offset the potential negative effects of this emotional work.

Research underlines the importance of these theories for workplace wellbeing. For example, Monroe et al. (2021) discovered that healthcare staff who practised mindfulness, a key aspect of self-compassion, reported greater job satisfaction and less burnout. This highlights the value of self-care and compassion in maintaining the wellbeing of library staff, helping them to innovate and serve effectively.

The theoretical structure for self-care and compassion in libraries is reinforced by psychological safety, self-compassion and emotional labour theories. Backed by research, these theories provide a solid basis for appreciating the need for such practices in the challenging, dynamic environment of libraries.

Practical applications

Building on the theoretical foundation of self-care and compassion, we now explore practical strategies that can be implemented in libraries. These approaches foster a culture of wellbeing and resilience among library staff, effectively translating theory into action. Offering a range of activities is essential, as no one size fits all:

- Mindfulness training: implement regular mindfulness sessions, such as guided meditation or breathing exercises, to help staff manage stress and enhance focus (see the self-compassion pause below).
- Peer support groups: establish peer support groups for staff to share experiences and coping strategies, fostering a sense of community and shared resilience. This is particularly effective if the group is made up of people from different teams and different grades.

- Professional development in emotional intelligence: offer training to improve emotional intelligence, aiding staff in understanding and managing emotions effectively.
- Flexible work schedules: provide flexible working hours to help staff balance personal and professional life, reducing stress and improving overall wellbeing.
- Regular check-ins and feedback: conduct regular wellbeing check-ins and provide platforms for staff feedback, promoting psychological safety and a sense of being valued.
- Wellbeing resources and workshops: offer access to wellbeing resources like counselling and self-care workshops, supporting staff mental health and resilience.
- Recognition and appreciation programmes: develop programmes to recognise and appreciate staff efforts, reinforcing their value to the organisation.
- Physical wellbeing initiatives: to address physical health, introduce physical wellbeing initiatives, including yoga classes or ergonomic assessments.
- Conflict resolution training: provide training in conflict resolution, equipping staff with skills to manage workplace conflicts with empathy.
- Library staff retreats: organise retreats or team-building activities to provide a break from routine and strengthen team bonds.
- Resilience workshops: conduct workshops on building resilience and teaching coping strategies for change, adversity and stress.
- Skills development opportunities: offer opportunities for staff to learn new or enhance existing skills, boosting confidence and a sense of accomplishment.
- Mindset and attitude training: facilitate sessions on developing a growth mindset and positive attitude, essential for resilience in challenging situations.
- Community involvement projects: encourage participation in community projects, which can provide a sense of purpose and connection, reinforcing resilience.

By integrating these strategies, libraries can create a nurturing environment that prioritises staff wellbeing, fosters resilience and promotes a culture of self-care and compassion. This holistic approach benefits the individual employees and contributes to the library's overall effectiveness and service quality.

Just as you can lead a horse to water but not make it drink, you can create and offer wellbeing initiatives and not everyone will interact. This is okay.

Self-compassion pause

A particularly effective mindful activity for cultivating self-compassion is the 'Self-compassion pause.' This activity is designed to be simple yet powerful, helping individuals foster a more compassionate and understanding relationship with themselves, especially during stress or difficulty. Here's how to practise it:

1 Find a quiet moment: begin by finding a quiet moment in your day. This could be a brief break during work or a quiet time at home. Sit or stand in a comfortable position.
2 Acknowledge the moment: recognise that you are experiencing a moment of difficulty or stress. This could be feeling overwhelmed, frustrated or anxious. Acknowledge this feeling without judgement.
3 Place a hand over your heart: gently place a hand over your heart. The physical touch is a powerful way to bring kindness to your experience. Feel the warmth of your hand and the gentle pressure on your chest.
4 Breathe deeply: take a few deep, slow breaths. Inhale compassion and kindness for yourself and exhale any tension or harshness you might be feeling.
5 Speak kindly to yourself: silently offer yourself some kind words, as you would to a good friend. You might say, 'It's okay,' 'I'm here for you,' or 'I am doing my best.' Choose phrases that resonate with you and offer comfort.
6 Expand your awareness: remind yourself that you are not alone in these feelings. Others have felt this way before and it's a shared human experience. This perspective can reduce feelings of isolation.
7 Release and return: take a few more deep breaths, then gently release your hand from your heart. As you return to your day, carry this sense of self-compassion with you.

Application in libraries: in a library setting, staff can use the self-compassion pause during challenging interactions, when faced with setbacks or simply as a regular practice to maintain a compassionate stance towards themselves. This practice can be particularly helpful in managing the emotional labour often involved in library work. By regularly engaging in this exercise, library professionals can cultivate a more compassionate and understanding attitude towards themselves, enhancing their overall wellbeing and ability to provide empathetic services to others.

Mindset and attitude training

An effective exercise for mindset and attitude training, focused on developing a growth mindset and positive attitude, is the 'Challenge-Response-Reframe' exercise (adapted from *Reframing Unhelpful Thoughts,* NHS, n.d.). This exercise encourages individuals to reframe challenges as opportunities for growth, fostering resilience and a positive outlook in the face of adversity. Here's how to conduct it:

Objective: to transform how individuals perceive and respond to challenges, shifting from a fixed mindset to a growth mindset.

Materials needed: notebook or journal; pen or pencil.

Steps:

1 Identify a challenge: start by identifying a recent challenge or a situation that felt difficult. It could be a work-related issue, a personal setback or any situation that prompted a negative response.
2 Describe your initial response: reflect on your initial response to this challenge. How did you feel? What thoughts went through your mind? Write these down in your notebook. Be honest and don't hold back – this is for your eyes only.
3 Analyse the fixed mindset: look at your written response and identify any signs of a fixed mindset. This might include thoughts like 'I can't do this,' 'It's too hard,' or 'I'll never be good enough.' Acknowledge these thoughts.
4 Shift to a growth mindset: now, challenge yourself to reframe these thoughts from a growth mindset perspective. For each fixed mindset thought, write a corresponding growth mindset response. For example, instead of 'I can't do this,' write 'I can learn how to do this with time and effort.'
5 Visualise a positive outcome: imagine facing this challenge with your new growth mindset responses. Visualise how you would act and feel differently. Write down what a successful outcome might look like.
6 Reflect on learning and growth: finally, reflect on what you can learn from this exercise. How can this challenge help you grow? What skills or strengths can you develop through this experience?
7 Regular practice: make this exercise a regular practice. Whenever you face a new challenge, take a moment to go through this process. Over time, it will help shift your mindset and attitude towards challenges.

This exercise can benefit staff dealing with evolving technologies, changing user needs or any work-related challenges in a library environment. Facilitating group sessions where staff can share and discuss their reflections can further enhance the collective growth mindset and foster a supportive, resilient workplace culture. By consistently practising the Challenge-

Response-Reframe exercise, library professionals can develop a more resilient and positive approach to challenges, transforming obstacles into opportunities for personal and professional growth.

Self-care isn't self-indulgence

Self-care and self-indulgence, though sometimes mistaken for one another, are distinct concepts with different impacts on an individual's wellbeing, especially in high-demand environments like libraries.

Self-care is a deliberate activity that we engage in to provide our physical, mental and emotional wellbeing with proper nourishment and care. It's about taking the time to attend to our personal needs in a way that replenishes our energy and strengthens our ability to cope with the challenges of our roles. This includes adequate sleep, healthy eating, physical exercise, mindfulness practices and setting boundaries to maintain a healthy work–life balance.

Self-indulgence refers to actions or behaviours often driven by immediate gratification or escapism rather than long-term wellbeing. These activities might provide temporary relief or pleasure but do not address the underlying needs for personal growth or emotional resilience. Examples include excessive shopping, overeating or binge-watching TV shows, which might feel good at the moment but don't meaningfully contribute to our overall wellbeing.

In the context of library professionals, recognising the difference between self-care and self-indulgence is crucial. While self-indulgence might offer a temporary reprieve from stress, self-care equips us with the resilience and energy to be effective in our roles and maintain our mental and emotional health. Self-care practices help deal with the demanding nature of library work, including managing stress, preventing burnout and fostering a positive and supportive work environment. These self-care strategies enable library professionals to remain committed and effective in their roles, contributing positively to transforming library spaces into inclusive, kind and nurturing environments.

The importance of boundaries, saying no and managing workload

Understanding and implementing boundaries becomes essential in creating a more compassionate and well-functioning library environment. Boundaries are not just crucial for personal wellbeing; they are also vital to maintaining a productive and positive workplace. Alongside setting boundaries, the ability to say 'no' and effectively manage workload significantly prevents burnout. It fosters a culture of respect and understanding.

Boundaries in the workplace are the limits we set on what we will and will not do, tolerate or accept. These boundaries are vital for several reasons:

- Preservation of energy and focus: by establishing clear boundaries, library staff can better manage their energy and focus on tasks that align with their roles and goals.
- Prevention of resentment and burnout: clear boundaries help prevent feeling overwhelmed and taken for granted, common precursors to burnout.
- Encouragement of mutual respect: when staff members articulate and respect each other's boundaries, it cultivates an environment of mutual respect.
- Enhancement of professionalism: boundaries help maintain a professional atmosphere where staff members feel safe, respected and valued.

A good example of boundaries is around working out of hours. From a wellbeing point of view rest is essential but it is difficult to rest when you are always working. Importantly, it also ripples out; you find that you are sending e-mails at 9 p.m., your colleague replies at 9:30 p.m. and so on. The wellbeing of the whole team starts to implode. This also applies to working on annual leave. It is very important, whether you are a leader or not, that you adhere to your hours. If you are worried about emergencies, the answer is not that you are on call checking e-mails at all times, it is that you have a disaster protocol which lays out what will happen in an emergency, so that when a call comes through you know it is an emergency – because, let's be honest, nobody tells you the library is on fire via an e-mail. E-mails may then be the way you communicate next steps but a disaster protocol allows everyone to relax.

The power of saying no

Saying 'no' is a critical component of setting boundaries. It involves understanding one's limits and conveying them assertively yet respectfully. Saying 'no' can:

- Manage workload: help maintain a manageable workload, ensuring quality over quantity in work output.
- Prioritise responsibilities: enable professionals to prioritise essential tasks that align with the library's objectives and their personal career goals.

■ Foster a culture of honesty: encourage a work culture where honesty is valued over agreeableness, leading to more realistic expectations and outcomes.

Saying 'no', especially to more senior colleagues, is a nuanced but essential skill in the workplace. It's about balancing respect for authority with the need to maintain personal and professional boundaries. The next section tells you how to do it effectively and why it's important.

Tips for saying no to senior colleagues

■ Understand your limits: before you can communicate your boundaries, you need to be clear about them. Assess your workload and responsibilities to understand what you can realistically take on.
■ Provide context: when saying no, it's helpful to explain why. For instance, 'I understand the importance of this task, but I am currently at capacity with [specific tasks]. Taking on more could affect the quality of my work.'
■ Offer alternatives: if you can't take on a task, suggest alternative solutions. 'I can't do this right now, but [colleague's name] has experience in this area. Would you like me to ask them?'
■ Use assertive communication: be clear and direct, but also respectful. Use 'I' statements to express your situation, like 'I am not able to take on any additional projects this week.'
■ Schedule a later follow-up: if it's a matter of timing, offer to revisit the request later. 'I can't commit to this right now, but I can schedule some time next week to discuss this further.'

Why it's important

■ Maintains quality of work: overextending yourself can lead to decreased quality in your work. Saying no helps maintain a high standard of output.
■ Ensures task prioritisation: it's crucial to focus on tasks that align with key responsibilities and goals. Saying no to less critical tasks allows you to prioritise effectively.
■ Builds professional respect: consistently saying yes can lead to being taken for granted. Saying no, when appropriate, can increase respect from colleagues, including senior ones, as it demonstrates a clear understanding of your role and capacities.
■ Promotes a healthy work culture: a culture where it's safe to say no without fear of retribution leads to more honest and effective

communication. It sets a precedent for realistic expectations and workloads.

■ Encourages self-care and wellbeing: saying no is often an act of self-care. It prevents burnout and ensures you have the bandwidth for both professional tasks and personal wellbeing.

By mastering the art of saying no, especially to senior colleagues, library professionals not only protect their wellbeing but also contribute to a more honest, efficient and respectful workplace culture.

Self-assessment tool for boundary-setting skills
Instructions: rate each statement on a scale from 1 (Never) to 5 (Always). Be honest with your responses to get an accurate assessment of your boundary-setting skills.

Boundary-setting skills
I can clearly articulate my work-related limits to my colleagues and supervisors.
1 2 3 4 5
I feel comfortable saying no to additional tasks when my workload is full.
1 2 3 4 5
I regularly communicate my working hours and stick to them.
1 2 3 4 5
I take regular breaks and encourage others to respect this time.
1 2 3 4 5
I ask for help or delegate tasks when I am overwhelmed.
1 2 3 4 5
I am able to separate work responsibilities from personal time.
1 2 3 4 5
I feel confident in addressing issues that violate my boundaries.
1 2 3 4 5
I respect the boundaries set by my colleagues.
1 2 3 4 5

Scoring:
35–40: Excellent boundary-setting skills.
25–34: Good, but there's room for improvement.
15–24: Fair; boundary-setting needs more attention.
Below 15: Consider developing stronger boundary-setting skills.

Managing workload

Effective workload management is a critical skill for library professionals. It's not just about getting through the to-do list but doing so in a way that aligns with the library's goals and your personal and professional development. Here's a deeper dive into the key components:

Prioritising tasks

- Understand the library's goals: align your tasks with the broader objectives of the library. What contributes most to the library's success?
- Evaluate impact and urgency: use tools like the Eisenhower Matrix (see description below) to categorise tasks based on their urgency and importance.
- Set clear objectives: start each day or week by setting clear, achievable goals. What are the top three tasks that need your attention?
- Reflect on personal career goals: Ensure that some of your high-priority tasks are aligned with your personal career advancement and learning.

Delegating effectively

- Identify delegable tasks: recognise tasks that can be handled by others. Not everything requires your direct input.
- Choose the right person: delegate tasks to colleagues whose skills and career goals align with the task at hand.
- Provide clear instructions and support: when delegating, be clear about expectations and offer support. Check in, but avoid micromanaging.
- Empower your team: delegating is also about trust. Allow team members to own their tasks and bring their unique perspectives.

Time management

- Use time blocking: allocate specific time blocks for different types of tasks. This could include deep work, administrative tasks, meetings and breaks.
- Limit interruptions: create periods of uninterrupted work where you can focus deeply on tasks. Inform your team of these focus times.
- Leverage technology: use digital tools for scheduling, reminders and tracking progress. Apps like Trello, Asana or even simple calendar tools can be highly effective.
- Regular reviews: at the end of each day or week, review what you've accomplished and what needs to be carried over. This helps in adjusting your plans and priorities.

Additional strategies

- Learn to say 'no': as discussed earlier, sometimes saying no is the best way to manage your workload.
- Seek feedback: regularly ask for feedback from your superiors and peers to ensure your workload aligns with team and library objectives.
- Continual learning: stay informed about new time management strategies and tools. Attend workshops or webinars that focus on productivity and workload management.

Effective workload management is about making strategic decisions on how to allocate your time and resources. It's a dynamic skill that evolves with your role and the changing needs of the library, ensuring that you remain productive, satisfied and aligned with your career trajectory.

The Eisenhower Matrix

The Eisenhower Matrix is a task management tool designed to help you organise and prioritise tasks by urgency and importance. It categorises tasks into four quadrants: tasks to do first, tasks to schedule for later, tasks to delegate and tasks to delete. This tool aids in distinguishing between urgent and important tasks, allowing for efficient workflows and prioritisation.

Reflective questions

To facilitate practical boundary setting and workload management, library professionals can ask themselves the following questions:

- Is this task essential to my role or the library's mission? This question helps in identifying the importance and relevance of a task.
- Does this task align with my professional goals and values? This helps in ensuring that the task contributes to personal and professional growth.
- What are the consequences of saying 'yes' or 'no'? This aids in understanding the impact of accepting or declining a task.
- Do I have the necessary resources and time to commit to this task? Assessing capacity and resources available is crucial for realistic commitment.
- How will this task affect my current workload and wellbeing? Understanding the potential impact on workload and personal wellbeing is essential.
- Can this task be delegated or shared? Identifying opportunities for delegation can help manage workload effectively.
- What would be an appropriate boundary to set in this situation? This helps in determining a reasonable and clear boundary.

■ How can I communicate my decision respectfully and assertively? It's essential to convey boundaries and decisions effectively.

Checklist for effective workload management
Use this checklist to evaluate and improve your workload management. Tick each item you currently practise.

☐ Prioritise tasks: I regularly prioritise tasks based on urgency and importance.
☐ Set realistic goals: I set achievable goals for each day or week.
☐ Use time management tools: I effectively use tools like calendars, to-do lists or digital apps for managing tasks.
☐ Delegate tasks: I delegate tasks whenever appropriate and feasible.
☐ Say no when necessary: I am comfortable saying no to tasks that I cannot handle.
☐ Take regular breaks: I ensure to take breaks to avoid burnout.
☐ Seek feedback: I regularly ask for feedback to ensure my workload aligns with team and library objectives.
☐ Review and adjust: I review my workload regularly and make adjustments as needed.
☐ Balance professional and personal time: I maintain a balance between my professional duties and personal life.
☐ Continuous learning: I am open to learning new strategies for effective workload management.

Reflection: If you have checked most of the items, you are effectively managing your workload. If several items are unchecked, consider which areas need improvement and seek resources or training to enhance these skills.

Setting boundaries, learning to say no and managing workload are not just self-care strategies but professional necessities. By incorporating these practices, library professionals can maintain their wellbeing, ensure job satisfaction and contribute positively to creating a kinder, more respectful and productive workplace. These skills are not innate; they require practice and commitment but are invaluable for personal and professional growth. They also need to be modelled at all levels: if the most senior people in an organisation don't model or, possibly more importantly, respect good boundaries then it can prove difficult to gain the benefits of them. Even if you work for someone who doesn't seem to understand boundaries it is really important you stand by yours, but it will take more work.

Integrating self-care and compassion: enhancing library staff wellbeing and effectiveness

This section explores how embedding self-care and compassion into the daily routine of library professionals not only enhances their personal wellbeing but also directly influences the quality of service they provide, the resilience they exhibit in the face of change and their long-term career fulfilment.

By emphasising mindfulness, self-compassion and resilience-building activities, we aim to demonstrate that the wellbeing of library staff is not just an individual concern but a cornerstone for creating a positive, dynamic and effective library environment. As we proceed, we will examine various strategies and practices that can be implemented to foster a culture of care and understanding within the library, ultimately leading to a more satisfying and productive workplace for all.

Elevating wellbeing and job satisfaction through self-care
Mindfulness and self-compassion in reducing stress

Mindfulness and self-compassion are vital components of self-care, playing a significant role in reducing workplace stress and preventing burnout. Practices like guided meditation and journalling enable library staff to take mindful breaks, providing them with opportunities to step back, reflect and regain their composure. This approach not only rejuvenates their energy but also renews their commitment and enthusiasm for their roles and responsibilities. By regularly engaging in these practices, staff can maintain a balanced perspective, effectively managing both personal and professional challenges.

Cultivating a positive library atmosphere

The practice of regular self-care routines contributes significantly to creating a positive and vibrant library atmosphere. When library staff engage in self-care, their improved wellbeing radiates throughout the library, influencing their interactions with colleagues and patrons. This creates a ripple effect, where the positive energy not only enhances the work atmosphere but also boosts overall productivity and morale. A library environment where staff feel cared for and supported is one where creativity and collaboration flourish, leading to improved services and a more fulfilling workplace.

Improving library service through staff wellbeing

The wellbeing of library staff is intrinsically linked to the quality of service they provide. Staff who regularly practise self-care and feel supported in their personal and professional growth are better equipped to engage with library users in an empathetic and attentive manner. This enhanced level of service improves the overall experience for library users, who benefit from interactions with staff who are present, attentive and empathetic. Such positive interactions not only enhance user satisfaction but also contribute to the library's reputation as a welcoming and supportive community space.

Resilience as a product of self-care and compassion
Adaptability in a changing environment

In the dynamic landscape of library services, characterised by continual technological advancements and policy shifts, resilience is essential. Self-care practices play a crucial role in building this resilience, enabling staff to effectively adapt to ongoing changes and challenges. This adaptability is not just about coping with change but also about embracing and thriving in it. Staff who practise self-care and compassion are more likely to view changes as opportunities for growth and innovation, thereby meeting the diverse and evolving needs of library users.

Maintaining high performance in challenging times

The resilience fostered through self-care and a compassionate workplace culture is pivotal in sustaining high performance, even in demanding situations. Library staff who have cultivated resilience are better prepared to handle high-pressure scenarios, ensuring that the library continues to provide uninterrupted, high-quality service. This resilience is a buffer against the stress and challenges that come with peak times or unforeseen circumstances, enabling staff to maintain a calm and effective presence.

Career sustainability and reduced turnover

Finally, self-care and compassion are key to long-term career sustainability in library services. Staff who are adept at managing stress through self-care practices are less likely to experience burnout and more likely to find ongoing satisfaction in their roles. This not only benefits the individual staff members but also contributes to a stable and experienced workforce, reducing turnover and building a strong, cohesive library team. The cultivation of a caring and supportive work environment, where self-care is prioritised, is essential for retaining talented staff and ensuring the continuous delivery of high-quality library services.

A note on the limitations of resilience

While increasing resilience among library staff is undoubtedly beneficial, it's essential to recognise that resilience is not a panacea for all workplace challenges. There are systemic issues in library environments – such as underfunding, staff shortages or lack of institutional support – that resilience alone cannot fix.

In some instances, the emphasis on resilience has been criticised for placing the burden of coping solely on individuals, potentially weaponising the concept. This happens when resilience is used to justify or ignore systemic problems, implying that staff should 'toughen up' in the face of any challenge, regardless of its nature or severity.

It's crucial, therefore, to balance the focus on individual resilience with efforts to address broader organisational and systemic challenges. Creating a supportive and sustainable library environment involves equipping staff with personal coping strategies and advocating and implementing institutional changes that address these broader issues.

In summary, while building resilience is critical to adapting to change, sustaining performance and ensuring career longevity, it must be complemented by efforts to tackle systemic challenges within library environments. This balanced approach ensures that resilience is a tool for empowerment, not a means to overlook deeper organisational issues.

Improved interpersonal relations in the context of self-care and self-compassion

Emotional intelligence training is vital for enhancing collaboration among library staff. It helps in appreciating diverse perspectives, leading to more effective teamwork. Staff learn to recognise and value different communication styles and approaches, fostering inclusivity and productivity in the team environment. Training in emotional intelligence often includes learning empathy and understanding, which are crucial for serving a diverse user base. This training equips staff to better understand and meet the community's varied needs, enhancing service quality. The diversity within library teams can be a source of creativity and innovation. Emotional intelligence training helps navigate and celebrate this diversity, leveraging unique backgrounds and experiences for enhanced service delivery.

Conflict resolution skills are essential in any workplace, including libraries. These skills enable staff to constructively address and resolve misunderstandings or disputes, preventing minor disagreements from escalating and maintaining a harmonious work environment. Effective conflict management also promotes a culture of open communication.

The development of trust and rapport is foundational to strong team dynamics. Emotional intelligence and conflict resolution skills contribute to interactions that build mutual trust and respect, encompassing active listening, empathy and constructive feedback. This leads to more supportive and co-operative team relationships. Staff interactions set the tone for the library environment. Positive interpersonal dynamics among staff benefit the team and influence the library's overall atmosphere. Such interactions serve as a model for users, fostering a welcoming, respectful and inclusive environment.

Self-care and self-compassion are not limited to internal processes; they extend to how we interact with others. When library staff practise self-compassion, they are more inclined to extend understanding and support to colleagues. This creates a more empathetic work environment and reduces workplace stress.

Positive interpersonal relations are a key component of self-care, fostering a sense of community and belonging that is vital for mental and emotional wellbeing. This holistic wellbeing approach acknowledges that personal health is deeply interconnected with our relationships, enhancing job satisfaction, morale and a supportive network. The improvement of interpersonal relations is integral to understanding self-care and self-compassion. These relations mirror and reinforce the principles of these practices, contributing to a healthier, more supportive and fulfilling work environment in libraries. This approach benefits individual staff members and enhances the library's role as a community hub.

Incorporating all these strategies results in a more resilient, satisfied and collaborative library staff, crucial for the effective functioning and positive evolution of library environments. Each element – from wellbeing and job satisfaction to resilience and interpersonal relations – plays a significant role in shaping a conducive work environment that reflects positively on library services and user experience.

Impact on the library environment

Implementing these strategies can cultivate a culture of kindness and understanding within the library, making it a more welcoming and nurturing place for staff and users. Staff who feel supported and valued are more likely to go the extra mile in providing high-quality service, leading to a better overall experience for library users. A psychologically safe environment, where staff feel comfortable expressing themselves and taking risks, is conducive to innovation and creative problem-solving, which improves the overall library environment.

Implementing them requires time, effort and possibly financial resources. Libraries must consider the feasibility of allocating these resources without impacting other essential services. Encouraging widespread participation among staff can be challenging. It's essential to communicate the benefits clearly and make these practices accessible to all. Establishing metrics to evaluate the effectiveness of the strategies is crucial. This might include staff surveys, feedback mechanisms and monitoring changes in staff turnover and user satisfaction. Each library is unique and strategies must be tailored to fit its and its staff's needs and culture. These strategies should be ongoing, with regular review and adaptation based on feedback and changing needs.

In summary, while implementing self-care and compassion strategies in libraries promises numerous benefits for staff wellbeing and service quality, it also requires careful consideration of resources, staff engagement and ongoing evaluation. The ultimate goal is to create a sustainable, nurturing work environment that supports the staff and enhances the library's role as a community hub.

Conclusion

This chapter underscores the transformative power of self-care and compassion in the library sector. By integrating Dr Kristin Neff's principles into library practices, a shift towards a culture of kindness and wellbeing is achievable, addressing both the individual needs of library staff and systemic challenges. Emphasising the balance between personal resilience and organisational change, the chapter envisions libraries not only as knowledge hubs but as exemplars of positive workplace culture, where staff wellbeing directly enhances service quality and positions libraries as pivotal community sanctuaries.

Exercises and reflective questions

Exercise for teams

Objective: to foster a sense of appreciation, connection and positive communication among team members.

Materials needed: none.

Steps:

1 Gather together: arrange for the team to sit in a circle, ensuring everyone can see each other.
2 Introduction to gratitude: start the session by briefly discussing the importance of gratitude in the workplace, highlighting how it can enhance team dynamics and individual wellbeing.

3   Sharing gratitude: each team member takes a turn to share something they are grateful for within the workplace. This could be an appreciation for a colleague, a successful project or any positive experience they have encountered.
4   Acknowledging contributions: as each person shares, others can offer acknowledgements or additional comments to build on the positive atmosphere.
5   Reflection: after everyone has shared, please take a few moments for the team to reflect on the shared gratitude and how it made them feel.
6   Regular practice: encourage the team to make this a regular practice, perhaps at the beginning of team meetings, to continuously cultivate a positive and supportive work environment.

Exercise for individuals
Objective: to encourage individual self-awareness, personal growth and self-compassion.
Materials needed: a journal or notebook and pen.
Steps:

1   Select a quiet space: find a quiet and comfortable space where you can sit undisturbed for a few minutes daily.
2   Daily reflections: dedicate a few minutes each day to write in your journal. Reflect on the day's events, focusing on your responses and feelings.
3   Identify challenges and growth: write about any challenges you faced during the day and how you responded to them. Reflect on what you learned and how you can grow from these experiences.
4   Practise self-compassion: for any negative experiences or mistakes, write down what you would say to a friend in the same situation. This practice helps in cultivating self-compassion and understanding.
5   Acknowledge successes: make sure to also write about your successes and the positive aspects of your day, no matter how small. This practice helps in recognising and celebrating personal achievements.
6   Review and reflect: regularly review past entries to reflect on your personal growth and patterns in your thoughts and behaviours.

By incorporating these exercises, teams and individuals in library settings can enhance their self-care and compassion practices, contributing to a more supportive, resilient and positive work environment.

Reflective questions

- How do you perceive the role of self-care and self-compassion in your professional life, especially within the library environment?
- In what ways have you observed the impact of emotional intelligence and conflict resolution skills on team dynamics and library services?
- How can psychological safety and self-compassion be integrated into daily library operations to enhance staff and user experiences?
- Reflect on a time when a resilience-building activity or mindset shift positively affected your approach to a challenge in the library. What was the outcome?
- Considering the holistic approach to wellbeing discussed in this chapter, what changes or initiatives would you propose to foster a culture of kindness, self-care and compassion in your library?

CHAPTER 7

Balancing Personal Growth and Wellbeing: A Key to Empowering Library Teams

Introduction

Be not afraid of growing slowly; be afraid only of standing still.

(Chinese proverb, quoted in Drummond, 2010, 294)

I really believe if we invest in our teams and ensure they are given every opportunity to develop and grow, we will be doing our best for them and the services we offer. Simply put, the world around us is developing constantly and if we invest in our teams, we will find that they become skilled, engaged and in turn their wellbeing will improve. This chapter explores the crucial role of personal development for library staff, emphasising how these aspects significantly influence their contribution to a positive workplace culture. It argues that nurturing individual growth benefits the staff and enhances the library's overall service quality and environment. It will also explain how to integrate key wellbeing models – ASSET, PERMA, JD-R and PsyCap – into library staff's personal development and self-care, exploring how these models can enhance their contribution to a positive workplace culture and improve overall wellbeing.

What happens if we don't invest in personal development?

A possible result of not investing in personal development is that our teams will rust out (Howard, 1989). Rust-out happens when someone is not feeling challenged or interested in their job anymore, causing them to be less productive and lose enthusiasm. Another result could be the team struggling to get roles elsewhere because they are deskilled and become increasingly resentful of the roles they are 'trapped' in, which can create negative ripples.

Understanding personal development in library work

Personal or staff development in the library encompasses a broad range of activities and processes to enhance an individual's skills, knowledge and effectiveness in their role. It is not limited to professional capabilities alone but includes personal growth, emotional intelligence and adaptability. This holistic approach recognises that the wellbeing and development of library staff are integral to the effectiveness and evolution of library services. The continuous process of learning, self-improvement and skill enhancement encompasses:

- Lifelong learning emphasises the importance of lifelong learning as a core component of personal development. This includes staying updated with the latest trends in library science, digital literacy and customer service excellence.
- Self-improvement initiatives encourage initiatives like attending workshops, participating in webinars and pursuing further education that contribute to professional and personal growth.
- Skill enhancement highlights the need for continuous upgrading of skills not just in traditional library skills but also in areas like technology, communication and leadership.

Understanding personal development in the library context involves recognising its broad scope, including the continuous learning process, self-improvement and skill enhancement.

Introduction to wellbeing models and their connection with personal development

This section revisits key wellbeing models – PERMA, Job Demands-Resources (JD-R) and PsyCap, all of which were discussed in Part 1 – highlighting their relevance to staff personal development in libraries. ASSET helps identify and manage unique stressors, such as adapting to digital changes. PERMA enhances job satisfaction by fostering positive emotions and meaningful work. JD-R balances job demands with resources, aiding in workload management. PsyCap, focusing on self-efficacy, optimism, hope and resilience, is crucial for adapting to the dynamic library environment. These models offer a roadmap for personal growth and resilience, enhancing job performance and contributing to a positive workplace culture.

The ASSET model is a framework for understanding and managing workplace stress in libraries. Strategies for implementation include conducting regular stress audits via surveys or workshops, organising stress management workshops tailored to library environments, establishing peer support groups and integrating stress management goals into personal development plans. Applying ASSET can lead to a healthier work environment and improved staff satisfaction.

PERMA enhances staff development by promoting positive emotions through activities like 'Happiness Jars', fostering engagement via professional development opportunities, building relationships through team activities, finding meaning in community projects and celebrating accomplishments. Practical activities include 'Feel-Good Fridays', themed workshops, 'Buddy Systems' and 'Star of the Month' programmes.

The JD-R model aids in staff development by balancing job demands with resources. Strategies include enhancing skills relevant to library demands, establishing mentorship and peer support networks, implementing regular feedback channels, integrating wellbeing and resilience training and providing workload management training. This approach creates a more supportive, capable and adaptive workforce, fostering long-term professional growth and satisfaction.

Developing PsyCap involves enhancing self-efficacy, optimism, hope and resilience. Methods include conducting training workshops, mentoring and coaching, providing regular feedback and recognition, creating a supportive work environment and facilitating peer support groups. PsyCap leads to enhanced staff performance, adaptability, job satisfaction and a positive work environment.

Incorporate ASSET, PERMA, JD-R and PsyCap into personal development plans by including regular stress audits, setting positive emotions and engagement goals, balancing job demands with resources and building self-efficacy and resilience. Offer online courses, workshops and mentoring for continuous learning and growth. Encourage regular check-ins, realistic goal setting, work–life balance and mindfulness practices to balance professional development and personal wellbeing.

Personal development and workplace culture

Personal development initiatives within libraries play a pivotal role in shaping a positive and inclusive workplace culture, as demonstrated in Case Study 7.1. Such initiatives often lead to improved staff communication skills, empathy and emotional intelligence, which are essential in strengthening team dynamics. This transformation makes the library a more collaborative and understanding place to work.

Case Study 7.1: Staff development groups

At Royal Holloway and the University of Westminster, I created staff development groups that encouraged ownership of staff development across the service. When colleagues shared skills through skill-sharing sessions, staff development was simple but effective. The colleagues who had the opportunity to share were empowered and gained experience in presenting and those who joined the sessions could develop new skills and, importantly, know who amongst their peers they could turn to for help, which helped build team cohesion.

Helen Rimmer

Furthermore, personal development programmes that incorporate elements of cultural competency and diversity training contribute significantly to creating an inclusive workplace culture. Staff become more aware of and sensitive to diversity issues, resulting in an environment welcoming to all users and colleagues.

Moreover, when library staff engage in personal development, it sparks a ripple effect that encourages a culture of continuous learning. This transforms the workplace into a dynamic and evolving environment, where learning and growth become integral parts of the daily routine.

The influence of leadership in promoting personal development

The role of library leaders is crucial in fostering an environment that values personal development. Leaders should model the behaviour they wish to see by actively engaging in their own personal development. This may involve pursuing qualifications, participating in leadership training or engaging in professional development opportunities. Importantly it needs to be relevant to their work and growth. Additionally, library leadership should strive to provide staff with the necessary resources and opportunities for personal development. This could include budgeting for training programmes, allowing time off for educational purposes and creating in-house development initiatives.

Creating a supportive environment is also vital. Leaders should recognise and celebrate achievements in personal development, supporting and encouraging staff in their growth goals. Such an approach ensures that personal growth is not just encouraged but becomes a fundamental part of the library's organisational culture.

Tools and resources for personal development in libraries

Libraries can offer various tools and resources to aid staff in their personal development. This includes organising or sponsoring workshops on a range of topics, from digital literacy to leadership skills, which could be conducted by external experts or experienced internal staff.

Providing access to online learning platforms that offer courses relevant to library work, such as information management and emerging library technologies, is also beneficial. Encouraging staff to join professional library associations and networks, both local and national, can provide valuable resources like webinars, conferences and networking opportunities. Establishing mentoring programmes where experienced library staff guide their less experienced colleagues can be instrumental in career advice, skill development and general support. Libraries might also consider creating a resource library that includes books, journals and online resources on personal development topics, ensuring it's easily accessible and regularly updated.

Guidance on balancing professional development with personal wellbeing

It's important to encourage a culture that values work–life balance (this is discussed further in Chapter 9). Library staff should be encouraged to manage their time effectively and set boundaries between work and personal life. Providing resources and training on mindfulness and stress management techniques can help staff handle work and personal life pressures healthily. Offering flexible learning opportunities, tailored to individual schedules and commitments, including online courses or recorded workshops for later viewing, is also crucial. Creating a supportive environment where staff feel comfortable discussing challenges in balancing professional development with personal wellbeing is essential. This could involve regular check-ins with supervisors or establishing peer support groups.

By providing these tools, resources and guidance, libraries can foster a culture of continuous learning and growth while also ensuring that staff maintain a healthy balance between their professional and personal lives.

Overcoming challenges and building a supportive culture for staff development in libraries

The journey towards effective staff development is often met with various challenges. From limited professional development opportunities to varied individual needs and perspectives, libraries face the task of creating an environment where every team member, regardless of their career stage or personal viewpoints on learning, can grow and thrive. This section explores the common challenges in fostering a culture of continuous library learning and development. It provides practical strategies to address these challenges, ensuring that staff development is inclusive, relevant and beneficial for all.

Whether it's overcoming resistance to new learning methods, managing time constraints or catering to diverse skill levels and interests, the goal is to build a supportive culture that values and promotes each staff member's professional and personal growth. By navigating these challenges thoughtfully, libraries can unlock the full potential of their teams, enhancing service quality and workplace satisfaction.

Common challenges

Addressing the challenge of limited opportunities involves allocating a budget for professional development and encouraging participation in diverse formats like online courses, workshops and conferences. There are creative ways for doing this, including encouraging people to apply for bursaries or finding low-cost one-day events to take part in. All of this allows for various development activities catering to different learning preferences and schedules.

To address resistance to new learning methods, especially among staff who may feel they don't need development or are approaching retirement, it's important to demonstrate the relevance of continuous learning. This can be achieved by highlighting how new skills can make daily tasks easier or more enjoyable and how they can contribute to personal fulfilment, even beyond the workplace.

Time constraints are another issue, because balancing work with development activities can be particularly challenging for busy library staff. Implementing flexible scheduling, creating dedicated time slots for professional development and integrating learning opportunities into regular work duties can help. It's also beneficial to recognise and validate the time spent on personal development as an integral part of job responsibilities. A good way forward is giving everybody time to focus on personal development or running staff training in a way that ensures everyone can attend or catch up, even if this means running things twice or in a hybrid fashion.

It is important to keep in mind that staff members have diverse skills, interests and motivations, which is why personalised development plans are crucial. For staff who may not see the immediate value in development or are nearing retirement, it can be helpful to focus on skills that enhance their current roles or prepare them for post-retirement activities. Asking people what their legacy will be often helps. It is also important to give people ownership over their personal development goals whilst encouraging them to make the goals ambitious and ones that will stretch them. Various learning options, including short-term workshops, mentorship opportunities or volunteer roles within the library, can cater to various interests and commitment levels.

Key to the success of a supportive workplace is an emphasis on the value of a learning culture that includes everyone, irrespective of their career stage or current skill level. Encourage an environment where learning is seen as a continuous, rewarding process that benefits both the individual and the library. Highlight stories or examples of staff from various backgrounds and career stages who have benefited from personal development to illustrate its broad relevance.

By addressing these challenges and promoting a culture that values continuous learning and growth for all staff members, libraries can create a more dynamic, skilled and satisfied workforce. This approach benefits the individual employees and contributes to the library's overall ability to adapt, innovate and provide high-quality service to the community.

Fostering a supportive environment for staff development

Fostering a culture that values and encourages continuous learning and development can be achieved by library leadership modelling learning behaviours, sharing knowledge and celebrating learning achievements or establishing mentorship programmes and peer learning groups. These initiatives facilitate knowledge sharing, strengthen team bonds and support networks within the library.

To help staff understand their growth areas and appreciate their progress, which enhances their development journey, implement regular feedback mechanisms and encourage reflective practices. This includes acknowledging and rewarding efforts and achievements in staff development. Recognition can be a powerful motivator and reinforces the value placed on personal and professional growth.

By addressing these challenges and promoting a culture of continuous learning and development, libraries can significantly enhance staff wellbeing and job satisfaction. A supportive environment for staff development benefits individual employees. It contributes to the library's ability to adapt, innovate and provide high-quality service to the community.

Guidance on having development conversations

Effective development conversations are critical for leaders and managers, as these discussions can significantly influence an employee's growth, motivation and overall job satisfaction. Here are some tips for leaders and managers to conduct these conversations effectively and stress their importance:

- Prepare thoroughly: before the conversation, review the employee's past performance, current responsibilities and any previous feedback or development plans. Be aware of their strengths, areas for improvement and career aspirations.
- Create a supportive environment: choose a quiet, private space for the conversation. Ensure there are no interruptions, so that the employee feels valued and respected.
- Open with positive acknowledgment: highlight the employee's achievements and strengths. Recognising their contributions sets a positive tone and builds confidence.
- Listen actively: encourage employees to share their thoughts, feelings and career aspirations. Listen actively, show genuine interest and avoid interrupting or jumping to conclusions.
- Discuss development opportunities: explore areas where the employee can develop. This could include new projects, training programmes or skill-building activities. Tailor these suggestions to align with their career goals and interests.
- Set SMART goals: help the employee set Specific, Measurable, Achievable, Relevant and Time-bound (SMART) goals for their development. Clearly defined goals provide direction and make progress measurable.
- Stress the importance of development: emphasise how personal and professional development benefits the individual and the organisation. Explain that continuous learning is critical to adapting to changing workplace demands and achieving long-term career success.
- Provide resources and support: inform the employee about available resources, such as training programmes, mentorship opportunities or educational materials. Offer your support in helping them access these resources.
- Establish a follow-up plan: agree on a timeline for reviewing progress. Regular check-ins ensure the development plan remains relevant and allows for adjustments as needed.
- Encourage reflection and self-assessment: motivate employees to reflect on their learning experiences and self-assess their progress. This fosters self-awareness and accountability.
- Be open to feedback: ask for feedback on how you can better support their development as a leader or manager. This demonstrates your commitment to their growth and builds trust.
- End on a positive note: conclude the conversation by reiterating your confidence in their abilities and your commitment to their growth.

Remember, development conversations are not a one-time event but an ongoing process. Regular, meaningful discussions about growth and development can significantly enhance employee engagement and job satisfaction. In developing conversations, asking the right coaching questions fosters reflection, insight and action.

Coaching questions

Here are five practical coaching questions that leaders and managers can use:

1 Reflecting on achievements and challenges: 'Can you share a recent accomplishment you're particularly proud of and a challenge you've faced? How did you approach these situations?' This question allows employees to reflect on their successes and difficulties, offering insights into their problem-solving approach and resilience.
2 Exploring aspirations and goals: 'What are your long-term career aspirations and how do they align with your current role and responsibilities?' This helps to understand the employee's career ambitions and identify ways their current role can support these goals, fostering a sense of purpose and direction.
3 Identifying development areas: 'What skills or knowledge do you feel you need to develop to achieve your career goals or to perform your current role more effectively?' This question encourages employees to self-assess their skill gaps and learning needs, setting the stage for a focused development plan.
4 Discussing support and resources: 'What kind of support or resources would help you in your professional development journey? How can I or the organisation assist you in accessing these?' By asking this, you open the door for the employee to express what they need to succeed, showing your willingness to support their growth.
5 Encouraging self-reflection: 'Looking back over the past year, what learning or experiences have been most valuable for your development? How have these contributed to your growth?' This question promotes reflection on past experiences and their impact on personal and professional growth, reinforcing the value of continuous learning and development.

These questions facilitate meaningful dialogue and demonstrate a genuine interest in the employee's growth, helping build a trusting and supportive relationship.

Conclusion

This chapter emphasises the critical role of personal development in creating a dynamic library workplace. Investing in staff development is vital to prevent 'rust-out' and maintain enthusiasm. Embracing models like ASSET, PERMA, JD-R and PsyCap, it advocates a holistic approach to staff growth, including emotional intelligence and adaptability. Prioritising lifelong learning ensures staff stay current and motivated. Incorporating wellbeing into development plans helps staff balance work and life, enhancing overall performance. Ultimately, continuous learning and development are essential for libraries to adapt, keep teams skilled and serve their communities effectively.

Exercises and reflective questions

Exercise for teams

Developing a staff development plan for the library

Objective: to collaboratively create a comprehensive staff development plan that addresses the needs, aspirations and wellbeing of all team members in the library.

Materials needed: Whiteboard and markers (or large paper sheets); sticky notes; pens; copies of current job descriptions; existing development plans; and access to a quiet meeting space.

Duration: approximately 2–3 hours.

Steps:

1 Preparation (15 minutes):
   ■ Gather the team in a quiet, comfortable space conducive to open discussion and creative thinking.
   ■ Distribute materials and briefly explain the objective of the exercise.
2 Individual reflection (30 minutes):
   ■ Ask each team member to reflect on their professional development needs and aspirations. Consider questions like:
      — What skills would you like to develop or enhance?
      — Are there areas in your current role where you need more support or training?
      — What are your long-term career goals and how do they align with your role in the library?
   ■ Have each team member write their thoughts on sticky notes.
3 Group discussion and sharing (45 minutes):
   ■ Go around the room and have each team member share their reflections. Encourage open and respectful listening.

- As team members speak, group similar themes or needs on the whiteboard or large paper sheets.

4 Identifying common and unique development needs (30 minutes):
- Review the grouped themes and identify joint development needs acrooo the team.
- Also, acknowledge unique needs that might apply to specific roles or individuals.
- Discuss how these needs align with the library's goals and objectives.

5 Brainstorming resources and opportunities (30 minutes):
- Brainstorm potential resources and opportunities that could address the identified development needs. Consider workshops, online courses, mentorship programmes, cross-training, conference attendance or in-house training sessions.
- Encourage creativity and inclusivity in suggestions to cover a broad range of interests and learning styles.

6 Drafting the development plan (30 minutes):
- Begin outlining a draft of the staff development plan. Assign a note-taker to document the discussion.
- Ensure the plan includes specific goals, the resources needed, timelines and who will be responsible for each part of the plan.
- Discuss how to integrate the plan with the library's overall strategy and how to measure its effectiveness.

7 Feedback and adjustments (15 minutes):
- Once a draft is created, invite feedback from all team members. Are there areas that need adjustment or refinement?
- Ensure the plan feels achievable and aligns with individual and library-wide goals.

8 Finalising and committing to the plan (15 minutes):
- Finalise the development plan based on the feedback.
- Discuss the following steps and set a date for the first review of the plan.
- Conclude by having each team member express their commitment to the plan and how they plan to contribute.

Follow-up: schedule regular check-ins to review the progress of the development plan, make necessary adjustments and celebrate achievements along the way.

This exercise not only fosters team collaboration in the planning process but also ensures that the development plan is tailored to the unique needs and goals of the library staff, enhancing overall engagement and effectiveness.

Individual exercise
Integrating wellbeing models into your personal development plan
Purpose: this exercise will help you integrate the ASSET, PERMA, JD-R and
   PsyCap models into your personal development plan, focusing on stress
   management, positive wellbeing and professional growth.
Materials needed: Notebook or digital document for planning; access to any
   current personal development plans or goals; and a quiet space for
   reflection.
Steps:

1 Self-Assessment and reflection:
   ■ Take a few moments to reflect on your current work situation and
     personal wellbeing.
   ■ Ask yourself: What are my main stressors at work? How do I
     currently handle them? What aspects of my job bring me the most
     satisfaction and which are the most challenging?
2 Incorporating ASSET:
   ■ Perform a mini-stress audit. List down the stressors you identified in
     Step 1.
   ■ For each stressor, think about possible ways to reduce or manage it.
     Consider factors like job control, support from managers and peers
     and clarity of your role.
3 Applying PERMA:
   ■ Set goals for each PERMA element: Positive emotions, Engagement,
     Relationships, Meaning and Accomplishment.
   ■ Example: For Positive emotions, you might set a goal to start each day
     by noting one thing you're grateful for in your work.
4 Balancing with JD-R:
   ■ List your main job demands and the resources you currently have or
     need. This could include time, support, skills or tools.
   ■ Develop strategies to balance these demands with your resources. For
     example, a resource could be time management training if a demand
     is high workload.
5 Building PsyCap:
   ■ Identify ways to enhance your Psychological Capital – focus on
     developing self-efficacy, optimism, hope and resilience.
   ■ Set small, achievable tasks that help build these areas. For example,
     tackle a challenging task to build self-efficacy or reflect on past
     successes to foster optimism.
6 Creating your personal development plan:
   ■ Combine the insights from the previous steps into a cohesive personal

development plan. Include specific actions, timeframes and how you'll measure progress.
- Remember to incorporate elements that balance professional development with personal wellbeing, such as mindfulness or work–life balance strategies.
7 Regular review and adjustment: plan regular reviews of your personal development plan (e.g., monthly or quarterly). Adjust your plan as necessary based on your experiences and changing circumstances.

Conclusion: This exercise guides you in creating a holistic personal development plan, integrating key wellbeing models. It encourages ongoing learning and growth while focusing on your overall wellbeing.

Reflective questions
Here are five overarching reflective questions that can help in evaluating the effectiveness and direction of staff development initiatives:

1 How effectively are current staff development initiatives meeting our library team's diverse needs and career aspirations?
2 How has integrating wellbeing models (ASSET, PERMA, JD-R and PsyCap) impacted the work environment and staff performance?
3 What changes or improvements can be made to our staff development plan to better align with the evolving needs of the library and its staff?
4 How effectively are we balancing the professional development of our staff with their personal wellbeing and what adjustments might be necessary?
5 What success stories or challenges have we encountered in implementing our staff development initiatives and what lessons can we learn from them?

These reflective questions aim to provide a comprehensive assessment of staff development efforts, helping library leaders and managers to continuously refine their approach and better support their team's growth and wellbeing.

CHAPTER 8

Creating a Culture of Kind Communication in Libraries: The Importance of Non-Violent Communication

Introduction

> Kind words do not cost much. Yet they accomplish much.
>
> (Blaise Pascal)

Kind communication, closely linked to concepts of civility and non-violent communication, is a way of interacting with others that emphasises respect, compassion and empathy. It's not just about what is said, but also how it's said. It's essential in any workplace, but it's vital in libraries. In a library, staff work together to help a wide range of people and manage lots of information. Talking to each other and the people who come into the library in a kind way makes the library a better place to work and visit.

Library staff often have to work as a team, help people who come in and keep learning new things. All this depends a lot on how well they communicate. Communication can help staff in different parts of the library work better together, make the library more friendly and create a welcoming environment.

In this chapter, we will look at why kind communication is so important in libraries. We'll focus on non-violent communication as a structured way of being kind. We'll see how it can make the library a better place to work and make the people who visit it happier. We'll also share some good ways for library staff to communicate kindly daily. We aim to help everyone in the library – staff and visitors – feel more welcome and happy. This chapter is here to help library workers and leaders understand how to make their library a place where kindness is a normal part of everyday life.

The foundations of kind communication

Kind communication is about talking and listening to others in a friendly, understanding and respectful way. It's not just about what we say but how we say it. This means using positive and encouraging words and being thoughtful about the feelings of others. When we communicate kindly, we're more likely to get along well with our colleagues and those visiting the library.

But why is kind communication so important? Talking to others kindly is good for our minds and those we speak to. Psychologists have found that being kind can make us happier and more satisfied with our lives. It can also reduce stress and help us get along better with other people (Pitts and Socha, 2013). In a workplace like a library, this is really important. Kind communication can make the library a better workplace, which means happier staff and visitors.

Reflect on a genuinely memorable conversation you've had. Often, it's not the words themselves but how they made you feel that lingers in memory. This sentiment highlights the profound impact of positive communication. It leaves a lasting impression and promotes health and wellness for the speaker and listener (Pitts and Socha, 2013).

Staff communication can make a big difference in libraries, where people often seek help or information. If they speak and listen kindly, it can make people feel more comfortable and willing to ask for what they need. This makes the library more effective at what it does – helping people and sharing knowledge.

The basics of kind communication are simple: be friendly, be respectful and think about how your words affect others. By doing this, we can make our libraries and workplaces better for everyone.

Non-violent communication

Non-violent communication (NVC), a concept developed by Marshall Rosenberg (2015), is a transformative approach to interaction and conflict resolution. Centred on the pillars of empathy and understanding, NVC guides individuals to express themselves authentically and listen to others with compassion. This methodology is not about winning or losing but fostering mutual respect and understanding. It emphasises the importance of being aware of our own and others' feelings and needs and communicating them non-threateningly. NVC is particularly effective in resolving conflicts, as it encourages a focus on shared human values and needs rather than on blame or judgement. This approach is invaluable in diverse settings, including libraries, where clear, empathetic communication can significantly enhance service quality, teamwork and the overall work environment.

The core components of NVC offer a framework for constructive and empathetic interaction which underpins kind communication, particularly relevant in a library setting:

- Observations: this involves objectively describing situations, behaviours or events without attaching personal judgments or evaluations. In libraries, this practice encourages staff to communicate about issues or behaviours in a way that minimises defensiveness and misunderstanding, focusing instead on facts and shared experiences.
- Feelings: NVC teaches the importance of acknowledging and expressing feelings that arise from these observations. In a library, staff members saying how certain situations make them feel can lead to more empathetic and understanding interactions among colleagues and users.
- Needs: Central to NVC is the identification and articulation of needs that are linked to these feelings. In a library context, this could involve expressing needs for support, more resources or a better understanding from colleagues or users. This step moves the conversation from emotional reactions to constructive problem-solving.
- Requests: The final component involves making clear, specific and actionable requests to address these needs. In a library, this means asking for particular actions or changes respectfully and directly. This step is crucial, as it provides a clear path to constructively meeting the identified needs and resolving issues.

By integrating these components, library staff can foster a more supportive, collaborative and understanding work environment, aligning with the principles of kindness and wellbeing.

NVC has significant relevance in library settings, enhancing the overall environment in various ways. Firstly, it fosters positive interactions among staff and users, creating a more welcoming and friendly atmosphere. Secondly, NVC is instrumental in effective conflict resolution. Encouraging understanding and empathy helps in peacefully resolving misunderstandings or disagreements. Thirdly, it improves collaborative work among library staff by promoting clear and respectful communication.

Additionally, NVC is crucial in enhancing customer service, ensuring interactions with users are more understanding and responsive to their needs. Finally, NVC helps build a culture of respect, empathy and kindness within the library, contributing to a more positive and productive workplace. This approach aligns with values essential for creating a harmonious and supportive library environment.

In practical application, NVC principles can be effectively integrated into everyday library scenarios:

- Handling customer queries: for instance, when a user expresses dissatisfaction, staff can use NVC by first observing the situation without judgement (e.g. noticing the user's tone), then acknowledging their feelings (e.g. understanding frustration) and finally addressing their needs with empathetic responses and clear solutions.

- Addressing team conflicts: NVC can be utilised to address disagreements among staff by encouraging open, judgement-free dialogue about each person's observations, feelings and needs, leading to mutually agreeable solutions.
- Managing stress and workload: when discussing workload issues, staff can express their feelings and needs clearly (e.g., feeling overwhelmed and needing support), leading to constructive discussions on workload management.

Library staff can practise simple NVC exercises like role-playing scenarios or reflective listening. These activities enhance their ability to apply NVC principles in real situations, thereby improving communication and collaboration within the library.

An exercise on NVC

A short reflective listening exercise based on NVC principles can be conducted as follows:

1 Pair up: library staff members pair up.
2 Scenario practice: one person shares a recent, real-life situation where they felt a strong emotion (e.g., frustration with a problematic user).
3 Reflective listening: the listener then reflects on what they heard, identifying the speaker's feelings and needs. For example, 'It sounds like you felt overwhelmed because you need support handling challenging interactions.'
4 Feedback: the speaker provides feedback on the accuracy of the reflection and clarifies if needed.
5 Role reversal: the roles are then reversed.

This exercise helps staff practice identifying and articulating feelings and needs, a key component of NVC, enhancing their communication skills and empathy.

Integrating NVC with existing communication practices in libraries can significantly enhance how staff interact and resolve issues. NVC complements kind communication strategies by adding depth to empathetic listening and expression. It encourages staff to be more attentive to what is being said and the underlying feelings and needs. This integration can improve problem-solving approaches, making them more centred on mutual understanding and respect. Incorporating NVC into regular training sessions or staff meetings ensures that its principles become a natural part of daily interactions, further enriching the library's communication culture.

NVC can be particularly effective in handling difficult conversations. It encourages openness and empathy, which are crucial in sensitive discussions. By focusing on expressing and acknowledging feelings and needs without judgement or aggression, NVC facilitates a deeper understanding between parties. This approach helps in de-escalating tension and fostering a collaborative atmosphere where solutions can be found that respect everyone's needs. NVC's emphasis on clear, empathetic listening and expression aids in transforming potentially confrontational situations into opportunities for growth and understanding.

The role of leadership in fostering kind communication

Library leaders are crucial in creating a workplace where kind communication is the norm. They're not just in charge of running the library; they also set the tone for how everyone communicates. Leaders can encourage everyone in the library to do the same by showing kindness in their communication.

Leaders can start by being good role models. This means they should always talk to their staff and library visitors in a friendly, understanding way. When leaders communicate like this, it shows everyone else that this is the right way to talk to each other. This is backed up by Goleman (1998), who discussed the importance of emotional intelligence in the workplace. Emotional intelligence includes being aware of your emotions and those of others, which is a big part of kind communication.

Library leaders can also set up policies that promote kind communication. For example, they could have training sessions for all staff on how to talk to each other and visitors in a kind way. They could also ensure that when people communicate well, they get recognised and rewarded for it. This could be part of their performance evaluations, as suggested by Porath and Pearson's work on workplace civility, which will be covered later in this chapter.

Another good idea is for leaders to encourage feedback. They should ask their staff how they feel about communication in the library and what could be done better. This shows that leaders care about their staff's opinions and are willing to make changes to improve things.

Leaders should also be ready to step in if there are any problems with communication. If someone is not being kind, they must address it immediately. This will help keep the library a friendly and respectful place for everyone.

In summary, library leaders are crucial in ensuring everyone communicates kindly. They must set a good example, make policies supporting kind communication, encourage feedback and handle problems quickly. By doing all this, they can make the library a great place to work and visit.

Systemic team coaching and communication

Systemic team coaching (Leary-Joyce and Lines, 2018) is a powerful approach that can significantly improve how library teams work and communicate. This approach goes beyond individual coaching by focusing on the team as a whole and how its members interact with each other and the broader organisation. By integrating the principles of systemic team coaching into library settings, we can enhance team dynamics and communication. Library teams can enhance their communication, work more cohesively and better serve the needs of their users and communities. This approach improves team performance and contributes to a more positive and productive library workplace.

Principle 1: Understanding the system as a whole

In libraries, teams are part of a more extensive system that includes other teams, the library's users and the community. Systemic team coaching encourages teams to understand their role within this broader system. This awareness helps team members communicate more effectively with each other and with different parts of the library, ensuring that their actions contribute positively to the library's overall goals.

Principle 2: Aligning team goals with library objectives

Systemic team coaching emphasises aligning the team's goals with the library's objectives. This alignment ensures that all communication and team activities are purpose-driven and focused on achieving shared outcomes. This might involve aligning team efforts with a library's community outreach, customer service improvement or digital transformation initiatives.

Principle 3: Encouraging open and honest communication

A key component of systemic team coaching is fostering an environment where open and honest communication is the norm. In a library setting, this means creating a safe space for staff to express their ideas, concerns and feedback without fear of judgement or negative consequences. This environment encourages innovation, problem-solving and a deeper understanding among team members.

Principle 4: Developing collective leadership

Systemic team coaching also involves developing collective leadership, where every team member feels responsible for the team's success. In libraries, this can transform how teams operate, with each member taking the initiative and demonstrating leadership in their area of expertise. This shared responsibility leads to more effective and efficient team collaboration and communication.

Principle 5: Reflecting and learning as a team

Continuous reflection and learning are essential in systemic team coaching. Library teams should regularly reflect on their communication patterns, decision-making processes and overall performance. This ongoing learning helps the team adapt and evolve, improving communication and effectiveness.

Addressing library-specific challenges through communication

Libraries face challenges that require effective communication strategies to manage successfully. These include catering to diverse user needs, adapting to digital transformation and handling sensitive issues like book bans or challenges. Kind communication plays a crucial role in addressing these challenges.

Addressing challenges
Catering to diverse user needs

Libraries serve a diverse community with varying needs, backgrounds and expectations. Effective communication involves understanding and respecting these differences. Strategies:

- Active listening: encourage staff to practise active listening, ensuring users feel heard and understood.
- Empathy: train staff to empathise with users' needs and perspectives.
- Clear and respectful responses: ensure communications are clear, respectful and tailored to individual user needs, whether in person, on the phone or via digital channels.

Adapting to digital transformation

The shift towards digital resources and services can be challenging for staff and users. Strategies:

- Transparent communication: keep staff and users informed about digital changes and how they will be implemented.
- Support and training: offer training sessions for staff and users, ensuring they are comfortable with new technologies.
- Feedback channels: create channels for staff and users to provide feedback on digital services and use this feedback to make improvements.

Handling book bans or challenges

Book bans and challenges are sensitive issues that libraries may face, often reflecting broader social or political tensions. Strategies:

- Open dialogue: foster an environment where staff can discuss and address these challenges openly and respectfully.
- Policy clarity: ensure all staff are clear on the library's policies regarding book selection and handling challenges and communicate these policies to users as needed.
- Conflict resolution: provide training in conflict resolution to help staff navigate difficult conversations with users who may challenge certain materials.

In all these situations, the key is maintaining a kind and respectful tone, even when dealing with complex or contentious issues. By focusing on empathetic, clear and constructive communication, library staff can better manage their unique challenges, ultimately leading to a more positive and inclusive library environment.

Practical strategies and exercises

Implementing kind communication in library settings requires practical strategies and exercises that library staff can use in their daily interactions.

Strategies

- Consider your intentions: reflect on the purpose of your communication and your goals.
- Active constructive responding: practise responding positively to others' good news.
- Active listening reflection: enhance listening skills through exercises focusing on encouragement, reflection and paraphrasing.

Interactive exercises

- Role-playing scenarios: create scenarios where staff role-play situations they might encounter in the library. For example, handling a problematic user query, resolving a misunderstanding among colleagues or introducing new digital services. This practice helps staff prepare for real-life situations.
- Communication workshops: organise workshops focusing on specific aspects of kind communication, like empathetic listening or constructive feedback. These workshops could include group discussions, expert talks and interactive activities.

Team-building activities

- 'Kindness circles': host regular team meetings where staff share positive feedback about their colleagues' communication and teamwork. This activity fosters a culture of appreciation and recognition.
- 'Communication challenges': set up weekly challenges for staff to practice specific communication skills, like giving constructive feedback or expressing gratitude to colleagues and users.

Reflective practice

Communication diaries: encourage staff to keep a diary where they reflect on their daily communications, noting what went well and what could be improved. This reflective practice can lead to greater self-awareness and improvement in communication skills.

By combining these practical strategies with interactive exercises, library staff can develop and enhance their communication skills, creating a more positive, efficient and welcoming library environment.

Navigating racial harassment: strategies for empathetic communication in libraries

Empathetic communication

Effective communication is a cornerstone of any positive work environment. In the context of libraries, this extends to how staff members interact with each other and library users, especially in sensitive situations like incidents of racial harassment. Training in empathetic communication is crucial for library staff. This training should focus on active listening, recognising emotional cues and responding sensitively to the needs and experiences of those affected by harassment. The goal is to equip staff with the skills to handle such situations with care, understanding and respect. Such training aligns with the recommendations from the Universities UK Report on

Tackling Racial Harassment in Higher Education (UUK, 2020), which emphasises the importance of proactive staff development in handling sensitive issues.

Creating safe spaces

Libraries should be safe havens where every individual feels welcome and respected. This involves more than just physical safety; it extends to creating an atmosphere of emotional and psychological security. Libraries should implement policies and practices that foster inclusivity and ensure that everyone – staff and users alike – feels comfortable discussing and reporting harassment.

Understanding impact

Understanding the impact of racial harassment is vital in shaping these support systems. Racial harassment can lead to severe emotional and psychological distress. Awareness of these impacts should inform the development of support mechanisms within the library. Staff should be trained to not only recognise the signs of someone experiencing harassment but also understand the broader implications it may have on their mental health and wellbeing. The UUK (2020) report provides insights into the institutional responsibilities in addressing these challenges, which can be adapted to the library context.

Diversity, inclusion and kind communication
Diversity and inclusion

Diversity and inclusion are vital in library workplaces, where staff and users come from various backgrounds, cultures and experiences. Kind communication plays a crucial role in supporting and enhancing these values in the following ways.

Recognising and valuing differences

Kind communication involves acknowledging and valuing the diverse perspectives and experiences of all staff and users. This means actively listening to different viewpoints and respecting cultural and personal backgrounds.

Creating an inclusive environment

Libraries should be welcoming spaces for everyone. By using inclusive language and avoiding assumptions about people's abilities, preferences or identities, staff can make everyone feel respected and included. This includes being mindful of language that is sensitive to different cultures, genders and abilities.

Addressing unconscious bias

Unconscious biases can affect how we communicate and interact with others. Training in kind communication can help library staff recognise and overcome these biases. This could involve workshops or training sessions where staff learn about the impact of unconscious biases on communication and how to avoid them.

Encouraging open dialogue

Libraries can foster open dialogue about diversity and inclusion issues. This could be through staff meetings, discussion groups or special events. Encouraging conversations about these topics can help staff understand different perspectives and experiences, leading to a more inclusive workplace.

Supporting diverse needs

Kind communication means adapting to the diverse needs of library users. This could involve providing materials in different languages, offering services for people with disabilities or creating programmes that cater to various community groups.

Conflict resolution.

In diverse workplaces, conflicts may arise from misunderstandings or different cultural expectations. Kind communication includes effective conflict resolution techniques that respect all parties' perspectives and seek a mutually beneficial resolution.

By focusing on these aspects, libraries can use kind communication to enhance diversity and inclusion, ensuring that the library is a welcoming, respectful and supportive environment for everyone.

Integrating communication strategies into wellbeing programmes

Integrating kind communication strategies into wellbeing programmes in libraries is a vital step towards creating a more positive and supportive workplace. Wellbeing programmes often focus on staff's mental, emotional and physical health and effective communication is critical to all these areas. By integrating communication strategies into wellbeing programmes, libraries can enhance their staff's overall health and happiness. Effective communication improves workplace relationships and contributes significantly to the mental and emotional wellbeing of everyone in the library. Here's how these strategies can be woven into existing or potential wellbeing programmes.

Wellbeing workshops and training

- Organise workshops that combine wellbeing topics with communication skills. For example, a session on stress management could include how kind communication can reduce workplace stress.
- Provide training on active listening and empathic responding, showing how these skills can improve relationships and personal wellbeing.

Mindfulness and communication

- Incorporate mindfulness techniques into communication training. Mindfulness can help staff become more aware of their thoughts and feelings during communication, leading to more thoughtful and kind interactions.
- Offer mindfulness sessions where staff can practise being present and attentive, skills that benefit personal wellbeing and effective communication.

Peer support systems

- Establish peer support systems where staff can practise kind communication in a supportive environment. This could involve setting up buddy systems or mentorship programmes where staff can discuss challenges and share advice.
- Use these systems to reinforce positive communication habits and provide a safe space for discussing workplace issues.

Regular feedback and reflective practice

- Encourage regular feedback sessions where staff can discuss communication strengths and areas for improvement. This practice promotes continuous learning and personal development.
- Implement reflective practices, such as communication diaries or debrief sessions, where staff can reflect on their interactions and identify ways to improve.

Health and wellbeing resources

- Include resources on kind communication as part of the library's wellbeing resources. This could be in the form of booklets, online modules or access to relevant online courses.

■ Provide resources that address communication challenges unique to library environments, such as dealing with difficult users or collaborating with diverse teams.

Recognition and reward programmes

■ Develop programmes to recognise and reward effective communication. Acknowledging staff who demonstrate excellent communication skills can motivate others to improve their skills.
■ These programmes can be linked to overall wellbeing initiatives, highlighting how positive communication contributes to a healthier work environment.

Incivility – the slow spread of unkind communication

Christine Porath and Christine Pearson's (2013) article 'The Price of Incivility' highlights the pervasive and escalating issue of rudeness in the workplace. They found that 98% of workers experienced uncivil behaviour, with half reporting such treatment at least weekly. This rise in incivility not only undermines wellbeing but also has tangible costs to businesses, including decreased employee effort, creativity and performance and damaged customer relationships.

Incivility can range from overt bullying to subtle disrespect, like ignoring someone or taking credit for others' work. Such behaviours lead to significant costs:

■ 48% of employees intentionally reduce their effort
■ 80% lose work time worrying about the incident
■ 78% report a decline in commitment to the organisation
■ 25% admit to taking their frustration out on customers.

Witnessing incivility also harms performance and team spirit, negatively impacting creativity and willingness to help.

Combating incivility with positive communication

Integrating Porath's and Pearson's insights with positive communication strategies can create a more respectful and productive work environment:

■ Promote awareness and accountability: leaders must recognise the cost of incivility and set a tone of respect. Encouraging feedback and self-awareness about one's own behaviour is crucial.

- Model positive communication: demonstrate empathetic listening, constructive speaking and positive non-verbal cues. Leaders should exemplify the behaviour they expect from their teams.
- Encourage civility in interactions: foster an environment where respect is paramount and uncivil behaviours are addressed. Create group norms that emphasise civility.
- Empower employees: equip staff with skills to handle incivility, such as de-escalation techniques, and promote a culture where they feel supported.
- Recognise and reward civility: make civility a part of performance evaluations. Acknowledge and reward behaviours that promote a positive and respectful work environment.
- Provide support and resources: offer tools and support for employees affected by incivility, including access to counselling and stress management resources.

Exercise: reflecting on incivility and positive communication
Objective: to understand the impact of incivility in the workplace and develop strategies for promoting positive communication.
Materials needed: pens; paper; a comfortable and private space for discussion.
Duration: approximately 60 minutes.
Process:

1 Group discussion on incivility: start by discussing the findings of Christine Porath and Christine Pearson regarding workplace incivility. Emphasise the impact of rudeness on employee wellbeing and performance.
2 Reflective questions: break into smaller groups and reflect on the following questions:
   - Understanding the impact of incivility
      — Have you ever experienced or witnessed incivility in the workplace? How did it make you feel?
      — How do you think incivility affects team morale and individual performance?
   - Forms and costs of incivility
      — Can you identify forms of incivility that might often go unnoticed in the workplace?
      — Reflect on the potential costs of incivility you've observed, such as decreased effort or commitment.

- ■ Combating incivility with positive communication
  - — How can we promote awareness and accountability regarding incivility in our workplace?
  - — In what ways can we model positive communication to counteract incivility?
- ■ Encouraging civility in interactions
  - — What group norms can we establish to emphasise civility and respect?
  - — Share an instance where positive communication helped resolve a tense or uncivil situation.
- ■ Empower employees and recognise civility
  - — Discuss how we can equip ourselves and others to handle incivility effectively.
  - — How can we recognise and reward civility in our daily work?
3 Group sharing and action plan:
- ■ Reconvene and share insights from the small group discussions.
- ■ Develop an action plan outlining the team's steps to combat incivility and promote positive communication. Include strategies for modelling positive communication, establishing group norms and recognising civil behaviour.
4 Follow-up: agree on a date for a follow-up meeting to review the progress of the action plan and make any necessary adjustments.

This exercise aims to enhance self-awareness and mutual understanding among team members regarding the impact of incivility and the importance of positive communication. Team members can work together to create a more respectful and productive work environment by engaging in this reflective process.

Conclusion

This chapter shows how important kind and non-violent communication is in libraries. It's not just about what library staff say, but how they say it. Kind communication helps them work better as a team and makes the library better for everyone. By exploring how leaders in libraries should set a good example and the ways systemic team coaching can support them, it demonstrates how this can improve the way teams work together. Overall, the chapter aims to help libraries become places where everyone talks to each other in a kind and helpful way, making them better for both staff and visitors.

Exercises and reflective questions

Exercise for teams

Kind communication reflection and action workshop

Objective: to apply the principles of kind communication in a library setting, fostering a more supportive and collaborative team environment.

Materials needed: Flip chart; markers; note cards.

Duration: 90 minutes.

Process:

1 Group discussion: begin with a brief recap of the key points of kind communication as outlined in the chapter. Emphasise non-violent communication, systemic team coaching and the role of leadership in fostering kind communication.
2 Reflective exercise: divide the team into small groups. Each group discusses and writes examples of how kind communication has positively impacted their work or how its absence has created challenges.
3 Idea generation: each group brainstorms ways to enhance kind communication in their daily interactions and responsibilities. Encourage creativity and practicality.
4 Sharing and feedback: groups share their reflections and ideas with the larger team. Other team members can provide feedback or additional suggestions.
5 Action plan development: select the most feasible and impactful ideas as a team. Develop a concrete action plan for implementing these strategies in the workplace.
6 Commitment and follow-up: each team member commits to specific actions. Schedule a follow-up meeting to review progress and make adjustments if necessary.

Exercise for individuals

Personal kind communication diary

Objective: to encourage self-reflection and personal development in kind communication skills.

Materials needed: a diary or journal for each individual.

Duration: ongoing, with periodic reviews (e.g. monthly).

Process:

1 Personal reflection: individuals reflect on their interactions at the end of each day. They should consider moments where kind communication was effectively used and moments where opportunities were missed.

2 Journalling: write down these reflections, focusing on what was learned, how they felt and what could be done differently in the future.
3 Goal setting: set personal goals for improvement in specific areas of communication based on the reflections.
4 Periodic review: every month, review the diary entries to assess progress towards the set goals. Adjust goals and strategies as needed for continuous improvement.
5 Sharing and learning (optional): if comfortable, individuals can share insights or learnings with their team or a manager, fostering a culture of open communication and continuous learning.

Reflective questions
- How have the principles of kind communication discussed in this chapter resonated with your own experiences in the workplace?
- What strategies can you implement to enhance kind communication within your team or organisation?
- What are the potential challenges in implementing kind communication in the library setting and how might you address these?
- How can adopting kind communication impact your personal wellbeing and that of your colleagues?
- How will you incorporate the learnings from this chapter into your ongoing personal and professional development?

CHAPTER 9

Flexible Working: The Key to Enhancing Wellbeing and Productivity in the Library Workplace

Introduction

Most of this book is about the how and why of wellbeing at work but this chapter will look at the when and where of work. A key to wellbeing is developing a partnership between people and, often, an organisation's attitude to the when and where we work and how it is implemented is fundamental to this. If you don't trust your staff to manage their own time (beyond the structure of rotas), you will find it hard to say you trust them elsewhere. This chapter will explore the future of work, looking at flexible, remote and hybrid work.

I was lucky that in my first library role at the University of Brighton, we had true flexibility (we could accrue flexitime and use it how we wanted) and it applied to all, so I have always struggled with the arguments that flexibility isn't able to work in libraries because the frontline teams can't do it and so it won't be fair. We did and loved it; it was fair and nobody took advantage. Stepping from a presenteeism culture of 9–5 to total flexibility is a big step. The compromise which we had at Royal Holloway and which I introduced at the University of Westminster was to have core hours (10–4) and then people had flexibility on how they managed their 35 hours over the week; there was also Time off in Lieu (TOIL) that could be accrued for work-related extra time, although unlike how we managed it at Brighton this TOIL had to be pre-agreed and generally related to events/teaching/projects. We were also unable to carry over our hours from week to week. At Royal Holloway and Westminster we called this Reduced Rigidity, which worked for our needs. It quelled worries and it was fair and, administratively, it was reasonably straightforward. This chapter is all about why I think we need to be more flexible.

Case Study 9.1: Flexible working

I requested a flexible working arrangement from my employer for the first time in 2007 when I was pregnant with twins. I was experiencing all-day 'morning' sickness and had a tricky commute that was making my symptoms worse. I discussed it with my GP and asked to work at home two days a week and went into the office the other three days. When I returned to work in 2008 I asked to carry on with the arrangement because the girls were in nursery three days a week. We simply couldn't afford for them to do more days (we were effectively paying for six days of childcare every week) and we didn't have access to help with childcare from family or friends. My husband does shift work, so I was able to work when he wasn't on shift, as he could look after the girls. I used to do a lot of late nights to make up the time. Some of my colleagues were really supportive but others 'jokingly' accused me of not doing any work on my home days.

Once I set a precedent for flexible working I felt more comfortable requesting it when I moved organisations. In 2009 I moved organisations and they were extremely supportive of my working pattern. In addition to continuing with the two-day/three-day split, I worked around my husband's shifts. One week I would work 'early' (8 a.m. – 4 p.m.) and the next week I would work 'late' (9.30/10 a.m. – 5.30/6 p.m.). This meant that we could divide the nursery and school pick-ups/drop-offs between us.

Initially I was one of the few people in the organisation with a flexible working arrangement but I noticed that over time more people requested it. By the time I left that organisation in 2019 most colleagues had a flexible working arrangement. This was all done informally, with agreement from the line manager.

I moved organisations in late 2019 and encountered a small amount of resistance to requesting a flexible working arrangement. My girls had just started secondary school and we wanted to make sure that one of us was around for them as they transitioned to a new environment. The organisation had a formal mechanism to request flexible working, which involved filling out two sets of forms. The request was granted but this felt like unnecessary paperwork, given that a precedent had already been set for flexible and hybrid working across the team.

The pandemic meant that everyone had to work from home as a matter of course. I know of friends and colleagues who really struggled with the concept of flexible working. However, because I'd been doing it for well over a decade, at that point it felt like everyone had finally caught on to my way of working.

I now do two days in the office and three at home, which is the expected ratio for all colleagues. I don't necessarily 'need' a flexible working arrangement now, but it is still hugely beneficial to my work/life balance.

Jo Wood, Innovations Knowledge Manager – New Hospital Programme:
Healthcare Innovation & Research, NHS England

The when – flexible working

For this chapter, **flexibility** refers to the adaptability and variety in working hours that accommodate library staff's diverse schedules and needs. This concept involves offering librarians and other library personnel the opportunity to choose or negotiate their work hours within the framework of the library's operational needs and service commitments. It includes options such as:

- Variable start and end times: staff can adjust their start and end times within certain limits for personal convenience.
- Compressed workweeks: employees work standard weekly hours over fewer days, such as longer hours for four days with a day off.
- Part-time schedules: reduced or part-time hours are available for those unable to commit to full-time for personal reasons.
- Shift swapping or self-scheduling: staff can swap shifts or influence their shift schedules, enhancing autonomy and co-operation.
- Time banking or flexitime: employees can accrue extra work hours for future time off.
- Annualised hours: a set number of yearly hours are distributed flexibly across weeks and months, helping manage peak and quiet times in libraries.

This approach to flexibility recognises the unique demands of library services and the varied roles within a library setting. It emphasises the importance of balancing the library's operational requirements with the staff's personal needs, aiming to enhance job satisfaction, work–life balance and overall staff wellbeing. By exploring different working hours, libraries can create a more dynamic, responsive and inclusive work environment that respects individual preferences and lifestyles while maintaining a high standard of service for their communities.

This is the when of library work; we will explore the where further in the section below on remote and hybrid working.

Why is flexibility in the workplace necessary?

Workplace flexibility is increasingly crucial as work dynamics evolve. Embracing flexibility, focusing on employee wellbeing and moving away from rigid structures allow organisations to support staff's personal and professional needs. This approach fosters a culture of trust, enhances productivity and helps attract and retain top talent. Ultimately, an organisation's success hinges on adapting to changing work trends and employee needs, making flexibility a key factor for future success.

How does flexible working improve wellbeing?

Workplace flexibility contributes significantly to equality and wellbeing by:

- Universal accessibility: offering flexible arrangements to all employees prevents perceptions of 'special treatment' and ensures everyone benefits, regardless of life stage or responsibilities.
- Normalising varied needs: universal access to flexible options normalises the diversity of employee needs, fostering empathy and support in the workplace.
- Reducing stigma: avoiding exclusive flexibility for those with caring responsibilities prevents stigma and workplace divisions.
- Promoting work–life balance for all: acknowledging that everyone has a life outside work, flexibility supports a healthier work–life balance, not just for caregivers.
- Encouraging equality in caregiving roles: universal flexibility facilitates equitable sharing of family tasks, challenging traditional gender roles in caregiving.
- Preventing resentment and burnout: equal flexibility reduces employee resentment and burnout, maintaining a positive work environment.
- Enhanced productivity and loyalty: employees who feel understood and valued are more committed and productive, benefiting organisational performance and retention.

Universal workplace flexibility is vital to promoting equality, removing potential resentments and creating an inclusive culture where every employee feels valued and supported.

The theory

Workplace flexibility aligns closely with the ASSET and PERMA models in positive psychology, enhancing employee wellbeing and satisfaction.

Integration with ASSET Model

- Autonomy: flexibility gives employees control over their schedules and environments, fostering freedom and self-determination.
- Organisational and supervisor support: flexible work practices demonstrate a commitment to employees' diverse needs and wellbeing.

- Empowerment: it entrusts employees with the responsibility to manage their work effectively, boosting job satisfaction and ownership.
- Training: flexibility may not be directly mentioned in the context of training but can be inferred to support continuous learning tailored to individual schedules.

Integration with PERMA Model

- Positive emotions: flexibility reduces stress and anxiety, uplifting positive emotions at work and personally.
- Engagement: tailoring work hours or locations enhances engagement, allowing work during peak productivity.
- Relationships: it supports personal relationship maintenance, which is crucial for wellbeing and reduces workplace resentment or burnout.
- Meaning: it demonstrates that employers value personal needs and wellbeing, helping employees find more purpose in their work.
- Accomplishment: it enables fulfilling professional tasks while managing personal lives, increasing a sense of achievement.

Workplace flexibility is key to enhancing employee wellbeing and fitting within the ASSET and PERMA models. It addresses the complex nature of employees' lives, benefiting individuals and the organisation by creating a harmonious and productive work environment.

How can you implement it?

To effectively implement flexible work arrangements, consider these questions:

- Necessity of traditional hours: why do we adhere to a 9–5 schedule and what evidence supports its necessity?
- Benefits of flexibility: how might flexible arrangements boost our service and employee satisfaction?
- Identifying flexible roles and tasks: what roles or tasks in our organisation are suitable for non-traditional hours?
- Ensuring accountability in flexibility: how can we maintain accountability and performance in a flexible environment?
- Trial and assessment of flexibility: how can we trial flexible work policies to evaluate their impact?
- Learning from others: what lessons can we learn from organisations that have successfully implemented flexibility?

- Impact on wellbeing and workforce: how does a strict schedule affect employee wellbeing and workforce diversity?
- Handling varied personal circumstances: how would we accommodate key team members needing non-traditional work hours?

Developing a flexible working policy

- Collaborative development: establishing a dialogue between management and staff to co-develop the policy.
- Acknowledging individual differences: ensuring the policy accommodates diverse personal circumstances and work styles.
- Service quality maintenance: balancing flexibility with high-quality service, setting clear performance indicators.
- Flexible but structured: defining essential policy elements for operational consistency while allowing individual negotiation.
- Adaptability and review: regularly update the policy to adapt to changing needs.
- Training and support: providing necessary training and resources for effective implementation.
- Communication and transparency: ensuring clear, transparent policy communication to all staff.

Points for individuals to consider

- Optimising productivity: identifying the most productive hours and structuring the day to balance work and personal wellbeing.
- Prioritising tasks: focusing on essential work tasks and setting boundaries to prevent work–life overlap.
- Maintaining team connection: planning communication strategies to stay integrated with the team.
- Measuring performance: using metrics or indicators to assess productivity and effectiveness.
- Creating adaptable routines: establishing a flexible yet structured routine.
- Addressing isolation: engaging in team activities and social interactions to mitigate isolation in remote or non-standard hours.
- Regularly adjusting schedules: reviewing and adjusting working patterns as needed.

A successful flexible work policy requires a collaborative, adaptive approach, respecting individual needs while aligning with organisational goals.

Realising potential: Sun Microsystems' journey in flexible working
According to Tsedal Neeley PhD, in the podcast 'Back to the Office? The Future of Remote and Hybrid Work' (Neeley, 2021), another compelling example of the benefits of flexible working can be found in the experience of Sun Microsystems, a company later acquired by Oracle in 1997. Sun Microsystems was an early adopter of remote work and working-from-anywhere models. Their experimentation led to significant insights: not only did they observe a remarkable increase in productivity, but they also recognised the need to re-evaluate their real estate holdings to support these new working arrangements permanently.

   This shift in working style at Sun Microsystems highlighted a crucial understanding: the increase in productivity was not a result of employees working longer hours. Instead, it was attributed to the value employees placed on their autonomy and flexibility. When employees operated in an environment that offered job satisfaction and flexibility, their performance naturally improved. This case clearly demonstrates that in a virtual, hybrid or remote work setting, the focus should shift from traditional process monitoring to outcome-based assessment. Success in such environments is not about the physical presence of employees in the office ('butts on seats'), but about achieving desired outcomes, fostering team cohesion and equipping staff with the necessary tools and support to succeed.

The where – remote and hybrid working

Looking at how Sun Microsystems used flexible working gives us a good starting point for this next topic. We've seen how Sun Microsystems led the way in moving towards more independent and adaptable ways of working. This kind of change became even more widespread when the COVID-19 pandemic hit in 2020. According to Quezada, Talbot and Quezada-Parker (2020), this crisis really pushed many organisations to embrace working from home, using methods like e-mails, phone calls and online meetings. But this quick change also showed us some problems, such as the way workers might feel lonely and cut off, as Aguilera-Hermida (2020) pointed out. These issues show us that it's important to find a balance in remote and hybrid work. We need to think about how to keep the good things about flexible work, like independence, while also making sure people can still connect and interact with others. In this section we're going to look into how organisations can deal with these challenges and learn from what the pandemic has taught us about the way we work together.

Types of remote and hybrid working

The concept of 'remote and hybrid working' refers to two distinct, yet increasingly common, modes of working in the modern workforce, particularly accentuated by the shifts during and after the COVID-19 pandemic.

Remote working

Remote working, as the term implies, involves employees working from a location outside the traditional office environment. This can be their homes, coffee shops or even while travelling. The main characteristic of remote working is that employees are not required to be physically present in a specific office location. The rapid advancement in technology, especially during the COVID-19 pandemic, has enabled widespread adoption of remote work. Employees typically communicate with their colleagues and supervisors via e-mails, phone calls and video conferencing tools like Zoom and Microsoft Teams. The advantages of remote working include flexibility, reduced commute times and the comfort of working in a preferred environment. Challenges such as feelings of isolation, difficulty in disconnecting from work and challenges in collaboration and communication have been noted.

Hybrid working

Hybrid working models blend in-office work with remote work. Employees in a hybrid setup can split their time between working at an office and working remotely. This model aims to offer the best of both worlds – the flexibility and independence of remote work and the collaboration and social interaction that come from working in an office. Organisations adopting a hybrid model often face challenges in harmonising diverse work preferences, ensuring efficiency and maintaining a consistent company culture. The key is to find a balance that allows for both flexibility and effective collaboration. Integrating a hybrid working model has its challenges.

Benefits and challenges
Benefits

The post-pandemic workforce requires leaders to harmonise diverse work preferences while ensuring efficiency and collaboration. A 2021 survey underscored this, with 61% of employees favouring permanent remote work over a considerable pay hike (GoodHire, 2021). A study (Buffer, 2021) involving over 2300 remote workers revealed that 97% of respondents would recommend remote work to others and would continue working remotely even post-pandemic. As cited by 32% of respondents, the primary advantage of remote work is flexibility. Another 25% valued the ability to work from their preferred location. Other positive aspects include avoiding the daily commute (22%) and spending time with family (11%).

Challenges

Despite the benefits, the study also highlighted remote working challenges. Before the pandemic, a lack of collaboration and loneliness were frequent concerns. In the 2021 Buffer Study 27% of participants cited difficulty in mentally disconnecting from work as the biggest challenge, followed by collaboration and communication difficulties and loneliness (both at 16%). Other issues included home distractions (15%), maintaining motivation (12%) and working in different time zones from teammates (7%). Nevertheless, as 74% of respondents stated their immediate teams work across multiple time zones, this arrangement is becoming more normalised.

Presenteeism and health

Another important aspect to consider is the health impact of presenteeism, particularly in spreading common illnesses such as colds, flu and COVID-19. 'Presenteeism' refers to the practice of coming to work despite not being well, often driven by a sense of obligation or a lack of flexible working options. This not only hampers the individual's recovery but also increases the risk of transmitting illnesses to colleagues. The spread of diseases in a workplace setting can lead to more staff falling ill, thereby affecting overall productivity and wellbeing. The COVID-19 pandemic has highlighted the critical need for workplaces to adopt flexible and remote working policies, not just for efficiency and employee satisfaction, but also as a means to protect the health of the workforce. By allowing employees the option to work from home organisations can significantly reduce the risk of disease transmission, ensuring a healthier and more resilient team.

We need to be careful that flexible working doesn't get misused whilst remote working can stop disease spreading. It's important that people aren't expected to work from home when they're not well. When someone is ill, they need proper rest and time to get better, not just a change of location from the office to their home. While it's great that employees can work remotely if they need to, we shouldn't let this turn into a situation where people feel they have to work even when they're sick. This kind of pressure can be bad for their health and wellbeing. It's crucial that employers encourage staff to take the time off they need for their health, rather than just switching to working from home. This approach helps ensure that everyone stays healthy and doesn't feel overworked or stressed. In Case Study 9.2, Michelle Brown offers some important insights into the environments we work in.

Case Study 9.2: Green spaces are kind spaces

How can people be expected to thrive in an environment where a plant wilts and struggles even to survive? An overlooked aspect of our workplaces is the physical environment; on average, people spend a third of their lives at work! Let's make the best of that time by creating spaces where the nurturing qualities of nature improve wellbeing and inspire kindness toward the environment and one another. Three steps to foster kindness and help staff thrive:

Assess the workspace
Evaluate the lighting, furniture and atmosphere of the workspace. Would a plant survive or thrive here? Natural lighting, comfortable equipment and plenty of organised space should exist. Make the changes necessary to support life and create an environment for staff to thrive.

Bring nature inside
Integrating nature into the workspace goes beyond mere aesthetics. It fosters kindness and wellbeing by providing a sense of calm, giving staff a shared commitment to environmental stewardship, fostering a sense of collective responsibility and providing a silent invitation to pause, breathe and connect with nature. Strategically place live plants around the workspace so that at least one is visible from every workstation. Have staff care for the plants together. To incorporate this into a teambuilding activity, discuss the similarities between plants and people and what each needs to survive versus thrive. You could also give plants as a welcome or appreciation gift. Live plants provide the most benefits. Artificial plants and pictures of natural landscapes also help reduce stress and improve mood.

Get outside
Just like a plant, humans need sunshine and fresh air. Spending even a few minutes outside daily, mindfully looking at the trees, grass and sky, can improve overall wellbeing and cultivate a sense of appreciation for nature. If your natural surroundings are limited, pay attention to changes in the weather and seasons. Think of ways for work tasks to be facilitated outdoors, like an icebreaker or team-building activity. These could be nature-themed, like a scavenger hunt, or simply take place outdoors. Hold a walking meeting where staff take their discussions on the go and walk outside while talking. Provide ongoing encouragement for staff to get outside by creating a nature wall where they can add treasures they found on

their outdoor adventures, like flowers or leaves. For remote work, create a digital board where staff share selfies or pictures of their finds.

Michelle Brown, Sacramento Public Library

How to be sure that a hybrid or remote working policy works for wellbeing

I have seen many times that when people navigate leading hybrid teams their knee-jerk reaction is to be prescriptive about when people need to come to the physical office when this is based on an operational need: for example, in-person teaching, team meetings, desk or building management and physical stock work that needs to be done on-site. Making these decisions in partnership with the team works much better than a blanket instruction that everybody should be in.

Below are some questions managers and individuals need to consider about being on-site.

Questions for managers to ask themselves

- Is the goal of in-office time clear, beneficial for collaboration and wellbeing and effectively communicated?
- Does our remote policy offer enough flexibility? How regularly do we seek and incorporate team feedback?
- Are remote workers included in all communications and decisions and what support is provided for their wellbeing?
- Are performance evaluations unbiased and do all employees have the necessary resources for practical remote work?
- How do we maintain team spirit and manage workload to prevent burnout among remote workers?
- Are remote workers given equal access to training and professional development opportunities?

Questions for individuals to ask themselves

- Am I maintaining a healthy work–life balance and is my home workspace conducive to productivity and wellbeing?
- Am I staying connected with colleagues and have I set clear work/personal time boundaries?
- Am I taking care of my physical and mental health, sharing feedback and seeking professional development opportunities?

■ How am I managing feelings of isolation, effectively using technology and assessing my productivity in remote settings?

The outcome of some of these questions may lead to people needing or wanting to be on-site more than expected; at this point, desk spaces and equipment may come under pressure and this needs to be part of planning.

Fairness and kindness are paramount in library and remote work environments, impacting everything from opportunity equality to resource allocation. Whether ensuring equitable access to career growth or providing necessary resources for remote workers and library staff, these practices contribute to a fair and supportive workplace.

Challenges and solutions

Challenges

■ Equity in opportunity and resource allocation: equitable tasks, role distribution and fair resource access are essential. This includes clear communication about role allocations and ensuring all staff have what they need to perform effectively.
■ Emotional support and recognition: emotional support and flexibility are key in high-stress environments like libraries, especially during peak times. Acknowledging and appreciating the efforts of both on-site and remote staff fosters a culture of kindness.
■ Perceptions of fairness: addressing perceived imbalances, isolation and inequity between on-site and remote staff is crucial. It is important to create an inclusive environment where every employee feels valued regardless of their work location.

Practical solutions

■ Staff training: implement positive psychology and wellbeing training to help staff navigate their roles effectively.
■ Regular team meetings: facilitate open discussions for all staff, allowing collective problem-solving and addressing feelings of unfairness.
■ Ongoing policy reviews: continuously update policies on fairness and kindness to remain relevant and responsive to all staff.

Strategies for remote working

■ Virtual social events: encourage informal interaction beyond work-related topics to maintain team cohesion.

- Mentorship and buddy systems: provide support and connection, especially for new hires or those feeling isolated.
- Flexible working hours: allow employees to work during their most productive times, balancing personal commitments.
- Professional development opportunities: offer online learning to keep remote workers engaged and growing with the organisation.

By emphasising fairness, kindness and inclusive practices, library professionals can create a supportive work environment conducive to personal and professional growth, regardless of team member's location. Regular engagement, open communication and flexible policies are key to adapting to the dynamic needs of a diverse workforce.

Case Study 9.3: Monthly Mentions: finding ways to share kindness in a hybrid-working era

Previously a very close-knit team, working in a hybrid manner meant that we often felt separated. That separation caused some to feel lonely, as well as making it difficult for some to keep up with the developments of the team. I wanted to come up with a way in which we could help people to feel close to one another, keep up to date with team developments and spread some kindness and positivity amongst each other. This is where our 'Monthly Mentions' were born.

An anonymous Microsoft Form allows members of our team to post 'shout-outs' to others. These can be thanks for a favour, appreciation of a job well done or a positive inspiring message about a colleague you love working with. Each month these are turned into an infographic and shared with the entire team. This not only allows us to share the kindness of the entries, but also gives people the opportunity to jump on the bandwagon, repeating the mentions and adding their own feedback. A train of kindness if you will!

This initiative has seen very positive feedback from staff at all levels, reporting that they feel more valued, appreciated and that it really cheers up their day when they're posted. Success has been such, that there's now talk of expanding this to cover the entire library staff network, rather than just our team. Even more opportunities to spread kindness!

Dean Brown, Reading List Support Administrator, University of Salford

Tips for leading hybrid working teams

If you are a leader reading this and still feeling overwhelmed by these changes, the following tips will help you improve your leadership.

- Recognise and reaffirm:
  - Team dynamics: regularly evaluate the impact of work mode changes on team dynamics, acknowledging challenges and successes.
  - Virtual culture building: use virtual activities and digital tools to foster a sense of belonging and community.
  - Open dialogue: encourage regular one-on-one and group discussions, focusing on coaching for personal and professional growth.
- Prioritise inclusion:
  - Inclusive meetings: ensure remote participants have equal input, possibly rotating meeting times for different time zones.
  - Team norms and clarity: develop shared norms and clear processes agreed upon by all team members.
  - Transparent communication: create a charter to define preferred channels and response expectations.
- Embrace adaptability:
  - Strategy review: continually adapt team strategies and objectives.
  - Employee wellbeing: integrate wellness programmes and mental health support.
  - Building resilience: provide resources and training for resilience development.
- Ensure direction, alignment and commitment (DAC):
  - Clear goals: communicate the organisation's vision and goals clearly.
  - Role alignment: use cross-functional teams to align on projects and goals.
  - Fostering commitment: recognise and reward individual and team achievements.
- Strengthen boundary spanning:
  - Cross-team collaboration: mix remote and on-site staff for projects to enhance co-operation.
  - Effective communication tools: invest in technology for smooth cross-location communication.
  - Integration activities: conduct regular virtual or hybrid team-building activities.

These strategies focus on inclusivity, adaptability and effective communication, which are key to fostering a productive and positive hybrid work environment.

The importance of trust in flexible, remote and hybrid working

Trust is critical to making flexible working successful and for ensuring people feel good at work. When leaders and managers trust their staff to manage their own time and tasks, it makes for a better and more positive workplace. Trust isn't just about thinking that people will get their work done. It's about valuing their ability to work well, no matter if they're in the office or working from somewhere else.

Trusting people at work means moving away from always watching over them and focusing more on the results they achieve. If people feel trusted, they will be more involved, eager and happy in their jobs. This leads to them feeling better mentally, being less stressed and being more productive. Trust also makes people feel more responsible and in charge of their work, which encourages them to come up with new ideas and take initiative.

But trust needs effort from both managers and staff. Managers should talk clearly, set sensible goals and give the support and tools needed. At the same time, staff should show they are dependable, communicate and meet their work goals. When both sides trust each other, flexible working can improve wellbeing and productivity.

Frei and Morriss's (2020) trust triangle (discussed in more detail in Chapter 10) gives us a model to understand trust in flexible workplaces. Frei and Morriss talk about three important parts of trust: Authenticity, Logic and Empathy. Let's look at how these fit into flexible working and wellbeing.

- Authenticity: in flexible working, being real means bosses need to be honest about what can and can't be done. They should be clear about what's expected and what might be hard in remote or hybrid working. Staff should also be open about their work situations and needs. When everyone is honest and open, it builds real understanding and respect between bosses and staff.
- Logic: this is about why decisions are made or why certain policies are in place. Bosses should clearly explain why they have certain remote working policies, what they expect and how they'll measure work. When staff understand the reasons, they're more likely to trust the way things are done and feel secure, no matter where they work.
- Empathy: In flexible working, caring means understanding that everyone has different challenges and needs. It's recognising that not everyone's situation is the same and so working solutions should be different for different people. When staff feel that their bosses understand and value their personal situations, it builds deeper trust and makes them feel more connected to their work.

By bringing these parts of the trust triangle into flexible work, we can create a well-balanced, productive and trusting environment. Bosses who show they are real, make sense and care in their flexible working policies are not just building trust. They are also supporting the wellbeing and happiness of their staff.

Work–life integration: beyond flexibility

As we've explored the tangible shifts towards flexible, remote and hybrid working models, let's explore the philosophical growth accompanying these changes: work–life integration. This approach moves beyond merely adjusting the 'where' and 'when' of work, advocating a more fluid blend of our professional and personal lives. It challenges us to rethink the structure of our workdays and the very nature of how we define work and life. As we consider transitioning towards a four-day work week, understanding work–life integration becomes crucial in reimagining a future where work enriches life and energy, in turn, fuels our work.

In an era where technology has blurred the lines between work and personal life, work–life integration offers a forward-thinking approach. This model recognises the intertwined nature of our professional ambitions and personal passions, advocating a seamless blend that enhances overall wellbeing and fulfilment. Unlike the traditional 9–5, work–life integration emphasises outcomes over hours, encouraging flexibility, autonomy and a shift towards measuring success by impact rather than time spent. It calls for leaders to foster environments that respect personal commitments through flexible working hours, support for remote work and open dialogue about workloads and personal needs. It also highlights the importance of clear boundaries to prevent burnout and the strategic use of technology to facilitate a smooth integration of work into our personal lives. This approach caters to the diverse needs and life stages of individuals and aligns with modern living realities, promising a richer, more fulfilling experience for both employees and organisations.

Work–life integration is seen as more adaptable than work–life balance because it aligns better with the fluidity of modern life. Unlike the balanced approach, which tries to allocate equal time and attention to work and personal life, integration allows for a more flexible merging of the two. This reflects the reality of today's always-connected world, where the strict boundaries between professional and personal activities are increasingly blurred. Integration acknowledges that work and personal interests can complement and enhance each other, leading to greater overall satisfaction and effectiveness.

The future: why consider a four-day working week?

The traditional 9–5, five-day working week is no longer suited to the needs of modern society.

The UK is among the nations working the longest hours in Europe (TUC, 2019), yet it has one of the least productive economics. The weekend concept, invented a century ago, needs a revamp.

A four-day working week is a four-day, 32-hour working week without pay reduction, which can benefit workers, employers, the economy, society and the environment.

Benefits of a four-day week include:

- For workers: improved work–life balance, better sleep and rest, more leisure time and financial savings.
- For employers: enhanced performance and profits, attracting and retaining talent.
- For the economy: lower unemployment, increased productivity and tourism growth.
- For society: better mental and physical health, gender equality and stronger communities.
- For the environment: sustainable living choices and reduced carbon footprint.

Among the challenges and strategies in libraries are:

- Staffing and scheduling: implementing longer shifts, staggered schedules, hiring part-time staff and rotating responsibilities.
- User services: enhancing digital access, increasing self-service options and providing remote assistance.
- Administrative duties: automating tasks, batching tasks and conducting virtual meetings.
- Monitoring and feedback: running a pilot phase, conducting regular check-ins and gathering community feedback.

The 4 Day Week Global (n.d.), UK's most extensive four-day working week pilot study, showed positive results, with 92% of participating firms maintaining the model. Benefits included reduced employee burnout, fewer sick days, improved job retention and increased job satisfaction. Businesses also reported revenue growth.

Despite positive trial outcomes, the UK government has expressed concerns regarding taxpayer value, advising against widespread adoption, and has opposed trials like those in South Cambridgeshire District Council, which reported improved performance, reduced staff turnover and lowered sickness rates.

Conclusion

This chapter underscores the significance of flexible working as a vital component in enhancing wellbeing and productivity in the library workplace. Highlighted are the positive impacts of flexible working arrangements, such as varied start and end times, compressed working weeks, part-time schedules and time banking. These measures not only address the unique demands and roles within a library setting but also balance operational requirements with staff's personal needs. The implementation of such flexible practices fosters a culture of trust, autonomy and inclusivity, contributing significantly to job satisfaction, work–life balance and overall staff wellbeing. This approach, resonating with the ASSET and PERMA models in positive psychology, shows that flexible working is not just a theoretical concept but a practical, beneficial strategy that can transform the library workplace into a more dynamic, responsive and fulfilling environment for all. It is an essential component of any kind culture.

Exercises and reflective questions

Exercise for leaders and teams

Collaborative flexibility mapping

Objective: to create a collaborative understanding and implementation plan for flexible working arrangements catering to individual needs and organisational goals.

Steps:

1   Group discussion: begin with a team meeting where each member shares their ideal working conditions, including preferred hours, remote working preferences and any personal constraints or preferences.
2   Flexibility mapping: on a large chart, map out the team's collective preferences and constraints. Include elements like preferred working hours, remote working days and essential in-office days.
3   Scenario planning: discuss various scenarios, such as peak work periods, project deadlines and emergencies. Develop strategies on how the team can adapt their flexible working arrangements to these scenarios while ensuring that work continues smoothly.

4 Policy drafting: draft a flexible working policy for the team based on the discussion. This should include guidelines on communication, core hours (if any) and how to handle changes in individual circumstances.
5 Trial period and feedback: implement the policy on a trial basis. Schedule regular check-ins to gather feedback and make adjustments as necessary.

Outcome: A team-based approach to flexible working that respects individual needs and maintains team cohesion and productivity.

Exercise for individuals
Personal wellbeing and productivity plan in a hybrid/remote working environment
Objective: to empower individuals to create a personalised plan that balances their work responsibilities with personal wellbeing, specifically tailored to the nuances of hybrid or remote working.
Steps:

1 Self-assessment: individuals reflect on their most productive hours and environments, considering how remote or hybrid working impacts their efficiency and energy levels. They should also assess personal commitments and wellbeing activities to incorporate into their routine.
2 Creating a hybrid/remote work schedule: using this assessment, individuals develop a weekly schedule that optimises their work tasks for remote or hybrid settings. This includes designating time blocks for focused work, considering remote collaboration needs, breaks, exercise and family time. The schedule should reflect the unique opportunities and challenges of working remotely or in a hybrid model.
3 Setting boundaries for remote work: develop strategies for delineating work and personal time, especially in remote settings. This could involve setting up a dedicated workspace, establishing 'offline' hours and using digital tools to signal availability to colleagues.
4 Communication plan for remote collaboration: create a plan to maintain clear and consistent team communication. This should include regular virtual check-ins, updates and collaborative sessions. Consideration should be given to how remote working affects communication dynamics and how to maintain team cohesion.
5 Weekly review and adjustment: at the end of each week, individuals should review the effectiveness of their schedule, focusing on productivity, work–life balance and overall wellbeing in a remote or hybrid context. Based on this review, adjustments should be made to improve the following week.

6 Adapting to remote challenges: include a step for identifying and addressing specific challenges of remote or hybrid working, such as feelings of isolation, managing distractions at home and ensuring adequate technical resources.

Outcome: A tailored plan that supports individuals in effectively managing their time and responsibilities, enhancing their productivity and wellbeing within the unique context of flexible, hybrid or remote working environments.

Reflective questions
■ How has my understanding of flexible and hybrid/remote working changed after reading this chapter? Reflect on any new insights or shifts in perspective you've gained about flexible and hybrid/remote working.
■ What are my key takeaways regarding the impact of flexible work arrangements on personal wellbeing and productivity? Consider the most significant lessons you've learned about balancing work and personal life in a flexible work setting.
■ How well do I manage work and personal life boundaries in a remote or hybrid environment? Think about the effectiveness of your current strategies in separating work from personal time, especially when working from home.
■ What challenges do I face in a hybrid/remote working setting and how can I address them? Identify any difficulties you experience, such as feeling isolated, managing distractions or communicating with colleagues, and consider potential solutions.
■ How effective is my communication with team members in a remote or hybrid setting and what improvements could be made? Reflect on your current communication practices and consider ways to enhance clarity, frequency and effectiveness.
■ How can I improve my work environment at home to boost my productivity and wellbeing? Think about the physical setup of your home workspace and any changes you could make to create a more conducive work environment.
■ How does my work schedule in a flexible arrangement align with my most productive times and what adjustments might be beneficial? Assess whether your current work schedule maximises your productivity and consider if any changes could align better with your natural energy levels.
■ What strategies can I adopt to better manage stress and maintain a healthy work–life balance in a remote or hybrid working setting? Think

about stress management techniques and work–life balance strategies that could be particularly effective in a remote or hybrid working context.

- How can I stay connected and engaged with my team and what role does technology play in this? Reflect on how you currently connect with your team and the role of technology, considering any improvements or additional tools that could enhance engagement.
- What personal goals can I set to continuously improve my effectiveness and satisfaction in a flexible, hybrid or remote work environment? Consider setting specific, measurable goals related to your work arrangements to help you grow and find greater satisfaction in your role.

CHAPTER 10

The Art of Kind Recruitment: Fostering Inclusivity and Empathy in Hiring Practices

Introduction

The start of everybody's journey working in a library is the recruitment process. Traditionally, this will have been stress-inducing, candidates unable to show their best side as they are trying to navigate unkind processes where adverts may close early, job application forms are all different, interviews are arranged at short notice with no idea who they are meeting or where to go. They are expected to be at their best when faced with questions they have no idea about and then, after all that, they wait days to find out if they have got the job. This can hugely impact the wellbeing of the candidate by stressing them out, especially as there may be many reasons that they are looking for a new job, some of which could be fundamental to their lifestyle such as financial or family needs.

We will address post-recruitment practices, highlighting the importance of feedback and relationship-building with candidates. Challenges and practical solutions to help implement kind recruitment in various organisational contexts will be discussed. The chapter will conclude with methods to measure the impact of kind recruitment on the organisation and its employees, ensuring that the practice of kindness remains a core element in the recruitment strategy. Additional resources and reflective questions will be provided to encourage the reader to engage actively with the concepts and integrate them into their own recruitment practices.

Reflective questions
- How does your current recruitment process align with the principles of kindness and fairness?
- Reflect on a recent recruitment exercise you conducted or participated in. In what ways could it have been more candidate-centred?
- What does 'kind recruitment' mean to you and why is it important in today's workplace?

- Can you identify any biases or barriers in your current recruitment practices? How might these impact candidates' experiences?
- How prepared do you feel your library is to implement kind recruitment strategies? What challenges do you anticipate in making this shift?

Definition of kind recruitment

Kind recruitment is a holistic approach to hiring that emphasises empathy, respect and consideration for all candidates throughout the recruitment process. It goes beyond merely assessing skills and qualifications; it's about creating a positive and inclusive experience for every applicant. This approach involves transparent communication, unbiased evaluation and a genuine commitment to the wellbeing of potential employees. Kind recruitment is not just a practice but a reflection of an organisation's values and culture, where kindness is foundational.

Differences between traditional and kind recruitment methods

- Approach to communication: traditional recruitment often involves standard, impersonal communication. In contrast, kind recruitment emphasises personalised and empathetic interactions, ensuring that candidates feel valued and heard.
- Candidate experience: traditional methods may focus primarily on the organisation's needs. Kind recruitment, however, emphasises the candidate's experience, aiming to make the process respectful and stress-free.
- Evaluation criteria: while traditional recruitment may primarily assess technical skills and experience, kind recruitment incorporates a more holistic view, considering a candidate's potential, personality and alignment with the organisation's values.
- Feedback practices: in traditional settings, feedback, if given, is often generic. Kind recruitment advocates constructive and thoughtful feedback to aid the candidate's growth, regardless of the hiring outcome.
- Focus on inclusivity: kind recruitment is inherently more inclusive, actively working to remove biases and barriers and ensuring all candidates feel welcome and respected.

Benefits of implementing kind recruitment for employers and candidates

The benefits for employers include:

- Enhanced employer brand: adopting kind recruitment practices improves an organisation's reputation, making it more attractive to top talent.
- Increased employee engagement and retention: candidates hired through kind recruitment processes are more likely to feel a strong sense of belonging and loyalty to the organisation, leading to higher retention rates.
- Diverse and inclusive workforce: kind recruitment naturally leads to a more diverse workforce, fostering creativity, innovation and various perspectives within the organisation.
- Improved workplace culture: integrating kindness into recruitment sets the tone for the overall workplace culture, promoting values of empathy, respect and collaboration.

The benefits for candidates are:

- Positive application experience: even if not selected, candidates are left with a positive impression of the organisation, which can encourage future applications or positive word-of-mouth.
- Reduced stress and anxiety: kind recruitment's respectful and transparent nature can alleviate the stress and anxiety often associated with job applications.
- Personal growth: receiving constructive feedback helps candidates develop personally and professionally, regardless of the hiring outcome.
- Sense of belonging: for those hired, the recruitment process begins their employment with a sense of being valued and respected, contributing to immediate engagement and job satisfaction.

In conclusion, understanding kind recruitment is about recognising its transformative potential for the hiring process and the organisation as a whole. It's a strategy that benefits everyone involved, laying the groundwork for a workplace culture that embodies kindness and wellbeing.

Case Study 10.1: Inclusive recruitment at the University of Westminster

The University of Westminster's Library and Archives Services initiated a recruitment enhancement project to foster a more inclusive hiring process, especially for autistic and neurodiverse candidates. This initiative sought to embody the University's commitment to equality, diversity and inclusion (EDI) by:

- creating a recruitment welcome pack, including panel details, role information, interview advice and questions and providing these to candidates beforehand
- ensuring job adverts communicated a welcoming stance towards diverse applicants, emphasising inclusive hiring
- involving neurodiverse student researchers in refining the welcome pack.

The goals of these methods included increasing transparency, aiding neurodiverse applicants in preparation, demonstrating the University's desire for candidate success and facilitating a comfortable interview environment where candidates could excel.

Despite initial concerns that pre-sharing questions might lead to less suitable candidates performing well or rehearsed responses, the team addressed these by:

- introducing unforeseen follow-up questions during interviews
- applying precise scoring criteria and expectations for each response.

Feedback was sought from both the panel and candidates. The panel noted varied candidate strengths despite advance question sharing and the effectiveness of follow-up questions in gauging the depth of knowledge. Candidate feedback was overwhelmingly positive, highlighting the University's commitment to EDI, reduced interview stress and a level playing field for all.

This successful approach led to more in-depth candidate responses and a less stressful interview atmosphere.

This innovative approach significantly contributes to applicants' wellbeing and mental health, fostering a supportive and inclusive work culture.

Daniela De Silva, Eleri Kyffin and Amy Stubbing, University of Westminster

Case Study 10.2: Inclusive recruitment at Lancaster University

Over the past year at Lancaster University, we have been developing our inclusive recruitment practices, which can also be termed as kind recruitment, as it places the applicants' experience at heart. Our work was inspired by colleagues at the University of Salford, who have developed an Inclusive Recruitment Checklist, and met members of our Library Management Team to discuss practicalities.

Across the library, we have paired up to examine job descriptions and person specs to ensure we aren't including library jargon and, where appropriate, making the requirements relevant to those who may not have worked in HE or libraries before, providing guidance on completing the application. We have discussed how applications from colleagues overseas (where English may not be their first language) may not be perfectly grammatically correct and to factor in whether that is important to the role. We have tried to make the interview process more friendly – by sharing photos of the interview location and panel (and their pronouns) in advance, sending out the interview questions at least 24 hours ahead of the interview and giving guidance on how to prepare for the interview (with the aim of the candidates being able to prepare in advance and take away the 'on the spot' challenge) and by thinking about the room layout – do we want the candidate to come into a row of interviewees? Or can we position the room so that it is less formal and, finally, be as welcoming and friendly as possible?

We have received informal feedback from those successful and unsuccessful at the interview that the process was as enjoyable as an interview can be and that having the questions in advance took the pressure off the situation:

'I cannot forget to thank you and your team for your professionalism and support and how you made me feel at ease throughout the interview. You reflected true ambassadorship for your organisation, which inspires me.'

Lesley English, Head of Library Engagement, Lancaster University

Pre-recruitment strategies
Creating job adverts with a positive tone

- Language use: words have power and the tone of a job advert can significantly influence a candidate's perception of the organisation. Avoid jargon and overly formal language that might seem intimidating.
- Highlighting opportunities: focus on what the organisation can offer to the candidate, not just on what is expected from them. This includes opportunities for growth, learning and personal development, which are key components of a kind and supportive workplace.
- Clarity and transparency: be clear about the role's requirements and responsibilities. Misleading or vague job descriptions can lead to confusion and mistrust. A kind approach is always straightforward and honest.

Ensuring diversity and inclusivity in job adverts

- Avoiding biased language: use tools or external reviews to ensure that the language in your job descriptions is free from unconscious biases that might discourage certain groups from applying.
- Representation matters: include statements or commitments to diversity and inclusivity, showing that all candidates will be valued and judged solely based on their merits.
- Working hours: be clear about the working pattern, what hours are people expected to work; if part-time are there certain days and if it is genuinely flexible be clear about that too. Also if the role is hybrid be clear about which days are on-site if there are set days.
- Accessibility: ensure that job postings are accessible to all, including those with disabilities. This includes the use of accessible website design and offering alternative application methods if needed.

The role of employer branding in attracting kind-minded candidates

- Communicating company values: use your employer brand to communicate your commitment to kindness and wellbeing in the workplace. This can be through stories, testimonials or examples of how these values are lived out in the organisation.
- Social media and online presence: leverage social media and your online presence to showcase your company culture. Post content that highlights employee experiences, community involvement and workplace initiatives that promote kindness and wellbeing.
- Employee advocacy: encourage current employees to share their positive experiences. Authentic stories from real employees can be powerful in attracting candidates who value kindness and wellbeing.

Implementing these pre-recruitment strategies sets the foundation for a kind recruitment process. It's about creating an initial impression that resonates with kind-minded candidates and ensuring that the organisation's values of kindness and wellbeing are clear right from the start. This approach not only attracts candidates who align with these values but also sets the tone for their entire journey with the organisation.

The recruitment process

The initial screening of candidates reflects an organisation's commitment to fairness and equality. Organisations should employ various structured screening methods to ensure this phase is conducted without bias. These

Kind recruitment self-assessment checklist
- Transparency:
  — Do our job descriptions clearly outline the role and its requirements?
  — Are our recruitment processes and timelines communicated clearly to candidates?
- Equity and inclusivity:
  — Have we audited our job adverts for biased language?
  — Do we actively encourage applications from diverse backgrounds?
- Respect for candidates:
  — Are we providing timely responses to all applicants, regardless of their selection status?
  — Do we offer constructive feedback to unsuccessful candidates?
- Empathetic and respectful interviewing:
  — Are our interviewers trained in empathetic interviewing techniques?
  — Do we ensure a comfortable and supportive interview environment for all candidates?
- Candidate experience:
  — Do we regularly seek feedback from candidates about their experience?
  — Are we making continuous improvements based on this feedback?
- Alignment with organisational values:
  — Is our recruitment process reflective of our organisation's core values and culture?
  — Do we assess candidates not just for skills but also for cultural fit?

This checklist will help you identify areas where your current recruitment practices align with kind recruitment principles and where there might be opportunities for improvement.

methods should exclusively focus on the skills and qualifications directly relevant to the job.

Training the recruitment team on recognising and mitigating unconscious bias is also essential. Workshops and training sessions help recruiters understand their biases, how they might affect their decision-making and strategies to counteract them. Creating a culture that values diversity and inclusivity at this stage sets the tone for the entire recruitment process and, ultimately, for the workplace culture.

Conducting empathetic and respectful interviews

The interview stage is a critical opportunity to assess candidates' suitability and forge a connection with them. An empathetic and respectful interview process is characterised by a warm, welcoming atmosphere where candidates are encouraged to be themselves and share their unique perspectives and experiences.

As highlighted in both the University of Westminster and the Lancaster University case studies (10.1 and 10.2), sending out interview questions in advance is good practice as it allows everyone to prepare, removing some of the anxiety involved in interviews and removing the advantage internal or experienced candidates have. It is up to the candidate if they wish to prepare in advance and it is recommended that you explain they will only have a certain amount of time per question so they can prepare.

Equity in the interview process is crucial. Ensuring all candidates receive the same information and are asked consistent questions is key to fairness. Additionally, interviewers should be prepared to make necessary adjustments for candidates with special needs, whether physical accommodation or adaptations to the interview format, in line with the principles of inclusivity and respect.

Providing constructive feedback to all candidates

Feedback is invaluable for candidates. Constructive feedback, when delivered thoughtfully, can provide candidates with insights into their strengths and areas for improvement. This feedback should be specific, focusing on aspects of the candidate's application or interview performance. It should always include positive and actionable suggestions.

Regardless of whether candidates are selected for the role, they should come away feeling that their time and effort have been respected and valued. This kind of feedback practice benefits the candidates in their professional development. It enhances the organisation's reputation as an employer who values and respects everyone who engages with them.

Incorporating fair and unbiased screening practices, conducting empathetic and respectful interviews and providing constructive feedback are not just recruitment strategies; they are manifestations of an organisation's commitment to kindness, fairness and inclusivity. This comprehensive approach ensures that the best candidates are selected based on merit and fit, fostering a positive and respectful experience for all applicants. When implemented effectively, these practices contribute significantly to a more inclusive, equitable and kind workplace culture.

Post-recruitment follow-up

The post-recruitment phase is crucial in maintaining the ethos of kindness and fairness established during the earlier stages of the recruitment process. This stage involves wrapping up the current recruitment cycle and setting the stage for future interactions with both successful and unsuccessful candidates.

Building relationships with potential future candidates

Candidates unsuitable for the current role may be perfect for future opportunities. Therefore, it's essential to maintain a positive relationship with these individuals. This can be achieved by expressing genuine appreciation for their interest in the organisation and encouraging them to apply for future positions that align with their skills and experience.

Organisations can consider creating talent pools, where details of promising candidates are retained (with their permission) for future opportunities. Regular communication, such as updates about new openings or organisational news, can help keep these candidates engaged and interested in the organisation.

Ensuring timely notification of recruitment delays

A critical aspect of the post-recruitment process is the timely communication with candidates regarding any delays in the recruitment timeline. It's vital to inform candidates promptly if there is a delay in notifying them of the outcome of their application. Failing to do so risks tarnishing the organisation's reputation for kindness and fairness and increases the likelihood of losing talented candidates to other opportunities.

In a world where candidates often have multiple options, how an organisation handles communication during recruitment delays can significantly impact a candidate's perception of the organisation. Promptly informing candidates about delays demonstrates respect for their time and consideration, reinforcing the organisation's commitment to transparency and fairness.

This practice of proactive communication is an extension of the organisation's ethos of kindness and wellbeing. The organisation builds trust by keeping candidates informed, even when the news isn't definitive. It maintains a positive relationship, which is essential for current and future recruitment efforts. It shows candidates that they are valued, not just as potential employees but as individuals, which aligns with the broader goal of transforming the world of work into a place where wellbeing and kindness are the norm.

Induction with kindness and support

The induction experience must align with the kindness and support demonstrated during recruitment. A kind and supportive induction process involves thorough preparation, clear communication and an empathetic approach to integrating new hires into the team.

New employees should be provided with all the resources and information they need to start their roles effectively. This includes a clear outline of their responsibilities, introductions to key team members and understanding the company's culture and values. Regular check-ins during the first few weeks can also help new hires feel supported and valued.

Induction is not just about the technicalities of a new job; it's about making new recruits feel welcomed and part of the team. Activities like team lunches or informal meet-and-greets can effectively build these connections. It's also essential to provide new employees with avenues for feedback and questions, ensuring they feel heard and understood.

In conclusion, the post-recruitment follow-up is critical in reinforcing the organisation's commitment to kindness and fairness. It involves providing constructive feedback to unsuccessful candidates, maintaining relationships with potential future candidates and ensuring a supportive induction experience for new hires. These practices enhance the organisation's reputation and contribute to a culture of continuous respect and empathy.

Enhancing diversity and inclusion through kind recruitment

Kind recruitment is integral in promoting diversity and inclusion within the workplace. This approach goes beyond traditional hiring practices by actively seeking and embracing diversity in all its forms. It involves creating an environment where candidates from all backgrounds feel valued and have equal opportunities to succeed. Strategies could include:

- Targeted outreach: implement strategies for actively reaching out to under-represented groups. This could involve partnering with organisations or communities that work closely with these groups, participating in job fairs targeting diverse candidates and advertising in media outlets that cater to these communities.
- Inclusive job descriptions: craft job descriptions that are welcoming to all. Use inclusive language and avoid criteria that could inadvertently exclude certain groups. Clearly state your commitment to diversity and inclusion in the job posting.
- Bias-free screening process: utilise tools and processes that minimise unconscious bias. This could include blind resumé screening, where

personal identifiers are removed, and structured interviews with standardised questions for all candidates.
- Diverse selection panels: ensure your interview panels are diverse, as this can help reduce bias in the selection process and provide different perspectives on a candidate's suitability.
- Accessibility and accommodations: make sure your recruitment process is accessible to candidates with disabilities. This includes providing materials in accessible formats and making reasonable adjustments during interviews.
- Cultural competence training: train your recruitment team on cultural competence and unconscious bias. This helps them understand and appreciate the value of diverse perspectives and backgrounds.

Kind recruitment can significantly contribute to a more diverse and inclusive workplace by focusing on these areas. This enriches the organisational culture and enhances creativity, innovation and understanding within the team.

Global perspectives in library kind recruitment

Understanding global recruitment perspectives is essential in the library sector, where community engagement and cultural diversity are pivotal. Libraries, as community hubs, often serve diverse populations, making it crucial to have a workforce that reflects and understands this diversity.

Internationally, libraries must adapt their recruitment to local cultural norms. For instance, libraries in regions with strong collective cultural values emphasise community involvement and teamwork in their hiring criteria. At the same time, those in individualistic societies focus on innovation and personal achievement.

Digital tools in library recruitment also require careful consideration of regional differences. For example, online recruitment platforms can be pivotal in areas with high internet penetration. At the same time, traditional methods may still hold sway in regions with less digital access.

For library systems operating in multiple countries, tailoring recruitment strategies to each region's cultural expectations while upholding the core values of inclusivity and community service is key. This approach ensures that libraries remain as inclusive and representative of their diverse user base as possible.

By embracing these global nuances, library recruitment can be both kind and practical, ensuring libraries worldwide continue to serve as inclusive, culturally aware community centres.

Challenges and solutions in implementing kind recruitment

Implementing kind recruitment practices often involves navigating through a range of organisational challenges. These can vary from deeply ingrained company cultures to logistical hurdles. However, with appropriate solutions and best practices in place, these challenges can be effectively tackled.

One significant obstacle is the resistance to change, particularly in organisations accustomed to traditional recruitment methods. Employees and management might show scepticism towards altering established practices. Overcoming this resistance is crucial for the adoption of kinder recruitment strategies.

Another issue is the need for more awareness or understanding of what kind recruitment involves and its benefits. This knowledge gap can be a significant barrier to effectively implementing these practices. Moreover, kind recruitment strategies can be resource-intensive. They may necessitate comprehensive training, potentially elongate the recruitment process and require developing new systems and tools, posing a significant challenge, especially for resource-strapped organisations.

Balancing fairness in the recruitment process with the organisation's immediate needs presents another challenge. This is particularly pronounced when there's an urgency to fill positions.

Measuring the impact and success of kind recruitment practices also poses a difficulty. Determining the effectiveness of these strategies and justifying the investment and effort involved can be complex for many organisations.

To address these challenges, several solutions and best practices can be employed. Building a culture of change within the organisation is fundamental. This involves fostering a continuous improvement and innovation culture and engaging employees at all levels, emphasising the long-term benefits of kind recruitment. Education and training play a pivotal role. Conducting training sessions and workshops to enlighten employees about the importance of kind recruitment and illustrating its positive impact through real-life case studies can be highly effective.

Efficient resource allocation is critical. Organisations might consider implementing kind recruitment practices in phases and utilising technology, such as AI, for initial screenings to reduce bias, thereby streamlining the process.

Maintaining a balance between fairness and organisational needs requires setting clear priorities and implementing structured and standardised recruitment processes. Developing clear metrics to measure the success of kind recruitment practices is crucial. Metrics such as candidate satisfaction surveys, diversity metrics, retention rates and time-to-hire can provide insights into the impact of these practices. Gaining the support of senior leadership is critical for successfully implementing kind recruitment practices. Leadership buy-in sets a positive tone throughout the organisation.

Establishing a feedback loop with candidates and new hires is essential for continuous improvement. This feedback should be actively sought, reviewed and utilised for ongoing enhancements to the recruitment process.

Finally, ensuring that recruitment practices align with the broader values and goals of the organisation is vital. This alignment facilitates the seamless integration of these practices into the organisational culture.

Organisations can successfully implement kind recruitment strategies by addressing these challenges with practical solutions and best practices. These strategies enhance the recruitment process and contribute significantly to creating a more inclusive, empathetic and respectful workplace culture.

Impact on company culture and employee retention

Kind recruitment practices significantly influence company culture and employee retention. These practices reinforce a culture that values respect, empathy and fairness, fostering a work environment that is both positive and inclusive. Organisations known for their kind recruitment are more likely to attract candidates who share these values, leading to a more harmonious and aligned workplace. This alignment between employee values and organisational culture is key to creating a cohesive and productive work environment.

Regarding employee retention, kind recruitment practices have been shown to contribute to higher retention rates (Abraham et al., 2023). Employees who feel they were selected for their skills and cultural fit are more likely to be satisfied and remain with the company long-term. Moreover, a kind recruitment approach enhances an organisation's employer brand, making it more appealing to prospective candidates. This positive reputation is a magnet for high-quality applicants, enriching the talent pool for future recruitment. Employees recruited through a process that respects their dignity and values tend to start their roles with higher engagement and motivation. This elevated engagement often translates into increased productivity and loyalty to the company, benefiting the organisation as a whole.

Kind recruitment in the digital age

Technology can reshape recruitment processes. Integrating technological tools and online platforms offers an opportunity to enhance the kindness and effectiveness of recruitment practices. This section explores how technology can be leveraged to support and augment recruitment strategies.

Leveraging technology to enhance kindness in recruitment

The digital transformation of recruitment processes has opened new avenues for incorporating kindness into every step of hiring. One significant area is using Artificial Intelligence (AI) and machine learning algorithms in initial candidate screenings. When programmed with an emphasis on fairness and inclusivity, these technologies can reduce unconscious bias, ensuring a more equitable selection process if they are utilised ethically.

Moreover, digital platforms enable more efficient and transparent communication between recruiters and candidates. Automated messaging systems, for instance, can keep candidates informed at every stage of the recruitment process, demonstrating respect for their time and efforts. This transparent communication fosters a sense of trust and respect, essential elements of kind recruitment.

Online platforms and tools supporting kind recruitment practices

Various online platforms and tools are specifically designed to support kind recruitment practices. Recruitment software that emphasises candidate experience can streamline application processes, making them more user-friendly and accessible. These platforms often include features for easy application tracking, scheduling interviews and providing timely feedback, all of which contribute to a positive candidate experience.

Social media platforms are also increasingly being used as tools for kind recruitment. They offer a way to showcase an organisation's culture and values, attract like-minded candidates and build a community around shared principles of kindness and inclusivity.

Additionally, online assessment tools prioritising ethical and fair testing methods are crucial. These tools can be designed to provide equitable assessments, ensuring that all candidates, regardless of background, have a fair chance to showcase their abilities.

The digital age offers remarkable tools and platforms to enhance the kindness of the recruitment process. By leveraging these technologies organisations can create more inclusive, fair and engaging recruitment experiences. This digital approach streamlines the recruitment process and aligns it with modern values of efficiency, inclusivity and respect, essential for attracting top talent in today's competitive job market.

Empowering candidates with technology in kind recruitment

In addition to the way technology is reshaping recruitment from an organisational perspective, candidates can also harness digital tools to enhance their experience and chances of success. The advent of AI-driven platforms for candidates presents new possibilities in preparing and refining their applications and interview techniques.

AI tools can now assist candidates in reviewing and optimising their resumés and cover letters. These tools analyse the content of an application against job descriptions, offering suggestions on how to tailor them to better match specific roles and highlighting key skills and experiences that align with the job requirements. This personalised feedback ensures that candidates present themselves in the best possible light, increasing their chances of making it through initial screenings.

Candidates can use AI-based interview preparation tools that offer practice questions, simulate real interview scenarios and provide feedback on their responses. These tools often use natural language processing to analyse speech patterns, offering constructive feedback on clarity, conciseness and even the emotional tone of responses. This preparation can be particularly valuable in boosting a candidate's confidence and interview performance.

Gamification and VR tools also come into play for candidates, allowing them to experience simulated work environments, understand the roles better and prepare more effectively for job-specific tasks. This level of preparation and engagement can significantly enhance a candidate's understanding of the job and the company, leading to more meaningful interactions during the recruitment process.

These technological advancements empower candidates unprecedentedly, giving them more control over their job search and application process. By utilising these tools, candidates can ensure that their applications are more aligned with the job requirements and reflective of their true potential, skills and experiences. As these technologies evolve, we expect to see a more level playing field in recruitment, where candidates are better equipped and more confident in presenting their qualifications and capabilities.

Legal and ethical foundations in kind recruitment

In the context of kind recruitment, it's crucial to intertwine legal compliance with ethical considerations. Adhering to specific laws and regulations of the country where recruitment takes place, especially regarding employment, data privacy and anti-discrimination, is fundamental. This includes being aware of and complying with regulations such as the GDPR in the EU or equivalent laws globally, ensuring candidate data is handled legally and ethically.

The ethical use of AI in recruitment needs careful attention. While AI can minimise human bias, ensuring these systems do not inadvertently introduce their own preferences is essential. Regular audits of AI algorithms for biases, maintaining transparency in AI use and keeping human oversight are key practices to uphold ethical standards.

Incorporating these legal and ethical practices into recruitment strategies ensures legal soundness and fosters candidate trust and respect. It reinforces the commitment to kind and ethical recruitment practices.

Conclusion

In this chapter, we've highlighted the vital role of kindness and fairness in recruitment. Emphasising kindness at every step, from job ads to induction, enhances candidate experience and workplace culture. The focus is not just on selecting the right candidate but also on how they're treated, with inclusive job descriptions, empathetic interviews, constructive feedback and supportive induction. Kind recruitment, far from a trend, signifies a deeper shift towards valuing human dignity in work environments.

Transitioning to the following chapter, written by Kirsten Elliott and Darren Flynn from the Fair Library Jobs campaign, we will see how these principles are practically applied, demonstrating the real-world impact of these approaches in library recruitment. This next chapter offers a detailed exploration of how such strategies create equitable, empathetic workplaces, furthering the journey towards a culture of kindness and wellbeing in our professional world.

Exercises and reflective questions

Exercise for teams

Objective: develop a kind recruitment plan.

Instructions: in teams, create a detailed recruitment plan incorporating the principles of kindness and inclusivity. Focus on every stage of the process – from job advertisement to induction. Each team presents their plan, highlighting innovative practices to enhance candidate experience and fairness.

Exercise for individuals

Objective: personal reflection on recruitment practices.

Instructions: reflect on your past experiences with recruitment – either as a candidate or as a recruiter. Identify aspects where kindness and inclusivity were present or lacking. Develop a personal action plan to implement kind recruitment practices in future roles.

Reflective questions

- How do kind recruitment principles align with your values and experiences?
- Reflect on a situation where a recruitment process impacted your wellbeing positively or negatively. What lessons can you draw from this?
- How can you make the recruitment process more inclusive and empathetic in your current role or library?
- Consider a time you felt excluded or unfairly treated in a recruitment process. How could the situation have been improved with kind recruitment practices?

CHAPTER 11

Fair Library Jobs: Kindness, Empathy and Equity in Library Recruitment

Kirsten Elliott and Darren Flynn

Introduction

As we explored in the preceding chapter, empathy and equity stand as cornerstones in transforming library recruitment practices. The 'Fair Library Jobs' manifesto resonates deeply with these values. It echoes the call for empathy and extends it by embedding fairness and inclusivity in the fabric of library recruitment strategies. This chapter explores how the Fair Library Jobs approach operationalises these ideals, demonstrating practical ways to infuse empathy into every stage of the hiring process. By aligning our strategies with this manifesto, we take significant steps towards creating a more compassionate and equitable library recruitment environment.

Fair Library Jobs is a grassroots organisation that aims to improve recruitment and employment practices in the UK's library sector. It was founded by the two authors of this chapter and a third member, Harriet Notman. The group was inspired by the work of Fair Museum Job and groups campaigning for equity in the sector, such as DILON and Intersectional GLAM. However, we were also motivated by our personal experiences of positive and negative recruitment and those of our friends and colleagues in the sector. Our guiding document is the Fair Library Jobs Manifesto, which we developed to outline recruitment practices that we see as promoting equity, respect and transparency. The full text of our manifesto with additional explanatory points can be found on our website (see 'Useful resources' at the end of this chapter).

In writing this chapter, we've decided to structure it in two parts. Firstly, we want to provide an overview of the wider situation in general recruitment and specifically in libraries. We use critical theory, which helps to understand and shed light on the power dynamics and ranking systems in the recruitment process. Secondly, we share our own experiences of applying for jobs. This helps us to think about the role kindness plays (or doesn't play) in how libraries hire people and how important it is to include this value for the benefit of applicants. We reflect on real-life experiences of dominating power. This reflection aims to increase awareness of our roles in these power structures and suggest ways to bring about change that is fair and equal, as suggested by Freire (1996).

Our views are shaped by our own life experiences and personal traits. While we have learned from talking to other library workers, we can't say our stories are typical – and we hope they aren't in many ways. Through deep understanding and empathy, we notice that some practices might leave out or disadvantage people who are different from us. But there are still areas we can't fully address. For example, the predominance of white people in UK libraries (Kinetiq, 2023) and experiences shared by library workers of colour (Haimé, 2023; Ishaq and Hussain, 2022) show us that racism is a regular and widespread problem in libraries (Leung and López-McKnight, 2021).

By recognising what we can and cannot understand based on our own experiences (Coghlan and Brydon-Miller 2014), we outline our standpoint regarding this work and the topics we're discussing.

Reflective questions

■ Reflect on your own experiences or observations in recruitment. How have you seen empathy and equity demonstrated or neglected in these processes?
■ Consider the impact of personal experiences on shaping professional practices. How do your own experiences influence your approach to recruitment and employment?

Positionality statements

Before we go into the core of our discussion, it's crucial to first introduce ourselves, not just by name, but through our positionality statements. These statements are more than just biographical details; they are an essential framework that shapes our perspectives and insights throughout this work.

By sharing our backgrounds and experiences, we aim to bring authenticity and transparency to our analysis. Our individual journeys – Kirsten, as a white, bisexual, cisgender woman with a history of chronic illnesses and Darren, as a white, cisgender male, identifying as gay and Queer with a working-class background – deeply influence how we perceive and interpret the subject matter at hand.

Acknowledging our biases and perspectives is not just an exercise in self-disclosure; it's a critical step in establishing the lens through which we view our topic. This process of self-reflection and openness paves the way for a more trustworthy and relatable narrative. Our readers can better understand where we are coming from, potentially seeing reflections of their own experiences or gaining insights into perspectives different from their own.

Furthermore, our positionality is vital in challenging systemic issues within the library profession. By openly discussing our identities and experiences, we aim to highlight and confront issues such as racism, classism and ableism within recruitment practices. This approach not only enriches our analysis but also emphasises the importance of diversity and inclusivity in shaping a more comprehensive understanding of the topic.

In summary, these positionality statements are not just introductory notes; they are foundational elements that set the stage for a deeper, more nuanced exploration of our subject. They remind us and our readers, that behind every analysis are individuals with unique backgrounds and experiences, each contributing to a richer, more diverse discourse.

Kirsten

I am a white bisexual, cis woman. Though I am not currently disabled, I have a history of chronic illnesses, which have, at times, had enough of an impact to act as disabilities. I am culturally middle-class and financially stable but have experience of underpaid and precarious employment. I do not have any caring responsibilities.

Darren

I am a white cis male and identify as gay and Queer. I am not currently disabled, though I have a history of mental health issues that have, at times, impacted my academic and professional life. I am socio-culturally and materially from a working-class background. However, I was fortunate not to experience severe levels of deprivation growing up. I remained the first in my family to continue my education past the age of 16. In my working life, I have generally benefited from financial security with relatively few experiences of precarious employment. I do not have any caring responsibilities.

Recruitment and power

Of all workplace interactions, the recruitment and selection process represents the starkest and most unequal power balance between applicant and recruiter. The source of these power imbalances is manifold.

Most statutory rights relating to employment exist only between current workers and employers, with potential applicants generally having recourse only to non-discrimination, data protection and data access rights. For an applicant, demonstrating that they have been discriminated against (based on a protected characteristic) is notoriously hard to prove and can be emotionally and financially costly. Moreover, in the context of the relatively small and interconnected world of libraries, the applicant may have a legitimate reluctance to raise issues for fear of reputational damage. In addition, many recruitment practices can undoubtedly result in unequal or inequitable outcomes but fall below the threshold required for legal redress.

In addition to legal power disparities, a significant information inequality exists between applicants and recruiters. In most cases, mainly where the applicant is external, the recruiter has far more information at their disposal and, more importantly, more information than they divulge to potential applicants. They have a greater knowledge of the process, who they envisage in the role, how criteria will be interpreted and judged and the details of the role and workplace. In systematically reviewing job vacancies, it's startling how even basic information, such as salaries, working hours, locations or criteria, is withheld by recruiting organisations. While some information may be intentionally and actively withheld, as insidious and harmful to just outcomes, the routine use of implicit knowledge in recruitment can be problematic. This might manifest as an assumption that the applicant will be aware of organisational or sectoral norms, the (unnecessary) use of jargon where more accessible terms might be used or assuming all candidates will know the employer's expectations regarding applications or interviews.

Finally, there is a material and affective power imbalance between the recruiter and the candidate. The recruiter has something (a job) that the candidate wants or needs that is within their gift. Literature and discourse often fall back on the line that recruitment is a two-way process, that candidates are testing the organisation as much as the organisation them and while theoretically this may be true, the reality is that this is rarely the case. By the point at which a candidate has applied or interviewed for a role, it is generally safe to say they want or need the job and declining an offered role is a privilege few enjoy. In this regard, candidates can be intensely disempowered and often vulnerable. They may be experiencing financial difficulty or un/under-employment, they may be in work but experiencing an unhealthy or abusive workplace or they may be desperate to change or progress their career.

An acknowledgement that power imbalances exist in recruitment is not the same as an accusation that recruiters enjoy or abuse this position of power in most cases. Instead, a hegemonic position of power exists as a persistent overarching context within recruitment. Within the library sector, it is also important to acknowledge that few libraries exist as independent employers rather than within a larger organisation. In the latter case, while the power imbalance still exists, the recruiting manager is, in some respects, bound by the requirements of the larger organisation through HR policy and accepted practices.

In recognising this fact, recruiting managers must ask themselves how they chose this power, what it says about their beliefs and priorities and how it may impact those applying for roles with them. In using power, person-centred values and the principles of kindness can do much to lessen the impact of hegemonic power. Few managers (we hope) set out to cause harm, distress or inequity when recruiting; rather, it can occur through thoughtlessness, an adherence to dated values and practices or a focus on process over people.

As emerging adults, we are often cautioned that, when it comes to applying for jobs, every aspect of our behaviour, appearance and communication is subject to judgement and censure; if we're not sufficiently well turned out, if we're at all late, whatever the reason, or if we say or do the wrong thing at any moment, then we will rule ourselves out of contention. It's unsurprising, therefore, that so many small inequities in recruitment go unreported or unquestioned. Applicants are understandably hesitant to question or challenge recruiter policies or behaviours for fear of being perceived as a problematic candidate. Already underrepresented and/or marginalised groups are often at heightened risk in this respect through negative stereotypes and hyper-visibility, such as the 'angry Black woman' trope. Achieving kindness in recruitment, though, also requires a step change towards radical empathy and a commitment to adopt the perspective of the disempowered applicant within the process. We hope tools such as the Fair Library Jobs Manifesto and the discussions below can help this journey.

Reflective questions
- How do you perceive power dynamics in recruitment processes?
- In what ways can these be addressed to create a more equitable environment?

Reflection on our own experiences

These reflections draw on both of our experiences. Whilst we have both been publicly critical of specific employers and librarianship organisations, the power imbalance above is still relevant: naming the particulars of poor treatment may have negative future career consequences. Moreover, it is not important details of each incident but the general themes that can be elicited from them. We have, therefore, amalgamated our stories and blurred particulars.

Scheduling

Case Study 11.1: Scheduling

A job I had applied for included the date of the interviews in the recruitment materials. Still, I had not heard anything by the week of the interviews. I telephoned HR to ask about the status of my application (partly because it was an HR department who had previously made a mistake in my e-mail address, so it felt plausible that I had missed an e-mail). They told me I would find out on the day of the interview if I would be interviewed. They implied I was demanding for wanting that information in advance. I found out later that I was the backup candidate and would have been called in at the last minute had someone else been unable to attend. That telephone call made me panic – I worked and needed to know whether to schedule a shift. If I'd been offered an interview on the day, I might not have been able to attend or even picked up the call. I did not know whether I needed to be preparing for the interview.

Attending an interview might require co-ordinating care arrangements or transport for other people. In Case Study 11.1, I happened to be in the same city, but buying train tickets at short notice, especially if, by necessity, in peak travel times, is expensive enough that many people would be prohibited from attending. Generally, the kind thing to do is give people adequate notice for all interviews. Honesty about the situation and providing the possible interview times would have been a kindness that saved me significant anxiety. Giving as much notice as possible will enable candidates to manage the practicalities of interview attendance.

Interviews

Case Study 11.2: Interviewing

I was invited for a two-part interview for a role in another city. The first part was a 10-minute presentation task scheduled for 9.30 in the morning. It was challenging to get there in time, but I managed it. The panel interview was the second part and was scheduled for 4 .00 in the afternoon. This meant I had six hours waiting and wandering around in another city, getting increasingly stressed about the interview. I couldn't really relax or do something else to distract myself. I had nowhere to go and after half-heartedly wandering around a gallery in the city, I spent about three hours sitting in my car. By the time of my panel interview, I was emotionally and physically exhausted.

Case Study 11.3: Interviewing

I was invited to a three-part interview where I had a staff panel, a teaching task and then a formal interview. I was put in a waiting room with the other candidates between the first two parts. It was uncomfortable to sit with the other candidates, knowing we were competing. Eventually, they called two of the other candidates through and they just disappeared. Evidently, they had yet to progress to the second round. After the teaching task, I was taken to the all-staff break room to wait for the final interview. It was someone's last day and they were having a small leaving party for them with cake and gifts. I just sat in a corner, super-awkwardly, unwilling or able to participate but also highly visible. A couple of people came over to speak to me, as I was obviously there for an interview. Still, I just desperately wanted to be somewhere else. I wanted to review my notes but wanted to avoid coming across as standoffish in case that filtered back.

Experiences like those in Case Studies 11.2 and 11.3 are evidence of a lack of thought about candidates' experiences. Ill-planned timings with long gaps and placing candidates in difficult social situations may have a more significant impact on neurodivergent candidates or those with certain health conditions such as anxiety. Many would worry that the informal interactions or responses were forming part of the assessment, due to unclear criteria.

In contrast, I had a positive experience at one of the first interviews I did the year after I finished university. It was at a highly prestigious institution and I was very nervous. I was applying to many jobs at the time and most rejected me without an interview. The first person I spoke to walked me to where the interview was taking place – a kindness in itself, to ensure I did not get lost. On the way, he told me the names of the three people interviewing me and their roles, that they were all very nice people and not to worry because it would be fine. It was almost 15 years ago. I still remember it because it was a moment of humanity and kindness when I needed it. When I've been in the role of doing meet and greets for interviews, I've tried to do the same thing – providing information that might be helpful and being as reassuring as possible.

The approaches taken in the case studies in the previous chapter from the University of Westminster and Lancaster University (10.1 and 10.2) are the opposite of 11.2 and 11.3: they took a people-centred and humane approach, enabling candidates to present themselves at their best. The provision of information packs formalises and goes beyond what that one person did for me, ensuring all candidates can have as minimally stressful an experience as possible.

Feedback and communication

Case Study 11.4: Feedback and communication

I've had multiple experiences applying for jobs and never hearing back about the status of my application. In one case, I sent a follow-up e-mail and received a rather terse reply implying I should have deduced that I had been unsuccessful from the time that had lapsed. The period of not knowing if I had been selected for the interview was very nerve-racking and increasingly bleak as I slowly lost hope. It took the reassurance of friends to feel that I was not in the wrong to reach out to the employer for confirmation of the decision because of the suggestion that I had somehow been unprofessional.

Case Study 11.5: Feedback and communication

I'd gone for an internal post and been interviewed. The interview went fine and I got a phone call later in the day saying I hadn't gotten the job. I was OK with this, but the person immediately went into giving me feedback before I'd really had a chance to process the information. All the 'feedback' I was given was about the other candidates, how they had more experience, how they were already working at that level and how they answered XYZ question better. There wasn't anything actionable on my part and rather than feedback, it felt that they were giving their justification for selecting the other person. After that, they talked about how they liked a couple of ideas I'd discussed in the interview and how they wanted to work with the successful candidate to make them happen. I was at a loss for words, as I felt it was insensitive and crass to say that to me at that moment, and later, angry that I felt I was being told, we don't want you, but we do want your ideas.

Unsuccessful candidates are vulnerable, experiencing the emotional and practical experiences of rejection. In any interaction with an employer, there is pressure to maintain a positive impression to avoid future professional consequences.

Informal generosity

Case Study 11.6: Informal generosity

I was successful in applying for a job in a new city. I had to find temporary accommodation there. Knowing this, the hiring manager sent me helpful information and recommendations for places to look, university accommodation and popular city areas. It was really useful to have that local knowledge. I was visiting the city to look at accommodation options and had some free time in the day. I asked about coming along to shadow the team that day so I'd be more prepared for my first day. The manager put together a really interesting day where I could see what I'd be doing, meet the team, etc. It helped remove some anxiety about starting a new role and helped me feel confident about what I'd be doing and who I'd be working with.

Case Study 11.7: Informal generosity

After the incident in Case Study 11.1, when an employer withheld information about whether I would have an interview, the manager sent me a lovely e-mail apologising. They commented on how lovely it had been to meet me when I had gone on an informal visit to the library and on some of the specifics of my application, meaning that I knew I had been seriously considered as a candidate. That moment of kindness made a difference, genuinely made me feel better and mitigated the negative view of the organisation I had developed.

In these cases, individuals took time and effort to consider their individual needs and experiences. They treated recruitment as the potential first step in an ongoing professional relationship – within that workplace or the broader librarianship community.

Reflective questions

Reflection on personal recruitment experiences: reflect on a time when you were involved in recruitment, either as a recruiter or as a candidate. Did you encounter any issues similar to those highlighted in the case studies?

- How did these experiences make you feel?
- What could have been done differently to improve the situation?

Reflection on interview experiences: think back to an interview experience you've had:

- Were empathy and kindness demonstrated during this process?
- If not, how could these elements have been better incorporated?
- Consider the impact this had on your perception of the interview and the organisation.

Feedback and communication: recall a time you received feedback following a job application or interview.

- Assess whether the feedback was constructive and helpful.
- Reflect on how the feedback process could have been improved.
- Think about how receiving effective feedback could have influenced your future job applications or professional development.

Impact of informal generosity: consider an instance where an act of kindness or generosity significantly impacted your professional journey.

- Reflect on the specific gesture and its impact on you.
- Think about how this experience influenced your perspective on professional relationships and workplace culture.

Application of Fair Library Jobs Manifesto principles:

- How do you envision the principles of the Fair Library Jobs Manifesto being implemented in your current or future workplace?
- What specific changes would you advocate for to align with these principles?
- Reflect on the potential challenges and benefits of implementing these changes.

Conclusion

The narratives we give above are a small selection of recruitment experiences from careers where we've applied for roles in the dozens if not hundreds. The selected stories represent archetypes (rather than representative examples) wherein kindness was shared or withheld. Examples of the 'everyday' experience of recruitment in libraries would inevitably show similar themes, albeit less acutely. Our broad experience of recruitment has been that, while progress can be claimed towards making the process (on the surface) more equal and objective, there is an unfulfilled promise to make the process kind and empathetic. The focus of library recruitment is to find the right candidate. At the same time, the core drivers for the manager are time and labour efficiency. In these, the candidate's experience is all too often overlooked. We wrote the Fair Library Jobs Manifesto to recentre and reorientate the background to that of the applicant, while balancing the statutory organisational and labour needs of the recruiter. Using its principles of transparency, equity and respect not only produces better outcomes and experiences for both parties but also allows the recruiter to demonstrate kindness and empathy for themselves and their organisation.

Useful resources

Fair Library Jobs, https://sites.google.com/view/fairlibraryjobs.
DILON: Diversity in Libraries of the North,
   https://libdiverse.wordpress.com.
Intersectional GLAM: creating a space for marginalised voices in Galleries,
   Libraries, Archives and Museums (GLAM).
   https://intersectionalglam.home.blog/intersectional-glam.
Fair Museum Jobs: highlighting good and bad practice in museum jobs and
   recruitment https://fairmuseumjobs.org.
Museum as Muck: a supportive network of working class museum people
   making change in the sector. http://museumasmuck.co.uk.

Appendix: Relevant sections of the Fair Library Jobs manifesto

6.11. Job adverts must have a clearly stated closing date and time.
6.12. Vacancies should not close early due to volume of applications. If the
       closing date is extended, the extension and the reasons for it must be
       clearly communicated to existing applicants.

Closing vacancies early is poor practice; it advantages those who have the
flexibility and time to put in early applications and disadvantages those that
would have submitted on time but closer to the original deadline. Applicants
may have many reasons for not submitting until the closing date and should
not be expected to drop everything and apply immediately. Further, some
may have started their application, invested several hours in writing it but
are waiting to proofread, do final checks etc. before submitting; closing the
application early has wasted their time.

   Where deadlines have been extended, existing applicants should be
informed and given a reason for this; this is courteous as they may be waiting
significantly longer than they anticipated for a response or assume their
application was unsuccessful and the post is being re-advertised.

8.2.   Candidates invited to interview, should they be unsuccessful, must be
       provided with meaningful feedback about their performance at
       interview.

Candidates who have completed an application and attended an interview
have invested substantial amounts of time, physical and emotional energy.
They should therefore rightly expect prompt notification of the outcome and
be given meaningful feedback that they can act on in future. To be useful,
feedback should not only be about the reason another candidate was

successful (e.g. another candidate was more qualified) but based on specific, actionable steps the candidate could make (e.g. you didn't have as much experience in XYZ aspects of the role).

8.3.   Job applicants, should they be unsuccessful in progressing to the interview stage, should be informed of the outcome of shortlisting in a timely fashion.

8.4.   Job applicants, should they be unsuccessful in progressing to the interview stage, should be provided with feedback regarding their applications.

Candidates who have completed an application have invested substantial amounts of time, physical and emotional energy to do so. They should therefore expect a prompt notification of the outcome of their application. Providing feedback at this stage for unsuccessful applicants is worthwhile; writing applications is a specific skillset, relies on large amounts of implicit knowledge and cultural capital. Candidates without this may be already disadvantaged and/or marginalised and should be supported for future applications. Wherever possible, recruiters should provide this feedback.

8.5.   Fair Library Jobs recommends not giving feedback at the same time as giving the recruitment outcome. Allow unsuccessful candidates time to absorb the result of the process before receiving feedback.

Completing a job application and attending an interview can be an emotionally fraught experience. An unsuccessful candidate might require time to process the outcome and not be emotionally prepared to receive feedback in a way that is useful to them. Scheduling a later call or offering feedback in a different format shows respect for the feelings of the candidate and may be more useful to them.

8.6.   Those giving feedback must ensure as far as possible that it is constructive, specific, actionable and honest.

For feedback to be useful, it must be constructive, based on how they might improve in future, specific, discuss specific areas of improvement and based on general terms such as 'less experienced', actionable, something the candidate can reasonably do in the future and honest; based on the true conclusions as discussed by the panel.

PART 3

Leadership Approaches to Enhancing Kindness and Wellbeing in Libraries

In this section, we explore the pivotal role leaders play in creating and maintaining an atmosphere of kindness and wellbeing within library settings. It emphasises the unique challenges and opportunities that library leaders face in fostering a culture that values and promotes these ideals. Through exploring various strategies and practical examples, this section aims to equip library leaders with the tools and insights necessary to effectively integrate kindness and wellbeing into their organisational culture, thereby transforming libraries into more nurturing and positive environments for both staff and patrons.

CHAPTER 12

Overcoming Challenges in Creating Kindness and Wellbeing in Libraries: Addressing Bystander Syndrome and Leadership Roles

Introduction

I have found prioritising kindness and wellbeing the most challenging thing I have done in libraries, both because of the myriad interpretations of what kindness and wellbeing mean and because people think it should be easy, when it is hard. This chapter looks at some difficulties libraries face when making their workplaces kinder and more focused on wellbeing. While it's a great goal, this book has identified many positive reasons. Several challenges can make it hard for libraries to do this successfully. We will explore these challenges and discuss ways to overcome them to help libraries be places full of books and where people feel supported and cared for.

We'll look at how the behaviour of others and the role of leaders in the library can affect bystander syndrome (Latané and Rodin, 1969) and suggest ways to help staff feel more confident and responsible, such as through mindfulness and promoting supportive leadership. We will discuss what causes the burden of caring for others and how libraries can help their staff through training, balancing personal interests with care for others and creating a work environment that supports their staff's wellbeing. We'll examine how wanting to succeed can sometimes lessen compassion and look at ways to encourage a more caring approach, including training for emotional skills, creating a culture that values kindness and changing how the library operates to support this.

Libraries, significantly smaller or less-funded ones, often need more money or staff to start wellbeing programmes. We will explore the effects of these limitations and suggest solutions like using their resources wisely, getting the community involved, developing low-cost wellbeing programmes and thinking carefully about how to use their funds.

Sometimes, how a library is run doesn't support kindness and wellbeing. This can be because of a gap between how leaders think they're acting and how their staff feels or because of how the library's culture is set up. We'll talk about ways to change this, like training for leaders, checking on the library's culture, encouraging open communication and building a supportive work environment.

By understanding these challenges and how to deal with them, libraries can become places where kindness and wellbeing are part of everyday life, making things better for the staff and the people who use the library.

Reflective questions

Reflect on your experiences in a library, either as staff or as a user. Have you noticed instances where kindness and wellbeing were prominently displayed or absent? Before reading about the specific challenges, what obstacles do you think libraries might face in integrating kindness and wellbeing into their environments?

Bystander syndrome in libraries

Bystander syndrome in libraries is a phenomenon observed where staff members hesitate to intervene in situations that require attention to wellbeing (Latané and Rodin, 1969). The reluctance to act often comes from a lack of confidence, fear of overstepping boundaries or uncertainty in dealing with wellbeing-related issues.

One key factor influencing this syndrome is the social influence and diffusion of responsibility. Staff in libraries, much as in other workplaces, may look to others for cues on how to react. This can lead to individuals waiting for someone else to act, particularly in ambiguous situations. This phenomenon hinders interventions against negative behaviour, such as incivility in the workplace, as highlighted by Jensen and Raver in 2021.

Recent research has expanded our understanding of bystander syndrome, particularly in professional settings. Scholars have started to explore the nuances of bystander behaviour in workplace environments, where power dynamics, organisational culture and group cohesion significantly influence individual actions. For instance, a study by Rosen et al. in 2018 revealed that in hierarchical organisations, employees are less likely to intervene in situations where they perceive a risk to their professional standing. This is particularly relevant in library settings, where the structure often dictates interactions and responses.

Furthermore, dal Cason, Casini and Hellemans in 2020 suggested that training programmes focusing on empowerment and ethical responsibility can effectively reduce bystander inaction in workplaces. By incorporating these findings, library leadership can develop targeted interventions to encourage proactive behaviour, reducing the prevalence of bystander syndrome. This could include workshops, scenario-based training and open discussions on ethical dilemmas faced in the library environment.

The role of leadership is crucial in mitigating the bystander effect. Leaders who are proactive and set a precedent for compassionate and responsible action can inspire staff to do the same. The diffusion of responsibility can be more pronounced when leadership roles are unclear or there's a sense of collective responsibility. This scenario highlights the need for a cultural shift to empower leaders and staff to feel secure in compassionate actions.

Addressing bystander syndrome in libraries involves several strategies. Mindfulness and empathic processing, as suggested by Condon et al. (2013), can be effective. By enhancing body awareness and attention regulation, mindfulness interventions can increase connection to others' suffering and reduce social influence, thereby encouraging personal responsibility. Empowering leadership is another key strategy. Developing leadership skills focusing on compassion and proactive intervention can set a tone for the entire staff. Training leaders to recognise and act in wellbeing-related situations can encourage others to model similar behaviour.

Reviewing and updating processes and procedures is essential. Libraries should ensure their guidelines and support systems promote kind communication and appropriate actions in intervention-required situations.

Lastly, cultivating a culture of responsibility is vital. This can be achieved through regular workshops, team discussions and fostering an environment that values and rewards compassionate actions.

By implementing these strategies, libraries can transform into more supportive and proactive spaces, enhancing the overall culture of wellbeing and kindness.

Burden of caring in libraries

The concept of the burden of caring in libraries centres on the emotional and psychological demands placed on library staff as they assist users and colleagues. This is particularly evident in libraries that serve diverse communities with a range of needs. Central to this burden is **compassion fatigue**, a type of stress that arises from continuous care for others, as identified by Figley in 2002.

Compassion fatigue in libraries is influenced by several factors. Library staff often engage in emotionally charged interactions, dealing with sensitive or complex personal issues of users. This constant emotional labour can lead to compassion fatigue, similar to what is observed in educational and other care-oriented professions. Additionally, secondary traumatic stress is a concern for library staff who build professional relationships with users experiencing traumatic events. This stress manifests in symptoms like intrusion, avoidance and arousal, linked to indirect exposure to trauma.

Addressing compassion fatigue in libraries requires a multifaceted approach. Workshops and training have been shown to be effective, as noted by Borntrager et al. in 2012. These programmes should focus on peer support, normalising experiences and educating on self-care strategies (Hydon et al., 2015). Balancing compassion with self-interest is crucial. Library leaders and staff often grapple with the conflict between acting compassionately and protecting their interests. Recognising and managing this conflict is key to maintaining a caring disposition and mitigating compassion fatigue.

Recent studies highlight the emotional labour inherent in librarianship, especially in school and public library settings, leading to compassion fatigue due to the caregiving aspect of the job layered on top of other responsibilities (Himmelstein, 2020). Libraries are adopting strategies such as training in mental health first aid, creating supportive work environments, offering mental health support, encouraging staff to set boundaries and providing access to counselling services to combat compassion fatigue among staff (Himmelstein, 2020).

Creating a supportive work environment is essential. This involves open communication, mutual support and acknowledging the challenges of compassion fatigue. Regular staff check-ins, mental health days and access to counselling services are practical steps in this direction. Promoting self-care among staff is another critical strategy. Practices like mindfulness, exercise, hobbies and maintaining a healthy work–life balance can help alleviate the effects of compassion fatigue.

Lastly, enhancing organisational policies can better support staff facing compassion fatigue. Libraries should consider flexible scheduling, providing mental health resources and establishing protocols for handling challenging user interactions. By recognising and actively addressing the burden of caring, library leaders can foster a more sustainable and supportive environment. This not only benefits the staff but enhances the quality of service and care provided to the community.

Self-interest in library management

Self-interest in library management can significantly affect the culture of kindness and wellbeing, as discussed by Keltner et al. (2014) and van Kleef et al. (2008). In a competitive environment, the pursuit of personal or institutional achievements may overshadow the focus on staff and user wellbeing. This often results in prioritising organisational goals over individual needs and neglecting the development of a compassionate work culture.

Several factors influence self-interest in libraries. Competitive motivations can grow stronger as individuals or institutions become more successful, potentially leading to decreased compassion if helping others is seen as a threat to one's self-interest. Leadership dynamics play a role: library leaders, often selected for their expertise in their field, may lack skills in leadership or compassion, which can exacerbate self-interest issues. They might focus more on professional advancement or the library's success, rather than nurturing a culture of kindness and wellbeing. Additionally, power dynamics within the library can affect compassion and empathy. As leaders gain more authority, their focus may shift towards maintaining their position and power, rather than the wellbeing of their staff and users.

To address self-interest in libraries, several strategies can be implemented. Training programmes that develop emotional skills and compassion can be effective. Such programmes help leaders and staff balance self-interest with genuine concern for others, fostering a more compassionate workplace. Workshops and peer support are beneficial. Workshops that encourage peer support and emphasise the need for self-care, as suggested by Paakkanen et al. in 2021, can assist staff and leaders in understanding the importance of balancing self-interest with the wellbeing of others. These workshops can normalise experiences and offer practical strategies for a compassionate approach.

Cultivating a compassionate culture is crucial. An organisational culture that values and rewards kindness and compassion can counter the negative aspects of self-interest. This includes recognising and celebrating acts of kindness and wellbeing within the library. Revising organisational policies to support a balance between achieving goals and fostering wellbeing is important. This might involve incorporating wellbeing metrics into performance evaluations or providing incentives for compassionate leadership. Encouraging reflective practice among staff and leaders can lead to greater self-awareness and more balanced decision-making that considers both organisational goals and the wellbeing of staff and users.

By addressing self-interest and promoting a culture that values both organisational success and the wellbeing of staff and users, libraries can evolve into more compassionate and supportive environments. This shift not only enhances the library's effectiveness but improves the experiences of both staff and users.

Resource limitations in libraries

Resource limitations in libraries, particularly those in smaller or underfunded communities, can be challenging. These challenges can be mitigated by implementing initiatives focused on kindness and wellbeing. The impact is more pronounced when transitioning from an abundance mindset, where resources are plentiful, to a mindset that carefully considers risk and scarcity.

One major aspect of resource limitations is financial constraints. Limited budgets can restrict libraries' ability to invest in programmes and training that foster a culture of kindness and wellbeing. This includes resources for staff training, development of wellbeing programmes and the creation of user support services. Additionally, under-resourced libraries may face staffing challenges, leading to increased workloads for existing staff. This can exacerbate feelings of burnout and compassion fatigue, as staff may struggle to balance their workload with the emotional demands of their roles.

With constrained budgets, access to professional development opportunities that could help staff manage the psychological demands of their roles may be limited. This includes training in compassion, empathy and stress management.

To deal with resource limitations, libraries can focus on maximising existing resources. This might involve reallocating budgets to prioritise wellbeing initiatives or seeking partnerships with local organisations for support and training. Engaging with the local community and encouraging volunteer support can help alleviate some of the resource constraints. Community involvement can foster a stronger sense of belonging and collective responsibility towards the library.

Adopting creative approaches to wellbeing programmes is another solution. Libraries can develop low-cost initiatives, such as peer support groups, mindfulness sessions or staff-led workshops, that require minimal financial investment. Additionally, seeking grants and external funding for wellbeing and kindness initiatives can provide necessary resources to implement these programmes. This can have the added benefit of involving team members from across the service. Case Study 12.1, an example from Lancaster University, demonstrates how wellbeing groups can support staff and users.

Case Study 12.1: A wellbeing group

The Library set up a wellbeing group which looks at the wellbeing of staff and students. Membership of the group is from across the library teams and has included student ambassadors. We have a monthly meeting as well as a team chat channel. As chair of the group I try to make the meetings enjoyable and productive. We are the wellbeing group, after all, so I want members to look forward to the meeting and not dread them! Having said this, the group covers a wide range of things from staff induction procedures to a paper on team wellbeing or arranging social events. We aim to have a range of events, so hopefully something appeals to everyone. Some are online some in person.

We look at the wellbeing offer for users of the Library; this again covers a wide range of things, in the hope that we can appeal to a broad spectrum of users. We have a leisure reading area, living walls, a range of spaces which all contribute to this. The group has collaborated with the University Parent Carer network with Easter egg hunts and stories, carols around the tree at Christmas and crafting and board game events. These are held outside of term when the Library is not as busy but an important place for those remaining on campus to come to and include staff and students.

Fiona Rhodes, Lancaster University

Transitioning to a more risk-aware mindset involves careful planning and prioritisation. Libraries need to assess which initiatives will have the most significant impact on wellbeing and allocate resources accordingly. Building resilience is crucial. Encouraging and training staff to cope with resource constraints can equip them with the skills to manage stress and adapt to challenging situations.

By acknowledging and strategically addressing these resource limitations, libraries can still effectively promote a culture of kindness and wellbeing. This requires a shift in mindset from focusing on what is lacking to making the most of available resources and opportunities.

Cultural and organisational barriers in libraries

Cultural and organisational barriers in libraries can significantly impede the integration of kindness and wellbeing initiatives. When existing organisational cultures do not prioritise or value these aspects, initiating meaningful change becomes challenging. This difficulty is further compounded when there is a lack of leadership support for wellbeing initiatives.

A key factor influencing these cultural barriers is the 'compassion gap'. This is where a disparity exists between how leaders perceive their own behaviour and how it is received by employees. Leaders might believe they are acting compassionately, but employees may not feel that this compassion extends to them. This gap can demotivate staff and foster a culture where kindness and wellbeing are not prioritised.

The influence of leadership in shaping organisational culture is paramount. Leaders who prioritise their position or self-interest over compassion contribute to a culture that devalues kindness and wellbeing. When leaders in a library setting demonstrate a lack of compassion, it sets a precedent that can influence the behaviour of other staff members.

To overcome these cultural barriers, several strategies can be employed. Leadership training and development that emphasises the importance of compassion and wellbeing is crucial. Leaders need to be equipped with the skills to effectively recognise and address their staff's and users' needs. Promoting compassionate leadership is essential. Encouraging leaders to practise and model compassion can help bridge the compassion gap, leading by example.

Organisational self-assessment is important for libraries to identify barriers to kindness and wellbeing. This can involve surveys, feedback sessions and discussions with all staff members. Encouraging open communication is another key strategy. Creating channels for open and honest communication allows staff to express their concerns and ideas about wellbeing. This includes providing platforms for staff to share their experiences with compassion fatigue and other related challenges.

Cultivating a culture of empathy within the library can help build a more inclusive and supportive work environment. This involves recognising the common humanity and shared experiences of all staff and users. Implementing workshops that address compassion fatigue and promote peer support can be an effective way to change the organisational culture. These workshops can normalise experiences related to compassion and wellbeing and recognise the need for self-care among staff.

By addressing these cultural and organisational barriers, libraries can create environments where kindness and wellbeing are integral to their operation and ethos. This not only benefits the library staff but enhances the quality of service and support provided to the users.

Conclusion

Libraries can overcome challenges like bystander syndrome, emotional burdens, management self-interest, limited resources and cultural barriers to become more supportive and caring. This requires commitment to continuous learning, policy adaptation, empathy and community engagement. By doing so, libraries are transformed into centres of wellbeing and kindness, enhancing experiences for staff and patrons and strengthening their community role. This journey demands dedication and creativity, but the outcome – a supportive, inclusive and compassionate environment – is immensely rewarding.

Exercises and reflective questions

Exercise for teams

The compassion circle

Objective: to explore and address bystander syndrome, compassion fatigue and cultural barriers within the library team.

Materials needed: flip chart; markers; sticky notes; and a quiet room with enough space for the team to sit in a circle.

Instructions:

1   Setting the scene: gather the team in a circle. Begin with a brief introduction about the importance of kindness and wellbeing in the workplace, referencing key issues from the chapter.
2   Issue identification: on a flip chart, write down the main topics from this chapter: bystander syndrome, burden of caring, self-interest, resource limitations and cultural barriers. Ask each team member to think about these issues in the context of their work environment.
3   Sharing experiences: pass around sticky notes. Ask each team member to write down one personal experience or observation related to any of the topics on the flip chart. Assure confidentiality and openness without judgment.
4   Group discussion: one by one, let team members stick their notes on the flip chart under the relevant topic and share their thoughts. Facilitate a discussion on each point, focusing on how these issues manifest in your library and their impact on the team.
5   Solution brainstorming: after discussing each topic, brainstorm practical solutions or strategies to address these challenges in your library as a group.
6   Action plan: conclude the exercise by creating an action plan based on the solutions discussed. Assign responsibilities and set deadlines for implementing these strategies.
7   Reflection and closure: end with a reflection round, where each team member shares one insight they gained from the exercise.

Exercise for individuals

The wellbeing journal

Objective: to encourage individual staff members to reflect on their personal experiences with workplace wellbeing and identify improvement areas.

Materials needed: A journal or notebook for each participant.

Instructions:

1 Introduction to journalling: provide each staff member with a journal. Explain that this exercise aims to reflect on their experiences and feelings related to workplace wellbeing.
2 Daily entries: instruct participants to make daily entries for a set period (e.g. two weeks). Prompts for each day could include:
   - Describe one moment today where you felt supported or unsupported by your colleagues.
   - Reflect on a situation where you could have intervened to support a colleague or patron but didn't. What held you back?
   - How did you balance your professional goals with the needs of your colleagues and patrons today?
   - Write about a time today when you felt resource limitations impacted your ability to perform your job or support others.
3 Personal reflection: at the end of the two weeks, ask participants to read through their entries and reflect on patterns or recurring themes.
4 Goal setting: encourage each individual to set personal goals based on their reflections. These could be related to improving their approach to teamwork, emotional wellbeing or how they engage with patrons.
5 Optional sharing session: organise a voluntary session where staff members can share insights from their journals and discuss personal growth strategies.

Both exercises aim to enhance understanding and implementation of kindness and wellbeing practices in library settings, fostering a more supportive and empathetic work environment.

Reflective questions
- New insights: what further information or perspectives did you gain about the challenges of incorporating kindness and wellbeing into libraries? Were there any challenges that particularly resonated with you?
- Bystander syndrome reflection: having read about bystander syndrome, can you recall any personal experiences where you or others might have demonstrated this behaviour in a library setting? How could the situation have been handled differently?
- Compassion fatigue awareness: reflect on the concept of compassion fatigue in the context of library staff. Why is it important to address this issue and how can libraries support their staff in this area?
- Resource limitations and solutions: after reading about the resource limitations that libraries face, what are some creative solutions you can think of that could help libraries overcome these constraints?

- Personal application: how can you apply this chapter's strategies and insights to your life or work environment, even if it's not in a library? Can you adopt practices or ideas to promote kindness and wellbeing around you?

CHAPTER 13

Creating a Culture of Kindness and Wellbeing in the Workplace: Challenges and Opportunities for Library Leaders

Introduction

You may have heard that 'culture eats strategy for breakfast', but what does it do to wellbeing? It eats it for lunch, dinner and every snack. During my working life, I've witnessed first-hand the profound impact that workplace culture can have on every part of a library – from the wellbeing of its employees to its overall effectiveness. Within an organisation, culture is not an abstract concept but a living, breathing entity that shapes our daily experiences and long-term outcomes. It can change and evolve and when leaders aren't mindful of this, it can often change for the worse, but toxic cultures are the focus of a subsequent chapter. This chapter explores the complex interplay between workplace culture and the twin virtues of kindness and wellbeing. I aim to show you the unique challenges and opportunities librarians and staff encounter when fostering a work culture rich in kindness and conducive to wellbeing.

Can culture really affect wellbeing?

In 2022, Huhtala et al. reported on a longitudinal study of the impact of ethical organisational culture on the wellbeing of leaders. In this study, they used the Conservation of Resources (COR) model (explored in detail in Chapter 2) to examine the impact of an ethical culture on the wellbeing of their leaders. Leaders in organisations with a strong ethical culture reported better wellbeing. Specifically, they experienced lower levels of ethical dilemmas, stress and burnout and higher levels of work engagement. Over time, these positive factors slightly improved. The improvements were not as substantial as the negative impacts seen in environments with weak ethical cultures. This aligns with COR theory, which suggests that positive gains in wellbeing are generally more fragile and less enduring than negative losses.

The ethical context of organisations is made up of two main components: formal and informal controls. Formal or 'hard controls' consist of concrete plans, policies and procedures designed to promote ethical behaviour (Huhtala et al. 2022). These often include ethics programmes that feature a code of ethics, training sessions, monitoring systems and whistle-blowing policies. Informal controls or 'soft controls' involve the less tangible aspects, such as the values, expectations and assumptions that prevail in the organisation. In business ethics, these informal elements are captured by two concepts: ethical climate and ethical culture. Ethical climate relates to the collective perceptions within the organisation about what is considered ethical or unethical behaviour. On the other hand, ethical culture focuses on the conditions that make ethical behaviour possible, representing the procedural aspects of the organisation's ethical context.

Checklist for library leaders: assessing workplace culture for kindness and wellbeing

Before we explore theory and practical solutions for creating kind cultures in libraries, it is worth taking the temperature of your own culture. This checklist is designed to help library leaders evaluate their current workplace culture in terms of kindness and wellbeing. It covers various aspects, including leadership, communication, employee engagement and organisational policies. Reflect on each statement and mark how often it applies to your library's environment.

- Leadership and management:
  - Leaders regularly communicate the importance of kindness and wellbeing.
  - Top management's clear commitment is to foster a positive work environment.
  - Leaders model kindness and wellbeing in their daily interactions.
- Communication:
  - Communication within the library is open and honest.
  - Staff feel comfortable sharing their ideas and concerns without fear of repercussions.
  - There are regular meetings where staff can discuss non-work-related issues.
- Employee engagement and relationships:
  - Staff members are encouraged to support each other's wellbeing.
  - There are opportunities for team members to build relationships outside work tasks.
  - Acts of kindness are recognised and celebrated within the team.

- Policies and practices:
  - The library has policies in place that support work–life balance.
  - Mental health days and wellbeing activities are part of the workplace culture.
  - There is an accessible and effective system for addressing grievances related to workplace culture.
- Training and development:
  - Regular training is provided on topics like emotional intelligence and conflict resolution.
  - Staff are encouraged and supported in their personal and professional development.
  - There is a focus on continuous learning and improvement in workplace culture.
- Feedback and evaluation:
  - There are mechanisms for regularly gathering feedback on workplace culture.
  - Feedback on culture is actively sought from all levels of staff.
  - There is a process for incorporating feedback into cultural improvements.
- Inclusivity and diversity:
  - The library actively promotes and values diversity and inclusivity.
  - All staff members feel they are treated fairly and with respect.
  - Cultural, ethnic and gender diversity is reflected in library policies and practices.
- Wellbeing and support:
  - The library offers resources and support for staff mental health and wellbeing.
  - There is an emphasis on physical health, including ergonomic workspaces and breaks.
  - Staff have access to professional support for personal or work-related challenges.
- Scoring guide:
  - Mostly yes: your library is on a strong path toward fostering a culture of kindness and wellbeing.
  - Mixed responses: there are areas of strength but key aspects that need development.
  - Mostly no: Consider focusing on areas that require immediate attention to improve your library's work culture.

This checklist serves as a starting point for reflection and discussion among library leaders and teams, guiding you in identifying areas of success and opportunities for further growth in creating a culture of kindness and wellbeing.

Case Study 13.1: Crafting a culture of kindness in libraries

It must have been ten years ago that I first read *The Happy Manifesto* (Stewart, 2013) and started thinking about how I could impact and 'make my organisation a great place to work'. I was fascinated by the concept and the disconnect between many people's reality (my own included) – that work is a bind, a means to an end and something to endure. Whilst its far from easy, I believe that strong leadership can go hand-in-hand with being kind and people-focused and that this is at the core of being a workplace of choice.

It doesn't detract from the need to make difficult decisions and have uncomfortable conversations and tackle poor performance or bad behaviour or change things that absolutely need changing to drive the service forward. But all of those things can be done with empathy and emotional intelligence, considering how each person might feel, anticipating the fear or anxiety or underlying emotions that determine people's responses. Many people are sceptical if senior managers are kind and some see it as weakness. All the more reason to amplify kindness and weave it into both the day-to-day and longer-term planning and decision-making.

How does this work on a day-to-day basis? It can be as simple as greeting all staff and making time to have a proper conversation and listen and understanding each person for who they are. It's about the little routines and rituals – chocolate Tuesday or openly recognising and thanking individuals for when they've moved beyond their comfort zone or made an extra effort, however big or small. It's about being human and admitting mistakes. It's about taking responsibility for addressing long-standing problems, about being clear on expected behaviours and a level of professional courtesy and respect. Ultimately it's about the most basic of human connections and when done well I truly believe it's at the heart of making an organisation a great place to work.

Ann-Marie James, Director of Aston University Library

Leadership commitment in library organisational culture

Leaders are crucial to shaping organisational culture, as Case Study 13.1 shows. Leadership attitudes, behaviours and values significantly influence the library's ethos. This influence aligns with the **Leader-Member Exchange (LMX) Theory**, which posits that leaders form unique relationships with each member, impacting the work environment and overall culture (Graen and

Uhl-Bien, 1995) and which will be the theory underpinning how we explore the interplay between leadership and organisational culture in libraries.

Key attributes of effective library leaders

Leaders with kindness, inclusivity and wellbeing as core values in libraries play a pivotal role in manifesting them. Kindness can be shown through regular recognition of staff efforts, attentive listening to their concerns and offering support in difficult times. Inclusivity involves ensuring equitable treatment, amplifying diverse voices and cultivating a work environment that reflects the varied tapestry of the community. Wellbeing is promoted by implementing policies that support a balance between work and personal life, heightening mental health awareness and providing developmental resources for staff. LMX theory suggests that such behaviours can lead to high-quality leader–member exchanges, characterised by mutual trust, respect and obligation (Graen and Scandura, 1987).

Leaders must be approachable, fostering an environment where staff feel comfortable sharing ideas and challenges. Empathy, a cornerstone of LMX theory, involves understanding and accommodating the unique situations of each team member, leading to the development of more robust, more trusting relationships (Graen and Scandura, 1987). The creation of an environment where every staff member feels valued is crucial. This can be achieved through regular team engagements, individual check-ins and maintaining an open-door policy. Recognising and supporting each team member's unique strengths and challenges, an essential aspect of LMX theory, is vital for effective leadership.

Leaders working on a kind organisational culture should ensure their actions and communications consistently reflect the library's values and mission. Such consistency is imperative for building trust and providing clear direction and standards for the team. Consistent leadership behaviours foster trust and predictability, which are vital for nurturing high-quality LMX relationships. When expectations from leaders are clear and reliable, staff members are more likely to feel secure, valued and understood, enhancing engagement and performance (Graen and Uhl-Bien, 1995). It's important to acknowledge and address inconsistencies. Leaders should transparently recognise any misalignments between their actions and the library's values and take corrective measures. This approach not only reinforces trust but demonstrates accountability.

If you are in a leadership role I encourage you to engage in personalised interactions with each team member, as advocated by LMX theory. Understanding and respecting individual goals, challenges and working styles enables tailored support and development (Graen and Scandura, 1987). Effective LMX relationships are founded on mutual respect and shared responsibility. Leaders should respect and utilise team members' unique expertise and contributions, fostering a reciprocal sense of loyalty and commitment to the library.

In conclusion, the critical attributes of demonstrating core values and maintaining consistency are indispensable for library leaders. Informed by LMX theory, these practices strengthen leader-member relationships and contribute significantly to a positive, productive and cohesive library work culture.

Reflective questions for leaders

- Exploring leadership influence: how do you perceive the impact of your leadership attitudes, behaviours and values on your library's organisational culture? Reflect on specific instances where your leadership approach has directly influenced the ethos of your library.
- Evaluating kindness and inclusivity: in what ways have you demonstrated kindness and inclusivity in your leadership role? Consider how these actions have affected staff morale and the work environment. Are there areas where you could improve or implement new strategies?
- Balancing wellbeing and productivity: reflect on the policies and practices you have implemented to promote staff wellbeing. How do you ensure these practices align with maintaining or enhancing productivity and service quality in the library?
- Consistency and trust in leadership: think about the consistency of your actions and communications with your library's values and mission. How has this consistency (or lack thereof) influenced trust and engagement among your team members?
- Personalised interactions and LMX Theory: how do you tailor your interactions with each team member to respect their individual goals, challenges and working styles? Reflect on how this approach has strengthened or could strengthen the leader–member relationships within your library, in line with LMX theory.

Building trust through transparency in library organisational culture

Transparency in leadership is pivotal for cultivating a trusting and open organisational culture in libraries. Leaders are encouraged to embrace openness, sharing information about decision-making processes, upcoming changes and existing challenges. Such transparency ensures that staff feel informed, involved and valued, laying the foundation for a trusting culture.

It's essential for leaders to not only communicate about positive developments but about difficulties and uncertainties, fostering an environment where honesty is valued and encouraged. Leaders are urged to practise clear and honest communication, even in challenging situations. Acknowledging uncertainties or admitting mistakes can significantly bolster trust and credibility among staff. Open communication needs to be a core aspect of the library's culture, offering staff a sense of security and stability. This approach helps build a reliable and trustworthy environment where staff feel confident about the information they receive and the transparency of their leaders. Moving beyond leadership, transparency should be a norm embraced at all levels within the library. It is crucial to create an environment where every staff member feels comfortable and safe to share their thoughts and feedback. This cultural shift ensures that open and honest communication is not just a leadership practice but a shared value amongst all staff, promoting a more inclusive and collaborative workplace.

Regular meetings and check-ins are essential for fostering open dialogue. These sessions range from formal team meetings and departmental briefings to informal coffee chats. They serve as platforms for staff to receive updates, provide input and share insights, enhancing the culture of open communication. Dedicated feedback sessions or open forums are recommended to allow staff to discuss broader topics, voice their ideas and raise concerns.

The effectiveness of these sessions hinges on them being safe spaces for open and respectful dialogue where all opinions are heard and valued. A key aspect of fostering a positive organisational culture is encouraging communication that flows from the bottom up. Leaders should actively seek and value inputs from all levels of staff, demonstrating that every team member's perspective is crucial. This approach fosters a sense of belonging and can unearth innovative and practical solutions to various challenges.

Open communication is a collective responsibility within the library. All staff members should feel empowered to discuss and share ideas and provide feedback. Training sessions focused on communication skills, including practical ways to give and receive feedback, can further strengthen this culture. Diverse channels for communication should be implemented, such as suggestion boxes, internal forums or regular surveys. These channels ensure that staff members have multiple avenues to voice their thoughts, catering to different communication preferences and encouraging widespread participation.

Encouraging open communication has a profound impact on the organisational culture of libraries. When staff feel heard and involved, it cultivates a sense of community, improves job satisfaction and fosters a more innovative and responsive workplace. It's crucial to recognise that fostering open communication is an ongoing effort. It requires continuous attention and adaptation to remain a fundamental part of the library's organisational culture, evolving with the changing needs and dynamics of the staff and the community it serves.

Collective responsibility in fostering kindness and wellbeing in library culture

The journey towards cultivating a culture of kindness and wellbeing in libraries is a collective endeavour. While leadership undeniably plays a pivotal role in shaping this culture, its true essence and sustainability come from the contributions of every individual within the organisation. This shared responsibility is vital for creating a positive work environment that benefits all (Cameron and Spreitzer, 2012).

Leaders act as catalysts in fostering an environment that values kindness and wellbeing. They set the tone and establish the norms. Still, the sustenance and growth of these values heavily depend on the engagement and actions of all staff members. Leaders who model kindness and wellbeing in their actions, decisions and interactions inspire similar behaviours across the organisation, as noted by Cameron and Quinn (2011) in their work on positive organisational scholarship.

Each staff member plays a crucial role in actively participating in and fostering a culture of kindness and wellbeing. This includes their everyday interactions, approaches to challenges and the support offered to colleagues. The influence peers have on each other is profound; recognising and celebrating acts of kindness and supporting each other's wellbeing can significantly strengthen this positive culture (Deci and Ryan, 2000).

Fostering an environment of openness and support is essential. Staff should feel comfortable sharing their experiences and challenges, as this openness builds community support and helps identify areas for cultural improvement. Organising activities that promote wellbeing and kindness, such as team-building exercises and wellness programmes, can be instrumental in building this community. These activities should cater to the diverse needs and preferences of the library staff, as diversity and inclusivity are key components of a positive work culture (Mor Barak, 2014).

Continuous communication and feedback among all levels of staff are critical. Regular check-ins, surveys and open forums can provide insights into the health of the workplace culture. Feedback should be viewed as a tool for growth and improvement in cultivating a kind and supportive work environment, a concept supported by London's theory on feedback and performance management (London, 2003).

Acknowledging and addressing challenges collectively is crucial. Solutions should involve input from all levels of staff, ensuring inclusivity and effectiveness. Training sessions focusing on empathy, effective communication and conflict resolution can be essential in maintaining and enhancing this culture (Goleman, 1998).

In conclusion, developing a positive library work culture is a shared responsibility. While leadership provides the vision and framework, the realisation of a culture rich in kindness and wellbeing is a journey that involves every individual in the organisation. This process requires continuous effort, reflection and adaptation to remain vibrant and effective (Schein, 2010).

The importance of psychological safety and trust in underpinning organisational culture

Psychological safety and trust are fundamental underpinning organisational culture, particularly within libraries. Amy Edmondson's concept of psychological safety describes an individual's perception of the safety of taking interpersonal risks in a work environment (Edmondson, 1999). Complementing this, Frei and Morriss's Trust Triangle Theory breaks down trust into three pillars: authenticity, logic and empathy (Frei and Morriss, 2020). These elements are critical in creating a workplace where employees feel secure and valued. It's essential to recognise that psychological safety is more than a 'soft skill' or a convenient addition to performance discussions – it is an integral part of the cultural fabric.

Psychological safety: beyond surface-level commitments

Library leaders must go beyond merely advocating psychological safety and actively cultivate an environment that truly supports it. This means creating a culture where expressing thoughts and ideas, especially unpopular ones, is encouraged and valued when done respectfully. It's about seeing mistakes not as failures but as opportunities for learning and growth, significantly enhancing psychological safety (Edmondson, 1999).

A crucial element is that even with all these efforts, psychological safety can still fall short if leaders do not genuinely commit to it. The metaphorical 'slap in the face' moment comes when we understand that while leaders can role-model authenticity, openness and empathy, there's still a gap. Psychological safety falls apart when there is no personal risk to the leader but significant risk to the employees who speak up, challenge or reveal vulnerabilities. This disparity can undermine the entire foundation of trust and safety.

To build trust, leaders and all people in libraries need to embody Frei and Morriss's Trust Triangle. Authenticity means being genuine in interactions and fostering trustworthiness (Frei and Morriss, 2020). Logic involves ensuring that decisions and their rationale are clear and understandable. Empathy requires understanding and addressing staff needs and concerns, reinforcing psychological safety.

Implementing psychological safety practically

- Regular check-ins and feedback sessions: implementing these sessions where staff can express concerns and ideas is crucial. Leaders must demonstrate vulnerability and openness during these interactions.
- Leadership training focused on vulnerability: training for library leaders should emphasise the principles of authenticity, logical decision-making, empathy and the importance of showing vulnerability.
- Transparent communication: this involves clarity in decision-making and demonstrating the leader's investment and risk.

Leaders must recognise that psychological safety is not a 'fad' or a set of 'clever words' but a critical, ongoing commitment. They must be willing to show their vulnerabilities and risks, demonstrating that their commitment to psychological safety is not just superficial. Failing to do so can lead to severe and lasting damage to individuals who take the risk of speaking up or showing vulnerability but are ultimately let down.

Integrating psychological safety and the principles of Frei and Morriss's Trust Triangle (2020) into library operations requires a deep and genuine commitment from leaders. It's about creating an environment where staff feel comfortable expressing themselves and trust that their leaders are equally invested and vulnerable. This level of commitment can lead to a truly inclusive, engaged and productive library environment.

Implementing kindness in organisations lacking a kindness ethos

Organisations with ingrained cultures focused on metrics, deadlines and the bottom line often overlook the significance of kindness and wellbeing. Fostering a culture of kindness isn't just a 'soft' value; it has tangible benefits for employee engagement, productivity and even profitability (Fredrickson, 2001; Lyubomirsky, King and Diener, 2005). The first step in implementing kindness is recognising the gap in existing organisational values. Many companies operate under transactional values, where employee interactions are seen merely as exchanges rather than opportunities for kindness (Cameron, 2011).

Evaluating psychological safety in your team: ten key questions
Psychological safety is integral to a positive and productive work environment, directly influencing team performance and cohesion. Assessing psychological safety doesn't require complex surveys or extensive research. Instead, reflecting on these ten straightforward questions can provide valuable insights into the level of psychological safety within your team:

1 Openness to unpopular opinions: how easy is it for someone to voice an unpopular opinion? Is there space for diverse viewpoints or are dissenting voices silenced?
2 Attitude Towards feedback: do team members fear receiving feedback? Is feedback seen as a threat or an opportunity for growth and learning?
3 Handling mistakes: are mistakes hidden or is the blame shifted to others? Or are errors treated as opportunities for improvement and learning?
4 Equal contribution: does everyone in the team have an equal opportunity to contribute or do some voices dominate while others are overlooked?
5 Inclusivity v. cliques: as a leader, do you tolerate the formation of exclusive cliques or do you foster an environment where everyone feels included?
6 Open-door policy for ideas: can anyone approach you with an idea and be assured that you'll listen sincerely?
7 Learning from failures: does the team reflect on mistakes constructively, seeking lessons rather than assigning blame?
8 Support for personal issues: can team members discuss personal issues affecting their work with their manager without fear of exposure or criticism?
9 Managerial support: do team members believe their manager will support them if something goes wrong?
10 True inclusivity: is the team genuinely inclusive, embracing people from diverse backgrounds and perspectives?

If you find yourself answering 'No' to any of these questions, it indicates that your team may lack psychological safety. Addressing these areas is not inconvenient: it's essential for fostering a healthy, effective and inclusive team environment. You can enhance your team's psychological safety and overall performance and satisfaction by actively working to improve these aspects.

Getting leadership to buy into the concept is crucial for successfully implementing kindness as an organisational value. Research shows that leadership style directly impacts organisational culture (Bass and Avolio, 1994). Leaders should be educated on the benefits of a kindness-oriented culture, such as increased employee wellbeing and potential boosts in productivity (Wright and Cropanzano, 2004). Kindness doesn't have to involve grand gestures. Sometimes, it's about people's day-to-day interactions within the workspace (Keltner and Haidt, 1999). Creating opportunities for 'micro-kindness' – small, everyday acts like expressing gratitude or listening attentively – can accumulate into a broader culture of kindness.

As mentioned previously, regularly solicit feedback from employees on the new initiatives. This can be done through anonymous surveys or open forums. Feedback is a valuable guide for making incremental changes and shows employees that their wellbeing is considered (Schaufeli and Bakker, 2004).

Continuous support systems and the role of job crafting

Establishing a culture that promotes kindness and wellbeing is not a one-time event but an ongoing process. Continuous support systems, such as mentorship programmes and learning initiatives, are key to sustaining this culture. Integrating the theory of job crafting (see Chapter 2) into these support systems can provide a more holistic approach to individual and organisational wellbeing. Job crafting refers to employees proactively altering aspects of their jobs to better fit their strengths, skills, interests and passions (Wrzesniewski and Dutton, 2001).

Implementing mentorship programmes
Peer mentorship

Pairing newer employees with more experienced peers can provide a nurturing environment where individuals can learn the ropes more easily. This is where job crafting comes into play. Experienced employees, through their own crafted roles, can guide newcomers in identifying opportunities for job crafting, thus helping them integrate better into the organisational culture.

Leadership mentorship

Senior leaders mentor middle management to create a trickle-down effect of the desired culture. They can use the principles of job crafting to empower middle managers to reshape their roles in a way that emphasises kindness and wellbeing, thereby becoming role models for their own teams.

Reverse mentorship

In this model, newer library staff, who may be more attuned to contemporary societal attitudes towards kindness and wellbeing, guide senior staff or management. This can be particularly effective in bridging generational gaps and introducing new ideas into the library's culture. Junior staff can share their unique perspectives on how the library can enhance its approach to wellbeing, potentially highlighting areas overlooked by more experienced staff. For example, they might offer insights into how digital tools can aid in promoting wellbeing or suggest fresh ways to engage with the community on these issues.

Through reverse mentorship, senior leaders are exposed to innovative ways of thinking about kindness and wellbeing, particularly from the viewpoint of younger generations or those new to the field. This approach can help reshape the library's strategies to be more inclusive and forward-thinking, ensuring that the institution remains relevant and responsive to the needs of all its stakeholders.

Combined with peer and leadership mentorship, reverse mentorship completes a holistic mentorship programme that ensures diverse perspectives are valued and utilised in fostering a culture of kindness and wellbeing in libraries.

Continuous learning initiatives
Workshops

Organising workshops on emotional intelligence, effective communication and conflict resolution can help employees develop skills contributing to a kinder workplace. Job crafting can be incorporated here as a workshop topic, educating employees on how to tailor their job roles to better align with organisational goals and personal wellbeing.

Online resources

Creating an internal portal with resources for continuous learning serves as an ongoing support system. Modules on job crafting can be included to guide employees in making incremental changes to their daily tasks, interactions and overall work structure, thereby contributing to their personal wellbeing.

Holistic connection with wellbeing

Job crafting serves a dual purpose. On an organisational level, it helps improve role alignment and performance. On a personal level, it contributes to individual wellbeing by allowing employees to focus on aspects of the job that they find meaningful and fulfilling. When employees craft their jobs to align more closely with their values and strengths, they will likely experience greater job satisfaction and less stress, naturally contributing to a culture of kindness and wellbeing.

In conclusion, job crafting isn't just a strategy for employee retention or engagement; it's a vital component for fostering kindness and wellbeing. By integrating job crafting into continuous support systems like mentorship programmes and learning initiatives organisations can ensure a more sustained and holistic approach to nurturing a healthy workplace.

Challenges and countermeasures to kind cultures

In our journey towards fostering a culture of kindness and wellbeing within libraries, one of the most significant barriers we encounter is resistance to change. This resistance is particularly pronounced in institutions with a long history and established routines. Accustomed to their traditional work practices, employees might view new initiatives with scepticism or discomfort, fearing disruption to their familiar work environment. Overcoming this resistance is critical to successfully implementing cultural changes that support kindness and wellbeing.

This section explores effective strategies to address and mitigate resistance to challenges. These strategies focus on three core principles: gradual implementation of changes, inclusive decision-making and transparent communication. Libraries can navigate resistance challenges by introducing changes incrementally, involving staff at all levels in the decision-making process and clearly articulating the rationale and benefits of these changes. This approach eases the transition and fosters a sense of ownership and engagement among staff, paving the way for a more harmonious and resilient workplace culture.

Six common challenges and their countermeasures

1. Resistance to change

Challenge: resistance to cultural change is a common hurdle, especially in long-established institutions. Staff may be sceptical or uncomfortable with new initiatives, fearing these changes could disrupt their routine or work dynamics.

Countermeasures:

■ Incremental implementation: introduce changes gradually to allow time for adjustment.

- Inclusive decision-making: involve staff at all levels in the planning and decision-making. This inclusivity can mitigate resistance by giving everyone a sense of ownership and control over the changes.
- Transparent communication: clearly communicate the reasons for changes and their benefits. Regularly share progress and successes to maintain momentum and enthusiasm.

2. Managing diverse perspectives

Challenge: in a diverse workplace, differing opinions and perspectives can create challenges, particularly when establishing a unified culture of kindness and wellbeing.
   Countermeasures:

- Facilitate open dialogues: create forums for staff to express their views and concerns. Actively listen and validate different perspectives.
- Customised approach: recognise that one size does not fit all. Tailor initiatives to accommodate diverse needs and preferences.
- Ongoing education: conduct workshops and training sessions to educate staff about diversity, inclusivity and the importance of multiple perspectives in enriching the workplace.

3. Maintaining consistency in practices

Challenge: ensuring consistent application of new cultural norms and practices across all levels of the organisation can be challenging, particularly in more extensive or segmented institutions.
   Countermeasures:

- Regular training and refreshers: offer ongoing training sessions to reinforce the new cultural values and practices.
- Leadership role modelling: ensure leaders consistently demonstrate the desired behaviours at all levels. Their actions set a precedent for the rest of the staff.
- Accountability mechanisms: implement systems to monitor adherence to new cultural norms, including regular check-ins and performance reviews incorporating cultural metrics.

4. Balancing wellbeing with performance goals

Challenge: aligning the focus on wellbeing and kindness with the need to meet performance goals and objectives can be a delicate balancing act.
   Countermeasures:

- Integrate wellbeing into performance metrics: develop performance metrics that include components of wellbeing and kindness, such as team collaboration and support.
- Emphasise long-term benefits: educate staff on how a positive work culture can enhance overall productivity and job satisfaction in the long term.
- Flexible goal-setting: allow for flexibility in goal-setting, recognising that a one-size-fits-all approach may not be conducive to promoting wellbeing.

5. Sustaining momentum

Challenge: there might initially be enthusiasm for cultural change, but sustaining this momentum over time can be difficult.

Countermeasures:

- Celebrate milestones: regularly celebrate achievements and milestones towards a kinder, more wellbeing-focused culture.
- Feedback loops: establish continuous feedback mechanisms to assess the effectiveness of initiatives and make adjustments as needed.
- Reinforce through storytelling: share success stories and testimonials from staff who have positively experienced the cultural shift.

6. Adapting to external changes

Challenge: external factors such as technological advancements, societal changes or economic pressures can impact the ability to maintain a certain workplace culture.

Countermeasures:

- Stay informed and agile: keep abreast of external trends and be prepared to adapt strategies accordingly.
- Build a resilient culture: foster a resilient and flexible culture that can adjust and thrive amidst change.
- Regular environmental scanning: regularly assess the external environment to anticipate and prepare for changes that may affect the workplace culture.

By addressing these challenges and implementing the suggested counter-measures, the next section will offer practical and actionable strategies for libraries to navigate the complexities of cultural transformation, thereby fostering a more sustainable environment of kindness and wellbeing.

Actionable steps for different hierarchical levels to foster a kindness and wellbeing culture

Creating a culture of kindness and wellbeing in libraries requires concerted efforts across all levels of the organisation. Here are specific actions tailored for different hierarchical levels:

Top leadership (directors, senior managers)

- Set clear expectations: communicate the importance of kindness and wellbeing as core values.
- Policy development: implement policies that support work–life balance and mental health.
- Resource allocation: ensure sufficient resources are allocated for wellbeing initiatives.
- Lead by example: model the behaviours and attitudes you wish to see throughout the organisation.
- Regular check-ins: hold frequent discussions with middle management to gauge the pulse of the workplace culture.

Middle management (department heads, team leaders)

- Encourage open communication: create a safe space for staff to voice concerns and ideas.
- Recognise and reward: acknowledge acts of kindness and contributions to team wellbeing.
- Team building: organise activities that foster team cohesion and mutual support.
- Personal development: support staff in personal and professional growth, including emotional intelligence and conflict resolution training.
- Feedback mechanisms: implement and utilise feedback systems to continuously improve the work environment.

Frontline and operational staff (librarians, assistants)

- Participate actively: engage in workplace culture initiatives and offer constructive feedback.
- Peer support: look out for colleagues' wellbeing and offer support when needed.
- Self-care: prioritise your own wellbeing and utilise available resources effectively.
- Embrace diversity: respect and celebrate diverse perspectives and backgrounds within the team.
- Collaborative efforts: work with colleagues to create a supportive and positive work environment.

Support staff (administrative, maintenance)

- Voice opinions: share your perspectives and ideas in meetings or through feedback channels.
- Respect and inclusion: treat everyone in the workplace with respect and inclusivity.
- Initiative taking: create a positive workplace, like organising a shared space for relaxation or informal gatherings.
- Self-advocacy: speak up about your own needs and wellbeing and seek support when necessary.
- Engage in learning opportunities: participate in training sessions promoting workplace kindness and wellbeing.

All staff

- Open-mindedness: remain open to new ideas and initiatives to improve workplace culture.
- Continuous learning: stay informed and engaged with the latest practices in workplace wellbeing.
- Constructive feedback: provide and receive feedback constructively.
- Celebrate successes: celebrate personal and team achievements in fostering a positive work environment.
- Reflect and adjust: regularly reflect on your role in the workplace culture and make adjustments as needed for continuous improvement.

By addressing the specific roles and responsibilities at each hierarchical level, libraries can create a more co-ordinated and practical approach to fostering a culture where kindness and wellbeing are not just values but daily practices.

Conclusion

This chapter has provided a comprehensive exploration of the intricate relationship between workplace culture and the essential virtues of kindness and wellbeing, especially within the library context. We have delved into the dynamics of ethical organisational cultures, highlighting their profound impact on employee welfare, engagement and ethical conduct. The role of leadership in shaping and sustaining these cultures has been underscored, emphasising the significance of embodying kindness, inclusivity and wellbeing in leadership practices. Moreover, the chapter has illuminated the importance of psychological safety and trust as foundational elements in cultivating a supportive and productive organisational culture. By integrating these insights into daily operations and interactions, libraries can enhance their internal environment and extend these virtues to their communities. As we move forward, it becomes evident that fostering a culture rich in kindness and wellbeing is not a passive process but an active, continuous journey requiring commitment, empathy and collaboration from every individual within the organisation.

Exercises and reflective questions

Exercise for teams

Discovering our core values

Objective: to engage library staff in a collaborative and reflective exercise to identify and define the core values that will shape their workplace culture.

Materials needed: flip chart or whiteboard; markers; sticky notes; pens.

Duration: 1 hour.

Procedure:

1 Introduction (10 minutes): begin by briefly explaining core values and their importance in shaping workplace culture. Emphasise how these values influence decision-making, interactions and the overall atmosphere in the library.
2 Individual reflection (10 minutes): distribute sticky notes and pens to each participant. Ask them to reflect on and write down the values they believe are essential for a positive and effective library work environment. Please encourage them to think about values that foster kindness, inclusivity and wellbeing.
3 Group sharing (15 minutes): have each participant take notes on the flip chart or whiteboard. Invite them to briefly explain their chosen values and why they consider them important.
4 Identifying common values (10 minutes): review all the values listed as a group. Discuss and identify common themes or values that multiple people have highlighted.
5 Defining core values (10 minutes): select 3–5 values the group agrees are most crucial. Work together to determine what each of these values means in the context of the library workplace. Discuss how these values can be embodied in everyday actions and decisions.
6 Action plan (5 minutes): conclude by brainstorming practical ways to integrate these core values into daily library operations. This could include specific behaviours, policy changes or new initiatives that reflect these values.

Debrief:

1 Summarise the core values and their definitions as agreed upon by the group.
2 Highlight the importance of everyone's role in upholding these values.
3 Discuss steps for implementing the action plan and how progress will be monitored.

Follow-up: consider creating a visual representation of these core values to be displayed prominently in the library, constantly reminding and inspiring all staff members.

Exercise for teams

Culture mapping workshop
Objective: to engage the entire team in identifying and mapping out the current state of their workplace culture, pinpointing areas of strength and opportunities for improvement in kindness and wellbeing.
Materials needed: large paper or whiteboard; markers; sticky notes; pens.
Duration: 1–2 hours.
Procedure:

1 Mapping the current culture (30 minutes):
   ▪ Draw a large map on the paper or whiteboard representing the library's workplace culture.
   ▪ Ask team members to place sticky notes on the map to depict various elements of the current culture, focusing on kindness and wellbeing.
2 Group discussion and analysis (45 minutes):
   ▪ Facilitate a discussion around the map. Encourage staff to share why they placed notes in certain areas and what those notes represent.
   ▪ Identify patterns, strengths and areas needing improvement.
3 Action planning (30 minutes):
   ▪ Based on the discussion, collaborate as a team to develop an action plan for enhancing positive aspects and addressing areas for improvement.
   ▪ Assign roles or create small working groups for specific initiatives.

Follow-up:

1 Regularly revisit the culture map in team meetings to track progress and adjust the action plan.

2 Encourage a culture of continuous feedback and openness to ensure the action plan remains relevant and effective.

Exercise for individuals
Workplace culture reflection diary
Objective: to enable individual library staff members to reflect on and understand their role in shaping the workplace culture, focusing specifically on elements related to kindness and wellbeing.
Materials needed: a diary or digital journal; pen or digital device for writing.
Duration: ongoing, with weekly reflections.
Procedure:

1 Initial setup (10 minutes):
   ■ Provide each staff member with a diary or instructions for writing a digital journal.
   ■ Introduce the concept of a 'Workplace Culture Reflection Diary', where they will record observations and reflections about the workplace culture each week.
2 Weekly reflection prompts (20 minutes per week):
   ■ Encourage staff to dedicate 20 minutes each week to reflect on specific prompts related to workplace culture. Prompts could include:
   ■ What actions did I take this week that contributed positively to our workplace culture?
   ■ Were there moments when I could have been more kind or supportive to a colleague?
   ■ How did I personally experience kindness and wellbeing in the workplace this week?
   ■ What aspects of our current workplace culture would I like to see improve?
3 Personal action steps (5 minutes per week): at the end of each weekly reflection, ask them to jot down one or two personal action steps they can take in the coming week to enhance the workplace culture.

Follow-up: monthly team meetings can include a voluntary share-out segment where staff members can share insights or positive changes they have noticed in the workplace culture from their reflections.

Reflective questions
   ■ Self-awareness in actions: 'In what ways have my actions and words this week contributed positively or negatively to the culture of kindness and wellbeing in our workplace?'

- Observation of environment: 'What behaviours or actions have I observed in the workplace that either promote or hinder a culture of kindness and wellbeing?'
- Response to challenges: 'When faced with a challenging situation at work this week, how did I respond and what impact did my response have on the workplace atmosphere and my colleagues?'
- Role in team dynamics: 'How do I perceive my role in the team and in what ways do I influence the team's culture through my everyday interactions?'
- Empathy and understanding: 'Have I made an effort to understand the perspectives and feelings of my colleagues this week and how has this affected my interactions with them?'
- Promoting inclusivity: 'What actions have I taken or could I take to ensure that everyone in the workplace feels included, respected and valued?'
- Feedback and growth: 'How do I handle receiving feedback and in what ways have I used it to contribute to a positive work environment?'
- Supporting others: 'In what ways have I offered support to a colleague in need this week and what impact did this have on their wellbeing and the overall team morale?'
- Personal wellbeing: 'How have I taken care of my wellbeing in the workplace and how does my wellbeing affect my ability to contribute to a positive work culture?'
- Future focus: 'What is one change I can commit to making in the upcoming week to further enhance the culture of kindness and wellbeing in our workplace?'

These questions encourage individual reflection and accountability, guiding library staff members in actively participating in and shaping a workplace culture that values kindness and wellbeing.

CHAPTER 14

Effective Conflict Resolution Strategies for Libraries: Prioritising Kindness and Wellbeing

Introduction

Conflict is inevitable in any workplace and libraries are no exception. Staff and users' diverse needs and expectations can often lead to misunderstandings and disagreements. This chapter explores effective conflict resolution strategies explicitly tailored for library environments. I aim to provide librarians and library staff with the tools and understanding necessary to address conflicts constructively, fostering an atmosphere of co-operation and respect. By prioritising kindness and wellbeing in our approach, we resolve disputes and strengthen the community bonds within the library setting. This is essential for creating a positive and productive work environment, ensuring that libraries continue to be places of learning, discovery and peaceful co-existence.

Overview of conflict in libraries

Conflicts in libraries can manifest in various forms and stem from many sources. Some of the most common types of disputes include:

- Staff conflicts; these arise from interpersonal issues between colleagues, differences in work styles or disagreements over responsibilities and duties. Such conflicts can stem from miscommunication, competition or varying professional opinions.
- User–staff conflicts: libraries serve diverse users, each with unique needs and expectations. Conflicts can occur over library policies, user behaviour, service quality or resource availability. These situations often require staff to balance policy enforcement with customer service and diplomacy.
- Policy-related conflicts: libraries operate under specific policies and guidelines, which sometimes can become sources of conflict. This includes disputes over censorship, privacy issues, resource allocation or

service access. These conflicts often involve balancing the needs and rights of individuals with those of the wider community.

■ Technology and innovation conflicts: as libraries evolve and adopt new technologies and methodologies, conflicts can arise from resistance to change, disparities in technological literacy among staff or users or disagreements over the direction of library development.

■ Cultural and diversity conflicts: libraries serve multicultural communities and conflicts can arise from misunderstandings or insensitivity to cultural differences. This includes language barriers, differing cultural norms and varying expectations of library roles in different cultures.

Understanding these types of conflicts is the first step in addressing them effectively. This chapter aims to guide library staff through recognising, understanding and resolving disputes in a manner that upholds the values of kindness, wellbeing and community service central to the library profession.

Reflective questions

■ Reflecting on staff conflicts: consider a recent conflict among staff members. What were the root causes and how might improved communication or understanding of different work styles have altered the outcome?

■ Handling user–staff conflicts: think about a challenging interaction with a user. How did you balance enforcing library policies with maintaining high-quality customer service and what could you learn from that experience?

■ Navigating policy-related disputes: recall a situation where library policies led to conflict. How did you balance the individual's needs with the community's and what insights did you gain?

■ Addressing technology and innovation challenges: reflect on a conflict caused by new technologies or changes in library practices. How did you handle resistance or differing opinions and what strategies proved effective?

■ Managing cultural and diversity conflicts: consider when cultural differences caused a misunderstanding or conflict. What steps did you take to resolve it and how has it informed your approach to creating an inclusive library environment?

These questions encourage critical reflection on various conflicts in libraries, aiming to enhance understanding and improve conflict resolution skills in line with the values of kindness, wellbeing and community service.

Principles of kindness and wellbeing in conflict resolution

Kindness is a practical and powerful tool in conflict resolution within library settings that transforms interaction dynamics. It's about understanding how people feel, being patient and respectful and really listening to different views. By being kind, you can calm down tense situations, help people understand each other and make sure everyone feels listened to and valued. This doesn't mean avoiding tough talks or just trying to keep the peace. It's about dealing with problems in a caring and sincere way, aiming to find good solutions for everyone. For example, if a library user is upset about a rule, staff can show they understand the person's feelings, explain why the rule is there and work together to find a solution that works. In Case Study 14.1, Sarah Ekey shows how having a planned approach and clear intention in these situations is important.

Case Study 14.1: Note-taking

Active note-taking and creating a conflict resolution script reinforces the intentionality of kindness. I want to actually understand the words people are saying. I don't just want to copy word for word during presentations. I will try to wrap my mind around the meaning and active note-taking forces that process. Most conflict comes from a place of misunderstanding and assuming, so intentionally listening already fixes many problems. For the remaining conflicts, other means are necessary. In times of conflict or surprise, I rarely find the right words, so prepping ahead of time with a script in mind helps me. It's actually something I have done for years. I can focus on the disagreement over personality differences or confusion. I'm not always perfect, but I do try.

Sarah Ekey, Metropolitan Community College – Longview

Emphasising wellbeing in resolution processes

Acknowledging the stressful and emotionally taxing nature of conflicts, it's crucial to concentrate not only on rapid resolution but also on the long-term emotional and psychological wellbeing of everyone involved, colleagues or library users. This holistic approach values mental and emotional health as much as tangible outcomes, safeguarding all parties in a conflict. It consists of providing staff with stress management training, offering emotional support to navigate challenging interactions and understanding colleagues and users as individuals with unique backgrounds and emotional needs. The organisation must take responsibility for the wellbeing of all parties. The post-conflict phase is critical, emphasising the need for a safe space for open dialogue without fear of reprisal, validating emotions and assisting in finding closure. Such an inclusive focus on wellbeing counterbalances the potential negative impacts of unresolved or ineffectively managed conflicts, benefiting each individual and the broader library community alike.

In addition to the strategies above, being vigilant about complaints raised in bad faith, particularly those among staff members, is essential. Such situations can escalate conflicts and create a toxic work environment if not appropriately addressed. Recognising and dealing with these complaints requires a sensitive yet firm approach. It involves establishing clear guidelines for evaluating the legitimacy of complaints and ensuring that all parties are heard fairly. Training in conflict resolution and ethical communication for staff can be instrumental. It's vital to foster a culture of honesty and transparency within the team, where raising concerns is done with the intention of constructive feedback rather than personal gain or detriment to others. This approach helps maintain a positive and respectful work environment and reinforces trust and integrity among colleagues. Effectively managing such situations can prevent unnecessary escalations and maintain a focus on promoting a positive and kind workplace aligned with the broader goals of wellbeing and mutual respect.

Synergy with wellbeing models

Having explored the foundational principles of kindness and wellbeing in conflict resolution, we now move into understanding how these concepts synergise with established wellbeing models. This integration offers a deeper insight into how kindness and wellbeing, when applied in library conflict resolution, align with broader psychological frameworks and contribute to a nurturing and positive work environment.

PERMA Model

- Positive emotion: kindness in conflict resolution nurtures empathy, compassion and satisfaction.
- Engagement: engaging staff in meaningful conflict resolution processes bolsters their sense of belonging and engagement.
- Relationships: effective communication and kindness in resolving conflicts reinforce interpersonal connections.
- Meaning: centring wellbeing in conflict resolution imbues the workplace with purpose and significance.
- Accomplishment: successfully overcoming conflicts enhances job satisfaction and a feeling of achievement.

JD-R Model

- Job demands: perceive conflicts as job demands and apply kindness-based strategies for effective management.
- Job resources: foster empathetic communication skills as key resources to alleviate the pressures of job demands.

PsyCap Model

- Hope: cultivate a hopeful outlook towards resolving workplace challenges through kindness and empathy.
- Efficacy: empower staff with confidence through comprehensive conflict resolution training.
- Resilience: encourage resilience among staff to manage and recover from conflicts effectively.
- Optimism: promote an optimistic work environment, encouraging positive perspectives in conflict situations.

Integrating these principles and models helps us address the immediate necessities of conflict resolution. It significantly contributes to the overall psychological wellbeing of library staff. This alignment with the broader goal of nurturing a work environment where wellbeing and kindness prevail underlines the essential nature of these principles in library conflict resolution.

Identifying and assessing conflict in library environments

Early detection: recognising the early signs of conflict

Effective conflict management in libraries hinges on early detection. Recognising early signs prevents serious disputes and keeps the environment harmonious. Key strategies include:

- Behavioural cues: staff should be trained to spot changes in behaviour such as irritability, withdrawal or overt frustration, indicating potential conflict.
- Communication patterns: be alert to shifts like increased complaints, sarcastic comments or breakdowns in regular communication, signalling issues.
- Workplace dynamics: watch for dynamic changes, including cliques, gossip or reduced collaboration and teamwork.
- Feedback mechanisms: regular, confidential feedback sessions allow staff to voice concerns early on.
- User interactions: observe user interactions for dissatisfaction or discomfort signs, which could lead to conflicts.

Assessing the severity

For assessing the severity and nature of identified conflicts, consider:

- Conflict mapping: this tool visually represents conflicts, showing involved parties, their interests and issues, aiding in understanding the conflict's complexity.
- Surveys and questionnaires: these gather information from involved parties and others, providing insights into perceptions and attitudes.
- One-on-one meetings: confidential meetings with each party offer deeper insights into their perspectives and feelings.
- Observation: monitoring interactions and dynamics in the library setting reveals the conflict's impact, including non-verbal cues and group dynamics.
- Severity scale: a scale categorising conflicts based on potential impact helps in deciding the appropriate response.
- Conflict diaries: staff logs of events and feelings can identify patterns and triggers.

In summary, detecting conflicts early and assessing them accurately is vital for effective conflict management in libraries, reducing escalation and fostering a positive work environment.

Conflict resolution process

This section outlines a structured, step-by-step process designed to effectively resolve conflicts in library settings. Each step is critical in ensuring a comprehensive approach to conflict resolution that aligns with principles of kindness and wellbeing.

1 Identify the conflict: start by clearly defining the conflict. Determine who is involved, what the conflict is about and what factors may have contributed to its emergence.
2 Create a safe space for dialogue: arrange a neutral, private space for discussion. Establish ground rules that promote respect, open-mindedness and confidentiality.
3 Understand each party's perspective: facilitate a conversation where each party can share their viewpoint without interruption. Use active listening techniques to ensure all parties feel heard and understood.
4 Find common ground: identify shared goals or interests that all parties can agree upon. This can help shift the focus from individual differences to collective objectives.

5 Brainstorm solutions: encourage all parties to contribute ideas for resolving the conflict. Aim for mutually beneficial solutions that align with library policies and values.

6 Agree on a resolution: reach a consensus on the best way forward. Ensure that the agreed upon solution addresses the concerns of all parties involved.

7 Develop an action plan: create a clear plan for implementing the resolution. Define specific actions, responsible individuals and timelines.

8 Monitor progress and follow-up: set up a mechanism to review the effectiveness of the resolution. Schedule follow-up meetings to ensure the conflict is fully resolved and address any emerging issues.

To illustrate these steps in action, Case Study 14.2 gives three anonymised examples of situations commonly encountered in library settings. Each details how the conflict emerged, the steps taken to resolve it and the outcome.

Case Study 14.2: Conflict resolution – three anonymised cases

1. Resolving staff workload disputes
Scenario: Two library staff members, referred to here as Alex and Tony, experienced a conflict over the distribution of workload. Alex felt overwhelmed with tasks, while Tony believed their workload was manageable. The situation led to tension and reduced collaboration between them.
Resolution process:

1 Open dialogue: a meeting was arranged for them to share their views in a safe, neutral environment.
2 Empathy and understanding: each staff member expressed their concerns and feelings. Alex discussed feeling overburdened, while Tony shared his perspective on managing workload efficiently.
3 Collaborative approach: they explored ways to balance the workload more equitably. This included redistributing tasks and adjusting schedules.

Resolution and follow-up: a new workload distribution plan was agreed upon, with a commitment to regular check-ins to ensure the arrangement continued to work for both parties.

   Outcome: the conflict was resolved amicably. Alex felt relieved and supported, while Tony better understood Alex's challenges. The resolution led to improved team dynamics and a more balanced workload distribution.

2. Managing internal conflicts over resource allocation
Scenario: the library management team faced a conflict regarding resource allocation. Different departments had competing needs, leading to tension among the management team members.
Resolution process:

1 Conflict mapping: the team used conflict mapping to visualise each department's needs and the areas of contention.
2 Brainstorming session: each department head presented their case in a collaborative meeting and the team brainstormed potential solutions.
3 Developing an action plan: a plan was formulated that considered the most pressing needs of each department while looking at future resource allocation strategies.

Outcome: the conflict was resolved through a balanced and strategic allocation of resources. This approach addressed immediate needs and set a precedent for future resource management, fostering a sense of fairness and collaboration within the management team.

3. Handling First Amendment auditors in public libraries
Scenario: in the USA, public libraries have encountered several instances of First Amendment auditors. These auditors visit libraries to test and assert their rights under the First Amendment, which includes freedoms related to religion, speech, press, peaceful assembly, and petitioning the government, often aiming to capture confrontational footage for online platforms. Unprepared libraries have faced challenges such as an influx of Freedom of Information Act requests, police involvement and potential lawsuits. Several library associations provide resources, including presentations on legal issues, to help libraries navigate these situations.

   Such developments, while deeply rooted in the US legal framework, resonate with global themes of freedom of expression and the public's entitlement to knowledge. Although the First Amendment is unique to American law, the essence of what it safeguards—liberties of speech, the press, and access to information—are echoed in international human rights statutes to varying extents. Libraries across the world serve as vital community hubs, committed to the dissemination of information, and therefore, they may confront similar challenges as those seen in the U.S. Understanding how different countries balance the individual's right to information with other collective rights and interests, including privacy and security, can provide valuable insights. Libraries can use this understanding to equip themselves for potential situations that test the limits of these rights, drawing on best practices and legal advisories tailored

to their local contexts. This global perspective reinforces the need for libraries to be prepared, proactive, and supported by their national and international bodies in upholding the principles of free and open access to information amidst rapidly evolving societal and technological landscapes.
Resolution strategies:

- Community engagement and education: engage with the local community to share experiences and strategies for dealing with First Amendment auditors. Educate staff and users about the auditors' typical behaviours and objectives.
- Staff training and preparedness: utilise resources such as various library associations' presentations to train staff. Empower them to handle these situations professionally, respecting the law and library policies.
- Understanding 'Limited Public Forum' protections: educate staff on the concept of the library as a 'limited public forum'. This understanding helps in managing activities that could disrupt normal operations. Understanding 'Limited Public Forum' protections refers to educating library staff about the legal concept that a public library, while a public space, does not necessarily provide an unrestricted platform for all forms of expression or activity. In US legal terms, a 'public forum' is a government-owned property open to public expression and assembly. There are different types of public forums and a 'limited public forum' is one where the government can impose reasonable restrictions on speech and activities based on subject matter and speaker identity, as long as these restrictions are not based on the viewpoint expressed.
- Professional and polite interaction: advise staff to maintain professionalism and politeness, ignoring the camera and treating auditors like any other user. Avoid engaging in confrontations that auditors may seek to instigate.
- Policy review and legal collaboration: review and clarify the library's policies regarding public use and First Amendment activities. Collaborate with legal experts to ensure the library's approach is legally sound and respects First Amendment rights.
- Minimising user involvement: protect users' privacy, especially minors, and ensure they are not inadvertently involved in such recordings.
- Positive spin on interactions: encourage staff to put a positive spin on any interaction with auditors, keeping in mind that footage can be edited and repurposed. Maintaining professionalism and respect in all interactions is key.
- Documenting encounters: keep records of First Amendment auditors' interactions for reference and use in training or legal situations if needed.

These three anonymised examples demonstrate the practical application of conflict resolution strategies in a library setting, showcasing how empathy, understanding and collaborative problem-solving can lead to effective and harmonious resolutions.

Helen Rimmer

Implementing solutions and follow-up in library conflict resolution

Action planning

Creating and putting into action a comprehensive plan is essential for effectively resolving conflicts in library settings. Here's a straightforward guide to crafting an efficient action plan:

1 Setting clear goals: start by precisely outlining the objectives of your action plan. Consider the specific outcomes you wish to achieve in resolving the conflict. What are the key issues to address and what would a successful resolution look like?
2 Delegating responsibilities: it's important to assign specific tasks and roles to individuals involved in the action plan. Who will handle which aspects of the plan? It's crucial that everyone understands their responsibilities and commitments clearly.
3 Establishing achievable deadlines: develop a timeline for each step of the plan, considering when each action should be completed. These deadlines should be realistic, providing enough time to effectively complete tasks while also allowing for some flexibility.
4 Allocating resources: determine what resources are necessary to carry out your plan. This could include staff time, budget allocation, materials or additional support. Ensure that these resources are available and can be accessed when needed.
5 Planning for communication: set up a communication strategy to keep everyone involved updated on the progress of the action plan. Regular updates are essential for maintaining momentum and ensuring that everyone is on the same page.
6 Documenting the process: finally, it's important to create a written document that clearly outlines the entire action plan. This document should be easily accessible to all parties involved and serve as a reference point throughout the implementation of the plan.

By following these steps, you can create a structured and effective plan to navigate and resolve conflicts in a library environment, ensuring a smoother and more harmonious workplace.

Monitoring and follow-up

Monitoring and following up on conflict resolution is essential for lasting success in a library setting. Regular check-ins are key, providing opportunities to assess whether the action plan is being followed and achieving its goals. This reflection ensures that the strategy is effective and heading in the right direction. Flexibility is crucial; be ready to adjust the plan based on feedback and observations. This adaptability helps in addressing any unexpected challenges, keeping the approach effective.

Once the action plan is under way, evaluate its overall impact. Determine if the conflict is resolved effectively and identify what was learned from the process. This evaluation helps understand the strengths and areas for improvement. Incorporate feedback from all parties involved, using surveys, conversations or feedback sessions. This feedback offers valuable insights into the resolution's effectiveness.

Documenting the lessons learned is vital for future conflict management. If the resolution is successful, celebrate this achievement to reinforce positive behaviours and boost morale. Finally, conduct a long-term review, months or a year later, to ensure the resolution's enduring positive impact. This step checks the long-term effects and allows for any necessary adjustments.

By following these steps, the library not only resolves conflicts but also enhances its overall conflict management, leading to a more harmonious and effective environment.

Fostering a conflict-resilient library environment

Preventive strategies

Preventing conflicts in a library setting calls for proactive strategies that tackle potential conflict sources before they escalate. While specific library-related peer-reviewed references are not readily available, insights from general organisational conflict management research highlight several effective approaches. Encouraging open and transparent communication, among staff and between staff and users, is crucial to prevent misunderstandings that might lead to conflicts. It's also important to establish and widely share clear policies and expectations, reducing ambiguities that could otherwise result in disagreements. Regular feedback sessions can be implemented, offering both staff and users a constructive platform to voice their concerns. Additionally, providing staff with training in cultural competency and diversity is vital. This helps in minimising conflicts that might arise from misunderstandings or biases, fostering a more inclusive and harmonious library environment.

Training and development

Continuous training and development in enhancing conflict resolution skills is crucial in creating a conflict-resilient environment. While specific peer-reviewed articles focusing on libraries were not available, these activities are widely recognised in the field of conflict resolution:

- Regular conflict resolution training: regular training sessions on conflict resolution techniques can equip staff with the skills to handle disputes effectively.
- Empathy and compassion training: empathy and compassion have been linked to more positive attitudes and a greater willingness to reconcile in various group interactions. (Klimecki, 2019).
- Role-playing and simulations: incorporate role-playing exercises and simulations in training to give staff practical experience in managing conflicts.
- Leadership development: train library leaders in conflict management and mediation skills, as they play a critical role in setting the tone for the way conflicts are approached and resolved.
- Ongoing skill development: encourage continuous learning and development in conflict resolution to keep up with best practices and emerging techniques.

Conclusion

This chapter concludes that conflicts in the workplace, including libraries, can be effectively managed with empathetic methods. It covers different conflict types, like staff disputes and user disagreements, emphasising the role of kindness, wellbeing and empathy. These principles help de-escalate tensions and promote an inclusive atmosphere. The chapter stresses the importance of mental and emotional health in conflict resolution, incorporating wellbeing models like PERMA and JD-R for a positive work environment. Real-world case studies demonstrate these strategies in action. Additionally, it highlights preventive measures and ongoing staff training as key to a conflict-resilient environment. Overall, the chapter guides library staff in conflict resolution, underscoring continuous learning and proactive approaches for a harmonious library setting.

Exercises and reflective questions

Exercise for teams
Collaborative conflict resolution workshop

Objective: to enhance team cohesion and collective conflict resolution skills through collaborative analysis and problem-solving.

Procedure:

1 Team gathering: bring the entire team together for a workshop session.
2 Presentation of scenarios: present a series of hypothetical conflict scenarios common in library settings, such as user–staff conflicts, policy-related disputes or issues arising from technological changes.
3 Small group discussions: divide the team into small groups. Assign each group a different scenario to discuss.
4 Analysis and strategy development:
   ■ Each group analyses its assigned scenario, discussing potential causes and impacts of the conflict.
   ■ Groups then brainstorm and develop a strategy for resolving the conflict, focusing on kindness, understanding and practical solutions.
5 Group presentations: each group presents its scenario, analysis and proposed resolution strategy to the rest of the team.
6 Feedback and group discussion: after each presentation, allow for a group discussion where other team members can provide input, alternative viewpoints or additional resolution ideas.

Outcome: This exercise aims to promote collaborative problem-solving, enhance understanding of various conflict types and develop collective strategies for conflict resolution in a supportive team environment.

This team exercise complements the individual reflective conflict analysis by encouraging personal and collective growth in conflict resolution skills, fostering a comprehensive approach to managing conflicts in library environments.

Exercise for individuals

Reflective conflict analysis

Objective: this exercise is designed to deepen your understanding of your personal approach to conflict resolution and identify areas for growth and development.

Procedure:

1 Select a past conflict: think about a specific conflict you've encountered in your work at the library. It could be a disagreement with a colleague, a challenging interaction with a user or a policy-related issue.
2 Reflective writing: using the following questions as a guide, write down your thoughts and reflections about the conflict:

- What was the nature of the conflict?
- How did you respond to the conflict at the time?
- What were the outcomes of your response?
- Looking back, what alternative strategies could you have employed?
- What lessons did you learn from this experience?

Be honest and thorough in your reflections. This is a personal exercise, so the more reflective and sincere you are, the more beneficial it will be.

3 Personal development plan: based on your reflections, draft a personal development plan. This should include:
   - specific steps you will take to improve your conflict resolution skills
   - any areas of learning or training you think would be beneficial
   - goals or milestones you would like to achieve in your conflict resolution abilities
   - ways you plan to apply these learnings in future conflict situations.

Outcome: This exercise aims to promote self-awareness and personal growth.

Reflective questions
By critically analysing your past experiences with conflict and planning for future development, you will be better equipped to handle conflicts effectively and empathetically. This contributes to your personal development and enhances the overall library environment, making it a more positive, productive and co-operative space.

- Reflect on how the principles of kindness and wellbeing can be integrated into your daily interactions and conflict resolution strategies in the library. How might these principles change your approach to future conflicts?
- Consider the conflict scenarios discussed in this chapter. Which scenario resonated with you the most and what key insights or strategies did you glean from it that you can apply in your professional practice?
- Considering the exercise on reflective conflict analysis, what is one significant area of personal growth you identified? How do you plan to implement changes or improvements in this area?
- How has your understanding of team dynamics and collective conflict resolution evolved through this chapter? What steps can you take to foster a more collaborative and supportive environment in your library?
- Reflect on the wellbeing models like PERMA, JD-R and PsyCap discussed in the chapter. How can you apply these models to enhance

your conflict resolution skills and the overall psychological wellbeing of yourself, your colleagues and users in the library setting?

CHAPTER 15

Leading with Impact: Transforming Library Culture through Diverse Leadership Styles and Effective Management

Introduction

> A manager's leadership style is responsible for 30% of the business's profitability.
>
> (Goleman, 2017)

Daniel Goleman's assertion that 'A manager's leadership style is responsible for 30% of the business's profitability' highlights the profound effect leadership has on organisational success. This is especially true in libraries, as they are made up of a variety of functions and greatly benefit from a variety of leadership styles. Each style brings unique strengths and influences to the workplace, impacting staff morale, motivation and the overall atmosphere. Before we go on, take a moment to think of all the different types of leader you have either currently in your organisation or have encountered throughout your career. Do any of them match these key types of leader?

Transformational leadership (Downton, 1973)

This style focuses on inspiring and motivating staff to exceed their usual limits and think innovatively. Transformational leaders in libraries encourage a culture of continuous learning and adaptability, essential in an environment where technology and information needs are constantly evolving. They focus on developing a shared vision, fostering an environment where creativity and problem-solving are highly valued. This approach helps library staff to adapt to changes and to be proactive in driving positive change within the organisation and the community it serves.

Transactional leadership (Bass, 1999)

While often contrasted with transformational leadership, transactional leadership has its place in libraries, especially in maintaining day-to-day operations. This style is based on clear structures and systems – rewarding staff for achieving specific goals and adhering to established procedures. In libraries, where organisational efficiency and adherence to policies are important, transactional leadership can ensure a well-structured and consistent service to the community.

Servant leadership (Greenleaf, 2007)

Servant leaders prioritise the needs of their team and the community they serve above their own. In a library setting, this might manifest as leaders who actively seek staff input on decisions, focus on the development and wellbeing of their team and make concerted efforts to meet the needs of the library's users. This leadership style helps to create a supportive and inclusive work environment, where staff feel valued and empowered. It's especially effective in fostering a sense of community both within the library staff and between the library and its users.

Democratic leadership (Lewin, Lippitt and White, 1939)

In this style, leaders encourage staff participation in decision-making, fostering a sense of ownership and collaboration among the team. This approach can be highly effective in libraries, where diverse perspectives can contribute to more innovative services and programmes. By valuing each team member's input, democratic leaders can create a more engaged and motivated workforce.

Laissez-Faire leadership (Lewin, Lippitt and White, 1939)

This hands-off approach can be beneficial in certain library contexts, particularly where staff are highly experienced and self-motivated. Leaders who adopt this style trust their team members to make decisions and work independently, which can lead to high levels of creativity and innovation.

Each of these leadership styles can be adapted to different situations within the library environment. The most effective leaders are those who can flexibly switch between styles, applying the most appropriate one depending on the situation at hand. This flexibility ensures that library leaders are not only managing their teams effectively but responding to the changing needs of the community they serve. By understanding and utilising these diverse leadership styles, library managers can create a positive and productive workplace, fostering an environment where staff wellbeing and motivation are paramount.

Management practices and their influence on wellbeing

Management practices, including communication methods and decision-making processes, play a crucial role in fostering a supportive culture in libraries. Effective conflict resolution strategies and a focus on ethical organisational culture, as outlined by Huhtala et al. (2022), are crucial for maintaining staff wellbeing. Libraries thrive when these practices support a positive work environment, where employees feel valued and heard.

Communication methods

- Open and transparent communication: effective communication channels are fundamental in libraries. Leaders and managers need to establish a culture of open and transparent communication where staff feel comfortable sharing their ideas, concerns and feedback. This includes regular team meetings, one-on-one check-ins and accessible communication platforms.
- Active listening: management should practise active listening, showing empathy and understanding to staff concerns. This approach not only helps in resolving issues more effectively but builds trust and respect within the team.

Decision-making processes

- Inclusive decision-making: involving staff in decision-making processes helps in creating a sense of ownership and empowerment. This can be facilitated through brainstorming sessions, suggestion boxes and committees that include representation from different levels of staff.
- Evidence-based decisions: utilising data and feedback to inform decisions can enhance the library's services and workplace environment. Management practices that emphasise evidence-based decision-making can lead to more effective and user-centric outcomes.

Conflict resolution strategies

- Constructive conflict management: effective conflict resolution is key in maintaining a healthy work environment. Adopting a constructive approach to conflict management, where differences are addressed through open dialogue and mutual respect, can prevent minor disagreements from escalating into major issues.
- Training and resources: providing staff with training on conflict resolution and communication skills can equip them with the tools needed to navigate disagreements professionally and effectively.

Ethical organisational culture

- Upholding ethical standards: as Huhtala et al. (2022) emphasise, an ethical organisational culture is essential for staff wellbeing. This includes fairness in treatment, integrity in operations and a commitment to the library's core values and ethical guidelines.
- Whistleblower policies: implementing clear policies and protections for staff who report unethical behaviour is important in fostering a culture of accountability and trust.

Recognition and feedback

- Regular feedback: constructive feedback helps staff understand their strengths and areas for improvement. It should be an ongoing process, not just limited to formal performance reviews.
- Recognition of achievements: celebrating successes and acknowledging individual and team achievements can significantly boost morale and motivation.

Work environment and work–life balance

- Supportive work environment: creating a physical and psychological work environment that supports staff wellbeing is crucial. This can include ergonomic workspaces, access to mental health resources and initiatives that promote a healthy work–life balance.
- Flexibility: offering flexible working arrangements, such as remote working options and flexible hours, can contribute to employee satisfaction and retention.

These management practices, when effectively implemented, can transform libraries into thriving workplaces. By prioritising communication, inclusive decision-making, ethical standards and staff wellbeing, library managers can create a supportive and productive work environment. This not only benefits the staff but enhances the quality of services provided to the community, reinforcing the library's role as a vital and positive community resource.

Creating a culture of kindness through leadership

The creation of a culture of kindness in libraries through leadership involves several key strategies and principles. Leaders must exhibit the behaviours they wish to see in their teams. This includes showing kindness, respect and compassion in their interactions. When leaders act with authenticity and integrity, it sets a powerful example for the staff to emulate. Leaders showing vulnerability, such as admitting mistakes or discussing challenges, can create a more open and trusting work environment. This encourages staff to be more authentic and supportive of each other.

Take time to recognise and reward kind behaviour. This can include acknowledgement programmes that recognise acts of kindness and collaboration among staff. In turn they reinforce these behaviours. This could be through awards, acknowledgements in team meetings or a simple thank-you note. Peer recognition can encourage peer-to-peer recognition and can strengthen a culture of kindness, as staff feel valued by their colleagues as well as their leaders.

Whenever possible encourage staff participation. This can be by inviting staff to participate in decision-making processes, especially those that affect their work or the library's services, which fosters a sense of belonging and respect. Remember to always include the people that 'do the do'. Establishing open channels for feedback allows staff to express their thoughts and suggestions, making them feel heard and valued.

Underpinning everything is empathy and emotional intelligence. This should include leaders practising active listening, showing genuine interest in their staff's perspectives and concerns. Being aware of and responsive to the emotional needs of staff is crucial. This involves understanding the impacts of work-related stress and providing support where needed.

A clear shared vision is vital for transformational leadership. Leaders should articulate a clear and inspiring vision for the library that aligns with the values of kindness and wellbeing. Offering support and encouragement tailored to individual staff members' needs and aspirations can foster a positive and motivating work environment.

Psychological safety, as discussed in previous chapters, is one of the key principles of kindness through leadership. Creating an environment where staff feel safe to express their ideas and concerns without fear of negative consequences is essential for a culture of kindness., whilst ensuring that any form of mistreatment or bullying is promptly and effectively addressed reinforces a commitment to a respectful and kind workplace.

Wellbeing initiatives including mental health support and work–life balance are key. Providing resources and support for mental health, such as access to counselling services or stress management workshops, demonstrates a commitment to staff wellbeing. Promoting a healthy work–life balance through flexible working arrangements or wellness programmes can contribute significantly to a culture of kindness.

Extending kindness beyond the library by encouraging and participating in community service or outreach programmes can further embed the values of kindness in the library's culture.

By integrating these practices, library leaders can create an environment where kindness is not just an abstract value, but a tangible aspect of the workplace culture. This not only enhances the wellbeing and satisfaction of the staff but positively impacts the quality of service provided to the library's users, thus fulfilling the library's mission in a meaningful way.

Challenges in management

Leadership and management in libraries involve navigating a complex array of challenges that demand strategic thinking and careful planning. The role of a library leader is multifaceted, addressing diverse issues ranging from budget constraints to staff morale.

A primary challenge is the effective allocation of limited resources. Leaders must judiciously balance funds between crucial areas like technology upgrades, collection development and staff training. Additionally, developing skills in fundraising and grant-writing becomes indispensable, as leaders must craft compelling narratives to attract external funding. Equally important is the ability to implement cost-efficient practices without sacrificing service quality, which often involves embracing digital solutions and forming strategic partnerships.

Another significant issue is managing staff turnover, which can affect library operations and team morale. To combat this, leaders should devise robust retention strategies, including offering competitive benefits, opportunities for professional development and nurturing a positive work culture. Succession planning is critical to maintain continuity in expertise and leadership. Efficient recruitment and comprehensive training programmes are vital to integrate new staff seamlessly.

Keeping pace with technological advancements is essential for libraries to remain relevant. Integrating new digital resources and services is an ongoing process, requiring continual staff training in these areas. Balancing this need with time and budget constraints presents its own set of challenges.

Understanding and meeting the expectations of a diverse user base is a cornerstone of effective library management. Leaders must ensure services are accessible and inclusive, catering to all community members, including those with disabilities.

Maintaining clear and consistent communication within a diverse team is crucial, particularly in the context of remote or hybrid working models.

Building team cohesion, fostering unity and encouraging collaboration among staff with varied backgrounds and expertise require continuous effort.

Implementing new policies, systems or organisational structures necessitates thoughtful change management to secure staff buy-in and minimise disruption. Leaders must adeptly balance the library's traditional roles with the need for innovation and change.

Navigating legal requirements and staying compliant with laws such as data privacy and copyright is critical. Risk management is a constant, with leaders needing to identify and mitigate risks associated with library operations.

Amid these myriad challenges, upholding a focus on kindness and wellbeing is vital but challenging. It is essential for creating a positive workplace culture. To effectively address these challenges, library leaders and managers need to cultivate a mix of technical expertise, strategic foresight, empathetic leadership and adaptability. Emphasising continuous learning, effective communication and a firm commitment to the library's core values is key to overcoming these hurdles and steering the library towards a successful and sustainable future.

The future of library leadership

The future of library leadership is being shaped by a confluence of technological advancements and evolving societal needs. To navigate this landscape effectively, library leaders must integrate emerging trends with foundational principles of kindness and wellbeing.

As libraries increasingly adopt remote or hybrid working models, leaders face the challenge of maintaining team cohesion and ensuring effective communication in a digital context. To build a supportive remote working culture, leaders are focusing on regular virtual check-ins, team-building activities and the efficient use of collaboration tools to keep staff connected and engaged, despite physical distances. This was discussed in more detail in Chapter 9.

In an age where digital transformation is key, library leaders are at the forefront of initiatives such as digitising collections, implementing digital literacy programmes and exploring cutting-edge technologies like AI and VR. A critical component of this digital leadership is ensuring that both leaders and staff continuously develop the necessary digital skills through ongoing learning and professional development.

Sustainability is becoming a central theme in libraries, with leaders exploring ways to minimise environmental impact through sustainable building designs and eco-friendly practices. Libraries are positioned as educational hubs for community awareness on environmental issues, leading the charge in promoting sustainability.

Future library leadership is characterised by a strong commitment to diversity and inclusivity. This commitment extends to staffing, programming and creating environments welcoming to all community members. Leaders are actively working to dismantle systemic barriers that hinder access to library services or career opportunities.

Data analytics are increasingly integral in library decision-making, helping leaders understand user needs and adapt services accordingly. This trend comes with the responsibility to balance the insights gained from data with the ethical standards of privacy and security of user information.

Recognising the importance of mental health, library leaders are focusing more on initiatives that support staff wellbeing, like mindfulness programmes and mental health days. Additionally, libraries are expanding their role in providing mental health resources and programming to the wider community.

As user expectations evolve, particularly among younger generations, library leaders must adapt services to stay relevant and engaging. This includes a shift towards community-centric services, outreach programmes and tailoring experiences to meet the needs of a diverse user base.

Investment in the development of future leaders is becoming a priority, with libraries focusing on mentoring and training programmes for emerging leaders. Alongside this, effective succession planning is crucial to ensure smooth transitions and continuity in leadership.

These emerging trends paint a picture of a dynamic future in library leadership, demanding adaptability, digital proficiency, inclusivity and a strong focus on sustainability and wellbeing. By staying true to their core values, library leaders can steer their institutions through this changing landscape, ensuring that libraries remain essential, responsive and inclusive community resources.

Evaluating leadership

Evaluating leadership effectiveness is vital for the growth and success of libraries. A comprehensive analysis can be achieved through various tools and methods, each offering unique insights into how leadership impacts the library environment.

Staff surveys

- Anonymous feedback: regular anonymous staff surveys are crucial. They

provide a safe platform for employees to share honest feedback about their experiences and views on leadership without fear of repercussions.
- Key areas of evaluation: these surveys delve into different aspects of leadership, including communication, support, decision-making and efforts to cultivate a positive work culture.

Performance metrics

- Quantitative measures: objective data on leadership impact comes from setting and tracking performance metrics aligned with the library's goals. Metrics could range from user satisfaction rates to service usage and operational efficiency.
- Balanced scorecard approach: adopting this approach, which includes financial, customer, internal processes and learning and growth metrics, offers a holistic view of leadership effectiveness.

360-degree feedback

- Holistic evaluation: this comprehensive method gathers feedback from various sources, including the leader's direct reports, peers, supervisors and, sometimes, library users, providing a well-rounded view of their impact.
- Developmental focus: the feedback serves as a foundation for personal and professional development, highlighting strengths and identifying areas for improvement.

Self-assessment:

- Reflective practice: leaders are encouraged to self-reflect, critically evaluating their own performance and leadership style.
- Personal development plans: based on self-assessment, leaders can create plans to enhance their skills and address any identified gaps.

Team performance and morale

- Staff retention and turnover rates: analysing these rates offers insights into the workplace atmosphere and the effectiveness of leadership.
- Team morale indicators: metrics like staff engagement, teamwork and conflict frequency provide clues about the health of the work environment under the current leadership.

User feedback
- Direct user surveys: feedback from library users is invaluable in understanding how leadership decisions affect user experience.
- Community engagement: the degree of community involvement in library programmes can reflect the effectiveness of leadership.

Review of strategic goals and objectives
- Alignment with strategic vision: assessing how well leadership actions align with the library's strategic goals is essential.
- Progress towards goals: monitoring advancements towards these goals aids in assessing leadership's role in driving the organisation forward.

Professional development and growth opportunities
- Staff training and development: the opportunities provided for staff development can signal the emphasis leadership places on growth and learning.
- Succession planning: effective leadership is evident in thorough succession planning and the cultivation of future leaders.

By employing this diverse range of tools and methods, libraries can acquire a nuanced understanding of leadership effectiveness. This approach aids in pinpointing areas for improvement, acknowledging successes and ensuring leadership practices consistently support the objective of fostering a positive and productive library environment.

Who looks after the leaders?
I have noticed that often in discussions about fostering a positive work environment and promoting staff wellbeing the wellbeing of the leaders themselves can be overlooked. Leaders play a crucial role in setting the tone and culture of the library, making their wellbeing equally important to that of everyone else. The following are suggestions of how the wellbeing of leaders can be supported and maintained.

Peer support and networking
- Encourage leaders to engage in peer support networks where they can share experiences, challenges and strategies with other leaders.

- Facilitate opportunities for leaders to connect with their counterparts in other libraries or related organisations for mutual support and learning.

Access to professional development and coaching

- Provide access to professional development opportunities specifically tailored for leadership roles, including workshops, seminars and courses on leadership and management.
- Offer coaching or mentoring programmes for leaders, focusing on personal growth, stress management and effective leadership strategies.

Creating a culture of openness

- Foster an organisational culture where leaders feel comfortable discussing their challenges and seeking support without fear of judgement.
- Encourage transparent communication about workload and stress, promoting a culture where it's okay not to be okay.

Work–life balance for leaders

- Recognise the importance of work–life balance for leaders and support them in achieving it. This could include flexible working arrangements or encouraging leaders to take time off when needed.
- Promote the understanding that taking time for self-care and family is not a sign of weakness but a necessary aspect of sustainable leadership.

Wellbeing resources and support systems

- Ensure leaders have access to wellbeing resources, such as counselling services, wellness programmes and health-related benefits.
- Implement support systems within the organisation that can assist leaders in managing stress and maintaining mental and emotional health.

Regular wellbeing check-ins

- Institute regular check-ins focused on wellbeing, where leaders can discuss their challenges and successes in a supportive environment.
- Use these check-ins not only to offer support but to identify any emerging issues that might impact the leader's wellbeing.

Encouraging self-reflection and mindfulness

■ Promote practices such as mindfulness and self-reflection, which can help leaders manage stress and maintain a balanced perspective.
■ Provide resources or training on mindfulness and meditation, which can be beneficial in developing resilience and emotional intelligence.

Feedback and recognition

■ Regularly provide constructive feedback to leaders, acknowledging their efforts and contributions.
■ Recognise the challenges of leadership roles and celebrate successes, both big and small.

By focusing on the wellbeing of leaders, libraries can ensure that their leadership teams are well-equipped, both mentally and emotionally, to guide their organisations effectively. This not only benefits the leaders themselves but sets a positive example for the entire library staff, reinforcing the importance of wellbeing at all levels of the organisation.

Reflection points

Here are five reflection points for leaders to consider as part of their self-assessment and personal development:

1 Peer support and networking:
    ■ 'How actively am I engaging in peer support networks and what value am I deriving from these interactions?'
    ■ 'Am I taking sufficient opportunities to connect with my counterparts in other libraries or organisations for mutual support and learning?'
2 Professional development and coaching:
    ■ 'Am I dedicating enough time to my own professional development, particularly in areas that strengthen my leadership and management skills?'
    ■ 'Have I considered seeking a coach or mentor to support my personal growth and help manage stress effectively?'
3 Culture of openness and communication:
    ■ 'How comfortable do I feel discussing my own challenges within the organisation and am I fostering an environment where open communication is encouraged?'
    ■ 'Am I promoting a culture where it's acceptable to talk about workload and stress, both for myself and my team?'

4 Work–life balance:
- 'Am I maintaining a healthy work–life balance and how am I modelling this balance to my team?'
- 'Do I prioritise self-care and family time and how does this influence my effectiveness and sustainability as a leader?'

5 Self-reflection and mindfulness:
- 'How regularly am I practising self-reflection and mindfulness to manage stress and maintain a balanced perspective?'
- 'Am I utilising available resources or training on mindfulness and meditation to develop resilience and emotional intelligence?'

Reflecting on the above questions can help leaders to identify areas where they need more support and can guide them in making necessary changes to ensure their wellbeing. This introspection is crucial not only for their personal health but for setting a positive example of wellbeing and balance for their teams. When leaders reflect on the answers to these points, it's important to translate these reflections into actionable steps for personal and professional growth. Here's what they should consider doing with their responses:

- Identify areas for improvement: use the answers to pinpoint specific areas where changes or improvements are needed. For instance, if a leader finds they are not engaging enough in peer networks, they can set a goal to join relevant groups or attend networking events.
- Develop an action plan: create a targeted action plan based on the reflections. This plan should include clear, achievable steps to address the identified areas for improvement. For example, if a leader realises they need more work–life balance, they could plan to delegate certain responsibilities or set boundaries for work hours.
- Seek resources and support: determine what resources or support systems are needed to implement these plans. This might involve seeking out professional development courses, finding a mentor or accessing wellbeing resources.
- Set goals and deadlines: establish specific, measurable goals and set realistic deadlines for achieving them. Goals should be aligned with the insights gained from the reflection points; for example, setting a goal to attend a leadership workshop within the next six months.
- Regular review and adjustment: regularly review progress against the set goals and be open to adjusting the action plan as needed. Reflection is an ongoing process and leaders should be flexible in adapting their strategies in response to new insights or changes in circumstances.

- Share insights with a trusted peer or mentor: discussing reflections and plans with a trusted peer, mentor or coach can provide valuable external perspectives. This helps in accountability and can lead to additional insights or advice.
- Practice self-compassion and patience: leaders should remember that personal and professional growth is a journey. It's important to practise self-compassion and patience, recognising that change takes time and persistence.
- Incorporate reflection as a regular practice: make reflection a regular part of the leadership routine. This ongoing practice helps in continuously aligning actions with personal values and professional objectives.

By actively engaging with the answers to these reflection points, leaders can make meaningful changes that enhance not only their personal wellbeing but their effectiveness as leaders, ultimately contributing to a more positive and productive work environment.

Actionable steps

I now want to offer some practical, actionable steps that library leaders can take to refine their management practices, with a focus on fostering environments of kindness and wellbeing. These steps are designed to guide leaders in transforming their libraries into nurturing and supportive community hubs.

Commit to continuous professional development

- Encourage and participate in ongoing learning opportunities focused on leadership and management skills.
- Stay updated with the latest trends in library science, technology and management to keep the library services relevant and efficient.

Cultivate empathy and emotional intelligence

- Develop and practise empathy by actively listening to staff and user concerns and understanding diverse perspectives.
- Conduct training sessions on emotional intelligence for leaders and staff, enhancing the ability to manage emotions and understand others.

Promote ethical leadership

- Adhere to high ethical standards in all decisions and actions. This includes transparency, fairness and accountability.
- Implement policies and practices that reflect the library's commitment to ethical behaviour and integrity.

Enhance communication strategies

- Foster open lines of communication within the team, encouraging feedback and collaborative problem-solving.
- Use various communication channels effectively, ensuring clarity and consistency in messaging.

Implement inclusive decision-making processes

- Involve staff at all levels in decision-making processes, ensuring diverse viewpoints are considered.
- Facilitate brainstorming sessions and workshops to gather ideas and suggestions from the team.

Focus on staff wellbeing and work–life balance

- Create initiatives that support staff wellbeing, such as flexible working arrangements, wellness programmes and mental health resources.
- Regularly assess the work environment and workload to ensure a healthy balance for staff.

Build a culture of recognition and appreciation

- Recognise and celebrate staff achievements and contributions regularly.
- Implement a system for peer-to-peer recognition, fostering a supportive and appreciative work culture.

Develop effective conflict resolution skills

- Equip leaders and staff with the skills to manage and resolve conflicts constructively.
- Promote a culture where differences are addressed respectfully and positively.

Foster community engagement and service

- Strengthen ties with the community by understanding and responding to their needs.
- Engage in outreach programmes and partnerships that extend the library's influence and impact.

Invest in leadership succession planning

- Identify and nurture potential future leaders within the organisation.
- Provide mentorship and leadership development opportunities to prepare the next generation of leaders.

By embracing these actionable steps, you can significantly enhance your management practices, leading to a positive transformation in your library. These changes will not only benefit staff by creating a more supportive and engaging work environment but enhance the experience of the users, solidifying the library's role as a cornerstone of community wellbeing and enrichment.

Conclusion

In summary, this chapter has highlighted the vital role of diverse leadership styles and effective management in shaping library culture. Emphasising the importance of adaptability, it shows how different leadership approaches can positively impact staff morale and library services. The focus on practices that promote staff wellbeing, open communication and ethical standards is crucial for creating a supportive work environment. Looking to the future, the chapter underscores the need for library leaders to stay adaptable and embrace emerging trends, particularly in digital transformation and mental health awareness. Evaluating leadership effectiveness through various methods is key to continual improvement. Overall, this chapter offers valuable insights for library leaders to create a positive and productive environment, benefiting both staff and the wider community.

Exercises and reflective questions

Exercise for teams

Collaborative leadership workshop

Objective: to foster understanding and appreciation of diverse leadership styles within the library team and explore how they can complement each other.

Instructions:

1 Pre-workshop preparation:
  ■ Each team member completes a brief questionnaire to identify their preferred leadership style.
  ■ Collect and summarise the results to get an overview of the diverse leadership styles within the team.
2 Workshop activities:
  ■ Group discussion: share the summary of leadership styles present in the team. Discuss how these styles are currently expressed in the team's work and how they can complement each other.
  ■ Role-playing scenarios: create scenarios that are common in library settings. Assign different leadership styles to team members for each scenario and act them out. Focus on how each style would handle the situation.
  ■ Strengths and challenges analysis: in groups, discuss the strengths and challenges of each leadership style, especially in the context of library management.
3 Collaborative strategy development: develop strategies on how different leadership styles can be integrated to enhance team performance, decision-making and conflict resolution.
4 Action plan for team development:
  ■ Based on the workshop's insights, create a team action plan to encourage the use of diverse leadership styles in daily operations.
  ■ Include regular check-ins and feedback sessions to monitor the plan's implementation and effectiveness.
5 Follow-up and review:
  ■ Schedule follow-up sessions to review the progress and make adjustments to the team action plan as necessary.
  ■ Encourage ongoing dialogue about leadership styles and their impact on the team's work and library environment.

These exercises aim to enhance individual and collective understanding of leadership styles and their practical application in library management, ultimately contributing to a more dynamic, adaptable and effective leadership approach within the library setting.

Exercise for individuals
Leadership style self-assessment
Objective: to identify and understand your predominant leadership style and its impact on library management.
Instructions:

1 Reflect on leadership styles: review the key leadership styles discussed in the chapter – Transformational, Transactional, Servant, Democratic and Laissez-Faire. Reflect on your management practices and consider which style or combination of styles resonates most with your approach.

2 Self-assessment questionnaire:
   ■ Develop a set of questions for each leadership style, focusing on how you interact with your team, make decisions and handle challenges.
   ■ Score your answers to identify which leadership style is most dominant in your approach.

3 Analysis and reflection:
   ■ Analyse the results to understand how your leadership style aligns with the needs and dynamics of your library.
   ■ Reflect on the advantages and potential drawbacks of your style in the current library environment.

4 Action plan: create a personal development plan to enhance aspects of your leadership style. Include goals to develop skills associated with other leadership styles that could benefit your team and library operations.

5 Implementation and review:
   ■ Implement the action plan and review your progress regularly.
   ■ Seek feedback from peers or a mentor to gauge changes and improvements in your leadership approach.

Reflective questions

■ Assessment of leadership style: reflect on your current leadership style. Which aspects of Transformational, Transactional, Servant, Democratic and Laissez-Faire leadership do you predominantly exhibit? How do these traits impact your team and the overall library environment?

■ Communication and decision-making: consider your approach to communication and decision-making. How effectively do you think you engage in open and transparent communication with your team? Are there areas where you could improve in actively listening and inclusively involving your team in decision-making processes?

■ Adaptability and change management: reflect on your adaptability to change and managing new initiatives within the library. How have you navigated recent changes or challenges and what have you learned from these experiences that could inform future strategies?

■ Culture of kindness and wellbeing: evaluate your role in fostering a culture of kindness and wellbeing. What actions have you taken to promote a supportive and positive work environment? Are there additional steps you could take to enhance staff wellbeing and create a more nurturing workplace?

■ Professional growth and development: contemplate your journey of professional growth. What areas of leadership development do you need to focus on? How can you align your personal growth goals with the evolving needs and objectives of the library?

CHAPTER 16

Kind Use of Data for Wellbeing and Leadership
Amy Stubbing

Introduction

The topic of data and its role in leadership has become both divisive and expansive over the past decade. As our access to data of all forms increases and tools to manage and analyse data have become more mainstream and accessible, naturally the use of data for management approaches and decisions has also grown. The issue arises in just how many approaches have been used to integrate data use into leadership and management and how many lack clear requirements of data literacy and ethics and good and compassionate leadership. These inconsistent and at times ill-informed approaches along with a widening gap in data literacy in the workplace have understandably encouraged a mistrust of data for leadership, hindering the ability for leaders to collect and use data even with the most effective approach.

Despite this context in which using data in leadership sits, and the clear challenges in this area, the ability to use data effectively is one of the most important skills a leader can have. Using data for decision-making can be a fundamental tool not just for achieving organisational goals, but crucially for enabling compassionate leadership and creating workplaces which truly focus on wellbeing and putting changes in place to enable the wellbeing of colleagues and service users. This chapter will explore why we need to use data in leadership and how we can go about this in a kind and compassionate way. We will explore how your approaches to data use can maximise your ability as a leader to create a genuinely compassionate workplace, giving you the tools to make decisions using data and bring colleagues along with you on this journey.

Reflective questions

- How do you currently perceive the role of data in leadership and decision-making?
- Can you identify any biases or preconceived notions you have about data-driven leadership?

Why we use data

The first thing we need to explore is the question of why we use data. As explored above, how we use data can be controversial, particularly in the conversations surrounding compassionate and people-centric leadership. However, there are myriad reasons why data is used and should be used and many benefits to making data-driven decisions.

Let's start by considering the benefits at a top-level view. The use of data for service development and decision-making is becoming an increasingly important topic in all sectors. In the current financial climate, where cutbacks and greater scrutiny on finances are becoming the norm, being able to develop within our means, to have evidence of the value of our services and to make better use of our current resources is fundamental to survival. Coupling this with increased focus on user satisfaction and the need to keep up with current trends and changing user needs, it has never been more important to learn how to develop without increased resources and to know how to make better use of the resources already held.

Even taking a more focused view, there are a number of core reasons why we continue to use data despite the challenges it can present:

- to examine and respond to the effectiveness and efficiency of our service
- to identify areas for improvement or areas of success which can be replicated
- to identify changing needs and trends and translate these into service development and strategy
- to articulate our strengths as a service and the importance of maintaining the services
- to identify areas of imbalance in workload
- to enable us to proactively identify issues before they escalate and impact wellbeing
- to encourage self awareness and self reflection.

The issue, of course, is that data can be and has been used incorrectly, inappropriately or lacking the considerations of the humans that it impacts. Because of this, there are many people who believe that using data for decision-making means removing the human element and understanding of a given situation. From the perspective of compassionate leadership, the idea of the removal of the human aspect of decision-making and management choices is naturally at odds with what we are trying to achieve as people-centric leaders. As such, a divide between engaging with data and this compassionate approach has been created. This is certainly a risk if we aren't making data-driven decisions correctly, but when we combine our approaches as

KIND USE OF DATA 273

compassionate and kind leaders with effective data approaches we can have significantly more impact. While we won't be covering the specific steps of implementing data-driven decisions in this chapter, an understanding of best practice in this area is fundamental to successfully implementing the ideas we will discuss. If you are interested in building your skills in the foundations of data-driven decisions you can explore this in my book: *Data-Driven Decisions: a toolkit for library and information professionals* (Stubbing, 2022).

Misusing data and data anxiety

Staff responses to using data

How your colleagues and staff respond to the use of data for leadership and decision-making can have a significant impact on the success of this work. However, by acknowledging and expecting the potential concerns and feelings that could arise for colleagues and combining the core skills of a compassionate leader in change management you will be able to overcome some of the hurdles change presents. While the reasons why colleagues may struggle with the idea of using data will be varied and complex, there are a few areas that come up consistently which you should be aware of:

Removal of the human element

In the introduction to the chapter we referred to the concern that data removes the human element of decision-making and management. This is a particularly interesting barrier for staff, as it undermines the perception of the value of the information and insights that data brings. Equally, it legitimises the wider concerns and fears towards a data-driven approach, leading us nicely to our next common concern:

Not trusting that data shows a real picture

This can be a difficult concern to unpick, as you are up against an idea which you need to disprove when the evidence you need to achieve this (data) is not trusted. Being cognisant of this, and understanding the impact it will have on any argument you make to prove the legitimacy of your data or insights from data, are vital to being able to respond effectively to this common barrier.

Feeling of being watched

Observation is an inherent part of data. It is not surprising, therefore, that one of the key concerns raised by people in regard to the implementation of using data for management is the feeling that they are being watched. This particular concern can cause issues for collecting accurate data (as staff may be disinclined to input data around their outputs and work), impacting morale and in some cases even feeding into presentism.

Understanding and responding to data anxiety

Overcoming these barriers is no small task and is often where organisations fall down on their data journey. When these barriers are not adequately dealt with we see that organisations which are using data for decision-making are unable to use their data effectively or, worse, the use of data begins to negatively impact wellbeing and morale.

This is really where our approaches to kind, brave leadership become a vital tool in enabling us to use and implement data for decision-making. With any implementation we need to be aware of change management and bringing staff on a journey through the change curve. The implementation and use of data for decision-making is exactly the same. If we start this journey with compassion, empathy and fundamental understanding of what our staff will be experiencing and feeling we will have significantly more chance of success.

Arguably one of the reasons these barriers are not overcome is a lack of true understanding of the deep emotional impact that something like using data can have on colleagues. As we can see from the barriers listed above, the root of most of these is fear. Fear is inherently an emotional response, meaning that the staff who do feel these things may be less likely to approach the topic or changes in a rational and distanced way. This is a phenomenon called the amygdala hijack (Peters, 2012). This is a situation where the amygdala, the part of the brain that deals with emotional processing, overtakes the neocortex, responsible for rational thought, leading to immediate and overwhelming emotional reactions rather than measured responses. It underscored the importance of addressing the emotional dimensions of workplace changes, not just the technical or procedural aspects. Understanding this is vital to successfully anticipating staff responses and to planning how you can bring colleagues back into a logical headspace.

Perhaps the emotional impact is not understood because when we consider things like implementing data collection and analysis we think first of the processes required and not necessarily the people completing these processes. However, when implementing data for decision-making we are not just changing processes, we are creating a new culture, a new way of understanding and engaging with our work and colleagues. Considering this kind of change as a culture change first and foremost dramatically shifts the approach we take to the implementation and change management required.

By approaching data for leadership and decision-making as a culture change and starting from a place of understanding what this experience and change will mean for your staff you have the foundations to truly overcome these identified barriers. These contexts, along with a focus on the emotional and cultural impact for staff in implementing data, are truly the key to enabling staff to move past the barriers they face, which will ultimately enable you to create a more positive and true understanding of how data can and will be used in your organisation.

Creating a data culture

The other core way we overcome these barriers is by showing and committing to good data practice. The act of demonstrating that data is being used in an appropriate way is a core tool in responding to the fears and anxieties listed above.

Part of creating a data culture is defining and sticking to a contract of sorts in how you use the data. You must demonstrate an understanding of the limitations of using data and show how you are engaging in the skills required to effectively use, handle and critically assess when data should be used.

With all of these topics, the demonstration is the important part. This is what creates transparency and trust with our colleagues, which is vital in achieving our goal of compassionate approaches to leadership. There are of course many ways in which you could achieve this, but one of the most effective and important ones is to create open conversations on these areas. You need to create space for disagreement, for questions and for staff to engage with the pitfalls of using data. This space is what creates the opportunity for staff to understand and build trust in your intentions. It also allows staff to build trust in *your* skills and *your* understanding. Often in leadership we expect respect and expect our staff to trust our abilities (which is not unreasonable!) but when the context of a subject is laced with fear we need to acknowledge the extra work required to gain and build this trust.

As well as the space to discuss data, your approaches and any concerns, you also need to engage staff in the development and creation of your data culture. You can create shared spaces for developing skills and data literacy, bring other staff on board for the analysis of data and create groups for staff to plan the data collection for the service. There are myriad ways in which to engage staff and you should be finding as many ways as possible if you are truly going to create a culture of data which is accepted and committed to by everyone.

Reflective questions
- How can you demonstrate good data practice in your leadership?

■ What steps will you take to involve staff in creating a data-driven culture?

Using data to enable kind and compassionate leadership

We've explored why we use data in a general sense and how we can take a more compassionate approach to implementing data in leadership. However, data can also be a fundamental tool in enabling us to lead in the most compassionate ways and improve wellbeing in our services.

Managing workloads and creating agile approaches to workloads

The ability to effectively manage workloads is fundamental to creating a workplace which responds to wellbeing needs. Many leadership approaches complete this task by speaking with colleagues or, more commonly, allocating workloads and tasks based on assumed time commitment. It is not unusual for these time commitments not to be reviewed and the assumed time and workload can be fairly arbitrary.

The benefit of using data to understand workloads is that you can combine individual perspective and testimony with a detailed picture of the actual time spent on tasks. It also enables you to unpick what are historic perspectives, where actually there is a misunderstanding of how time-consuming or onerous a task actually is. It essentially removes from the equation the guesswork and 'gut feeling' which can encourage us to make decisions which do not actually respond to the true situation. When we respond to an idea of a situation rather than the actual situation we are not really going to be addressing the problem in the most effective way.

Monitoring and gaining insights into workloads can be done in a variety of ways, but one of the most effective approaches is to log the time allocation across tasks. This approach enables us to gain a true understanding of the time spent on different tasks as a team and service and where different tasks may be taking more time for individuals. In having this information we can identify inconsistency in workloads, potential training needs, potential process issues and opportunities to redistribute work.

Identify what looks like capacity for each individual person

Approaches to examining workloads lead nicely on to the ability to examine the capacity of your staff. The major difference in taking a compassionate and data-driven approach to exploring capacity is that you can identify the expected capacity at an individual level rather than a bar for an entire team or service. This approach is fundamental to creating a safe and responsive workplace. The individual approach to leadership is a vital component to kind and compassionate leadership and data in this context is the tool which enables this approach to be successful. It can also facilitate individual conversations and self-reflection, which once again is an important component of creating a compassionate workplace.

By collecting data which examines workload and time allocation for different tasks by individuals we are able to monitor capacity at a much closer level and crucially be proactive in identifying individuals reaching or exceeding their capacity. When data is not used in this way then it is often reliant entirely on either a manager identifying warning signs or a colleague expressing that their workload is too high. By using data alongside these tools we have the opportunity to identify potential issues in workload and capacity before they escalate. We can also respond to individual circumstances and change individual capacity based on the specific needs and context which could affect a person's capacity. As a tool, the data here is important, as it can help you to identify where there is capacity elsewhere for these changes. Additionally by taking the combined approach, with data and insights involved, we can be more certain about the impact that changes to workloads, new projects and new tasks may have on an individual, meaning that we can be more sure of our decision-making in this area.

Another element of this work is the ability to identify the spread of tasks for an individual. As leaders we should be encouraging staff to be reflective of what tasks bring them energy (radiator tasks) and which ones drain their energy and enthusiasm (drain tasks). Naturally, all roles will have drain tasks, but by reviewing workloads and task allocation we can ensure that all staff have a balance of these tasks. This balance is vital to wellbeing, staff retainment and preventing things like burnout.

Identify overworking and making effective moves to address this when it is happening

A major benefit of using data to monitor and understand workloads is the ability to identify overworking. When we discussed fears and anxiety surrounding data earlier in the chapter we noted that one of the areas that comes up regularly is the fear of being watched. The assumption from many staff is that data will be used to identify where people aren't working enough. However, often a far more prevalent issue is that of overworking. With overworking this is hard to identify, particularly as many people will hide their overworking or at the very least hide the extent of it. By using data to examine workloads and time allocation of tasks we have the opportunity to identify where this is happening and respond to it. The data here is a tool for an open conversation with individuals on where they are overworking, why they may be working well over their hours and what may be causing this situation. The data then can also be used to shed light on the situation and identify where overworking is a product of workload being too high or where there may be individual issues which create this, for example not working efficiently, prioritising tasks which do not need to be prioritised or a sense of presentism. When you can work with your staff to understand where an issue may be arising from you are significantly more likely to be able to come up with an effective solution.

A tool for communication and self-reflection

Using data is key for wellbeing and creating open and trusting relationships between management and staff as decisions are made. One of the real benefits of using data in your leadership approaches is that it can facilitate the beginnings of open communication between management and line managees and within services as a whole. It can be crucial to enabling and solidifying self-reflective practice when used as a regular part of conversations where staff are encouraged to bring their own observations and insights based on the data and how it compares with how they are feeling or their experiences. This practice is important not just from a wider wellbeing perspective of temperature-checking and reflection, it also gives space for a culture of open and trusting relationships between staff and leadership. Equally, the ongoing review of data can support a wider culture of early discussion on management decisions and changes, enabling staff at all levels to be fully involved in change-making at the earliest points.

Horizon-scanning and agile approaches to annual cycles

As well as the individual approaches that using data can enable us to take, effectively collecting and reviewing data can also enable leaders to be proactive in wider service horizon-scanning. Horizon-scanning is the act of looking at past data to identify likely scenarios or situations for a service in the future. For example, is there a trend of busy periods of the year or an area of work increasing year on year? By reviewing this data, leaders can proactively plan and change approaches, workload redistribution or processes to avoid potential negative impacts on staff at peaks in a service. It can also be used to create more agile approaches to annual cycles and reflection on how tasks and work is completed.

A tool for advocating for your team

The use of data is a tool during difficult conversations or when senior management have ideas about the direction of your services. As leaders it is our role to advocate for our staff and our services, to help it grow and continue in a way that serves its purpose and change to respond to new or additional requirements. This is an extremely difficult job without good data and understanding of our services. The financial climate has been such that all sectors have had difficult conversations and decisions to make regarding staffing and budgets. Many leaders have experienced the situation of decisions being proposed or made by more senior leaders who do not and cannot understand all of the services they are making decisions for. By having a strong set of data and insights and being proactive to respond to changing needs, leaders are significantly more able to engage in these conversations at an early stage. Data can help us to accurately prove the value of a service and the actual capacity of the staff when responding to budget queries. It can also enable us to make changes early on to protect services before more drastic decisions need to be taken.

Balancing wellbeing, anxiety, time and the need for data (essentially people and data)

The balance between the need for data with the impact on staff anxieties, and the time required to collect good data, should be seriously considered when entering a data journey as a leader. All tasks and changes will inevitably have an impact (whether short- or long-term) on wellbeing and the close monitoring and management of this is vital to ensure your staff can positively engage with the change.

As we have explored throughout this book, wellbeing absolutely needs to be the priority in leadership. When wellbeing is focused on first, many other positive outcomes that leadership are trying to achieve will fall in line with this. However we need to be aware of the balance between wellbeing as a priority and working within a business where business needs cannot be ignored. We need to prioritise wellbeing of course, but in a way which ultimately makes sense for the context in which we sit in our services.

A focus on wellbeing does not mean making everyone happy or agreeing to everything that your staff ask. It is instead identifying and understanding what is feasible within business needs and being as flexible and open as possible to achieve this. After all, without the business working effectively you cannot protect jobs or enable the space required for things like wellbeing approaches. Another thing to remember is that sometimes the perspectives of individual members of staff on what will be positive for their wellbeing is not always the same and may conflict with each other. You are working within the context of a multifaceted team or set of teams with different needs and wants and in a business that needs to run effectively you ultimately need to make decisions which will not on the surface make everyone happy.

This is particularly important to be aware of when considering implementing data and a data culture in your leadership approach. For example, collecting and analysing data will naturally require time and create additional pressures for your staff. This could be perceived as a negative thing for the wellbeing of your staff, as it adds additional time and workload to colleagues who are already busy. When adding this to the anxieties we've discussed already it can be easy to assume that a data culture is not worth the wider impact on staff wellbeing. However, while time used towards collecting data may indeed be an additional pressure, it helps us to engage with and achieve the wider needs of the organisation and address other issues which impact wellbeing.

With all of this in mind, how you implement your data collection and analysis has a significant impact on their success and on minimising the stress and negative impacts of this change. We need to accept that a level of stress is guaranteed by the very nature of having additional tasks to complete, but by focusing on reducing and minimising the impact on our staff through effective planning and review of these processes we will likely create much more effective and lasting changes.

There are clear risks associated with disengaged staff or staff who do not see the benefits of collecting data compared to the perceived drawbacks and added stress. One of the key ones to be aware of is incorrect or inconsistent data input. This is one of the first signs of lack of engagement, particularly if staff are not invested in, or do not fully understand, the why of data collection and analysis. When we have incorrectly inputted data this reduces the validity and effectiveness of any of the data which is collected, meaning that the work and time that is put to it could be a wasted effort. Managing a lack of engagement really comes down to effective change management. In addition, though, you also need to work with colleagues to make it really clear how data will be used and what the expectations are in collecting data. Within this work you can really focus on what the impact of this lack of engagement in the collection or analysis will have on the wider goals you are trying to achieve. This honesty and transparency are vital to giving staff the space to engage effectively with the data culture you are creating and for your whole service to benefit from the opportunities that a data culture can offer.

Data transparency

The final area we're going to explore in this chapter is the transparency of your data. We've already explored the fears surrounding implementing data cultures and the issues this creates for enabling staff to engage in this work. Transparency is going to be a major way in which to address and deal with these.

Unsurprisingly, a core part of the engagement and change management approaches when considering using data to support kindness and wellbeing is transparency at all stages. Transparency in why we use our data, what data we are using and when we use it all build strong foundations which help us to unpick anxiety and fear and remove the mistrust that can come from these.

We must first and foremost build a foundation of transparency in our data approaches and culture. This means that where possible we should have all data accessible to all colleagues at all times. When data is shrouded in mystery and kept a secret, unsurprisingly staff begin to assume that the data is being used for something that does not support them. By having data available and visible to colleagues at all levels you can encourage data to be part of the daily conversation and decision-making and even enable staff to begin engaging with the data for their own day-to-day needs. This approach normalises the use of data and helps to remove the fear attached to it.

We also need to ensure that we are being transparent in when and how we are using the data. This means engaging with staff at the earliest stages of reviews and decision-making and informing them of what initial thoughts are being considered. Often we avoid sharing initial ideas and possibilities with staff as a way to avoid making them feel stressed by ideas which may never come to fruition. However, by speaking openly with colleagues about these we can normalise the ideas stage of leadership and open a door for colleagues to be involved in this. We may also be able to get new insights into what we are proposing and what the data says.

Of course, with transparency we do need to consider the need for confidential elements too. One area where this is prudent is when looking at individual staff data or outputs. In situations like this you can anonymise the data or have team analysis to enable the data to be examined by all staff but removing the individual nature of the data.

Reflective questions
- Reflect on the balance between data needs and staff wellbeing in your leadership approach.
- How can you ensure ongoing transparency and trust in data use?

Conclusion

In this chapter we have explored the wide-ranging benefits that using data to gain insights and make decisions can have on your service and leadership approaches. When used correctly, a data-driven approach to leadership can support the implementation of wellbeing initiates, enable effective and self-reflective conversations with staff and enable staff to engage with the leadership of a service at all levels (to name just a few benefits). However, if not approached in the right manner there are many ways in which these positives can be negated.

Committing to a culture of data-driven decisions is therefore not something that should be done without significant thought and planning. Two of the most vital parts of ensuring you are living the values of a kind, brave leader is to listen and engage. It is no different with this strand of leadership. If you work with your staff, hear their concerns and support them through the changes, concerns and possibilities you will have a truly transformative tool in using data for your service.

Exercises and reflective questions

Exercise for teams

Data-driven role play

Objective: to understand and empathise with different perspectives on data use in the workplace.

Instructions:

1 Form groups: divide into small groups of 4–5 members.
2 Assign roles: each member assumes a role (e.g., Manager, Data Analyst, Front-line Staff, HR Representative, IT Specialist).
3 Scenario development: each group develops a scenario where data use conflicts with staff wellbeing, such as implementing a new performance-tracking system.
4 Role play: members discuss the scenario within their roles, focusing on concerns, benefits and ethical implications of data use.
5 Group reflection: after the discussion, reflect as a group on the different viewpoints and how a balance between data use and staff wellbeing can be achieved.

Exercise for individuals

Personal data reflection

Objective: to encourage individual staff members to reflect on how their work contributes to the overall data culture and how data affects their wellbeing.

Procedure:

- Personal data tracking:
  - For one week, have each individual track their work tasks, time spent and any relevant outcomes or metrics.
  - Encourage them to also note their mood, stress levels and satisfaction at various points throughout the week.
- Reflection activity: at the end of the week, ask them to review their data and reflect on the following questions:
  - How does my work and the data I produce contribute to the team and organisational goals?
  - Are there areas where I feel data collection impacts my wellbeing, positively or negatively?
  - What changes could I suggest that might improve how we use data in our team?

Reflective questions
- Integrating data and wellbeing:
  - How can we integrate data practices in a way that enhances, rather than detracts from, staff wellbeing?
  - Reflect on a situation where data-driven decision-making might have conflicted with staff wellbeing. How was it addressed and what could have been done better?
- Transparency and trust:
  - What steps can I take to improve transparency in how data is used and discussed within the team?
  - How can I foster a culture where team members feel comfortable voicing concerns or ideas about data practices?
- Personal growth and data literacy:
  - In what ways has my understanding of data in leadership evolved throughout this chapter?
  - What personal steps can I take to further develop my data literacy and lead by example in this area?
- Future vision:
  - Looking ahead, how can I ensure that the principles of kindness and wellbeing are consistently integrated into our data-driven practices?
  - What are the key challenges I foresee in maintaining a balance between data needs and staff wellbeing and how might I address them?

PART 4

Embracing Kindness and Wellbeing in Library Cultures: Navigating Change and Toxicity

This section explores the transformative power of kindness and wellbeing in library environments, particularly amidst the challenges of change and toxic work cultures. It combines theoretical insights with practical strategies, illustrating how a culture rooted in empathy and support can revolutionise the library experience for both staff and patrons. By addressing the complexities of workplace dynamics and change management through the lens of kindness and wellbeing, these chapters offer a roadmap for creating more inclusive, resilient and nurturing library communities. This section is not just about overcoming adversity but about reimagining the role of libraries as beacons of positivity and growth in a rapidly evolving world.

CHAPTER 17

Nurturing Wellbeing in Toxic Work Environments

Introduction

> He perceives very clearly that the world is in greater peril from those who
> tolerate or encourage evil than from those who actually commit it.
>
> (Albert Einstein's tribute to Pablo Casals, Corredor, 1957)

The phrase 'I just did what anyone else would do' is often associated with acts of remarkable courage. The prevailing attitudes in many workplaces could be improved. Common refrains like 'You just need to be more resilient', 'It doesn't sound that bad', or 'You cannot win, just let it go' indicate a culture that shies away from confronting issues (Marcum and Young, 2019). Even in seemingly benign environments like libraries, I have seen first-hand how deep-rooted problems can undermine efforts to nurture wellbeing.

Despite organisational declarations of integrity and honesty, the harsh reality can be starkly different. It is startling that 69% of whistleblowers risk job loss and blocklisting, even with protective policies (Marcum and Young, 2019). This toxic atmosphere extends beyond whistleblowers, subtly affecting employee morale and causing moral distress. As Ahmad and Klotz (2020) observed, unethical behaviour tends to have a more profound effect on employee wellbeing than ethical behaviour, underscoring the importance of conserving resources for maintaining employee wellness. Any organisation is only as good as the worst behaviour it tolerates.

To counteract this toxicity, we must champion courage and kindness. Toxic workplaces, riddled with silence and fear, hinder open communication and personal expression, leading to a stifling work culture (Schilpzand, De Pater and Erez, 2016). This impedes organisational growth and drives away non-toxic staff, potentially leading to elevated sickness rates, as reported by the CIPD in 2022.

Leadership psychology offers hope. Research from De Smet et al. (2023) identifies six characteristics of kind managers: authenticity, compassion, gratitude, humility, humour and integrity. Leaders embodying these qualities foster a prosocial work environment, encouraging positive organisational citizenship behaviours.

Acknowledging the significance of workplace culture, companies rated as 'great places to work' credit their success to prioritising employee wellbeing, inclusion and empathy (Gautrey, 2022). In contrast, people can equate stress-inducing practices to a form of psychological slavery detrimental to both employees and the organisation.

This chapter explores toxic work environments, with a particular focus on libraries. Understanding how such hostile atmospheres can pervade spaces traditionally associated with kindness and wellbeing is crucial.

Strategies in a toxic culture

Today, ensuring people are happy and treated well at work is essential for the workers and the whole organisation. This is true for libraries – we want libraries to be great workplaces where kindness and wellbeing are central, not places where toxicity and bullying are rife. We will look at ways work can become unpleasant, how it affects people and the library and what can be done to improve things. The aim is not just to stop the bad stuff but to create a positive work environment that fits what libraries stand for – helping and supporting the community.

Case Study 17.1: Effects of a toxic culture

Jessica interviewed at a local library for a children's programming position but ended up obtaining a catalogue co-ordinator position that switched to dual catalogue co-ordinator and circulation assistant position before starting and soon found herself strategising ways to get out of a toxic work culture. Inconsistent leadership messaging led Jessica to complete a job with an unclear and always changing job description with no job performance expectations.

Jessica asked for training resources for her new position and was met with silence and no training. While Jessica worked there, she rolled with all of the changes in her job description, trying to complete all of her duties. Due to a lack of training and changing duties, Jessica made occasional mistakes when cataloguing, resulting in another change in her role to circulation assistant. Micromanaging started and Jessica's every task had to be checked for accurate completion. This instilled a feeling of disempowerment and insecurity in Jessica as she began to feel she could do nothing right in this job. Jessica resolved to be successful and tried to be proactive, asking more questions and being more cautious about the tasks she tried to complete. Jessica's efforts were met with silence, which she felt was a vote of no confidence in her abilities. After a year of working in this library, Jessica's mental health started to decline.

Jessica tried to get her schedule changed to accommodate her health. Jessica was told 'no', because her job description stated she needed to be available to work night and weekend hours. Finally, Jessica realised, despite all her efforts, that the position would not work out and her mental health needed to come first. Jessica decided to take the financial hit and resigned from her position.

Sarah E. Sporko, Circulation Manager, Marywood University

Recognising signs of a toxic culture

Toxic work environments in libraries can significantly impact staff wellbeing and service quality. Key characteristics of such environments include:

- Exclusionary practices: situations where favouritism or discrimination prevails, leading to unequal opportunities and a demotivated workforce. This is often linked to the Leader-Member Exchange (LMX) Theory, which explains how unequal relationships between leaders and subordinates can foster toxicity (Einarsen et al., 2020).
- Inconsistent leadership: frequent policy changes, unclear directives or absent leadership can create an unstable environment, paving the way for toxic behaviours (Bakker and Demerouti, 2007).
- High-stress scenarios: environments characterised by demanding workloads with little support from management can lead to employee burnout and disengagement (Deery, Iverson and Walsh., 2002).
- Gaslighting: this involves manipulation by supervisors or colleagues to make employees question their reality or sanity. It can manifest as denying or twisting information, dismissing concerns or shifting blame, leading to confusion and self-doubt among staff. Gaslighting can be particularly harmful, as it erodes trust and contributes to a hostile work environment.
- Upward bullying: this lesser-known form occurs when subordinates target their superiors. It can manifest as defiance, spreading rumours, malicious grievances or undermining authority. Upward bullying can disrupt the hierarchy, create a hostile work atmosphere and hinder effective management.

Understanding these signs is vital for addressing and preventing toxicity. By identifying these elements, libraries can proactively foster a more positive and supportive work culture.

Theoretical foundations
Psychological concepts in toxic work environments
Understanding toxic work environments, particularly in libraries, requires an exploration of various psychological theories and concepts. These concepts help identify the underlying causes of such environments and guide the development of strategies to mitigate them.

Psychological capital (PsyCap)
PsyCap, as explained in Chapter 4, can help staff to proactively and constructively address challenges, thereby, thereby minimising toxicity (Luthans, Youssef and Avolio, 2007).

Job Demands-Resources (JD-R) Model
The Job Demands-Resources (JD-R) Model, as cited by Bakker and Demerouti (2007) and explained in Chapter 2, is particularly effective for tackling specific types of workplace toxicity based on its focus on this balance. For instance, identifying imbalances in resource allocation can help address issues related to favouritism or a 'Boys' Club' atmosphere. Similarly, understanding disengagement in the context of high demands and low resources can inform strategies to improve engagement.

Psychological safety
The concept of psychological safety is essential in combating toxicity. Libraries must foster an environment where staff feel comfortable expressing concerns and ideas without fear of negative consequences. In a psychologically safe library, individuals are more likely to share ideas, voice concerns and engage in constructive dialogues, which are all essential for identifying and solving problems (Edmondson, 1999).

Understanding and implementing these psychological theories is critical in developing effective strategies against toxicity in libraries. They provide a theoretical understanding of the dynamics of toxic work cultures and practical approaches to creating healthier, more supportive library environments.

Common forms of toxicity
Toxic work environments in libraries can be manifested in various forms, each with distinct characteristics and impacts on staff and the overall work atmosphere. Understanding these forms is crucial for developing targeted strategies to address them effectively.

Toxic positivity

This refers to an environment where excessive optimism suppresses genuine emotions and challenges. This might look like consistently downplaying difficulties or enforcing a facade of happiness in libraries. Toxic positivity undermines honest dialogue and emotional expression, potentially leading to increased stress and burnout among staff. Library leadership must cultivate a culture that values emotional intelligence and allows for open expression of feelings (Tugade and Fredrickson, 2004; Kahn, 1990).

Cut-throat competition

This describes overly aggressive and unhealthy competition among colleagues or departments. It is characterised by practices where success is pursued without regard for ethical standards or the wellbeing of others. This type of competition often leads to a toxic workplace culture, where individuals or teams are more focused on outperforming each other rather than collaborating or contributing to the library's overall mission. It can result in strained relationships and decreased collaboration between colleagues. In some libraries, particularly in academic settings, intense competition for resources, academic recognition or professional advancement may exist. Such environments prioritise individual success over collective achievement, which can strain team dynamics and erode trust. Addressing this requires fostering a culture of teamwork and recognising collaborative efforts.

Inconsistent or absent leadership

Inconsistent leadership describes a situation where leadership behaviour and decision-making lack predictability, fairness and clarity. This inconsistency can stem from changing priorities without clear communication, arbitrary decision-making or erratic emotional responses from leaders. Such leadership creates an unstable work environment, where employees may feel unsure about expectations, lack trust in their leaders and face challenges in performing their roles effectively. This uncertainty can lead to increased stress, diminished morale and toxic behaviours as employees struggle to adapt to a continually shifting landscape without solid guidance or reliable support. Inconsistent leadership in libraries can lead to shifting priorities, role ambiguity and a lack of support for staff. This creates an environment of uncertainty and stress, paving the way for toxicity. Effective communication and stable leadership are essential in preventing these scenarios.

Exclusionary environments

Often characterised by a 'boys' club' atmosphere, these environments are marked by favouritism and discrimination, sidelining those who do not fit a particular profile. Such settings, which may be explained by the Leader–Member Exchange (LMX) Theory, lead to reduced job satisfaction and increased stress among those excluded. LMX theory is a concept in organisational behaviour that describes how leaders develop individualised relationships with each team member. These relationships can vary in quality, ranging from high trust and mutual respect to more distant, formal interactions. In the context of workplace toxicity, LMX Theory is relevant because it describes behaviour that leads to exclusionary practices. When leaders form closer bonds with some team members over others, it can create an environment where specific individuals feel marginalised or left out, potentially fostering a toxic work atmosphere. This uneven dynamic can impact team cohesion, employee engagement and workplace harmony.

High-stress, low-support environments

Characterised by demanding workloads without adequate support from management, these environments can quickly lead to employee burnout and disengagement. Libraries facing budget cuts or staffing shortages are particularly vulnerable to this toxicity.

Upward bullying

This common but little talked about form of bullying involves staff targeting their supervisors or managers. In library settings, this can manifest as insubordination, undermining decisions or spreading rumours, significantly impacting team morale and service quality.

Legacy toxicity

When toxicity becomes so ingrained that it forms the organisational culture, it is known as legacy toxicity. Legacy toxicity refers to the enduring negative culture or behaviours within an organisation that have been perpetuated over time, often passed down through successive leadership or entrenched in organisational practices. This type of toxicity is challenging to address because it becomes normalised and embedded in the workplace culture. It often requires significant effort to identify, understand and change, as it involves altering long-standing habits, attitudes and unwritten rules that have been accepted as the norm within the organisation. This issue is particularly prevalent in libraries, where employees might stay for decades. It can lead to resistance to change, closed-mindedness and hostility towards new initiatives or leadership. New leaders face the challenge of changing this deeply rooted culture.

Each of these forms of toxicity requires a tailored approach for resolution, considering the unique dynamics and needs of the library environment. By recognising and understanding these diverse manifestations of toxicity, libraries can develop more effective strategies to create a healthier, more supportive workplace.

Case Study 17.2: Addressing a toxic culture

When I first took on the role of Programming Co-ordinator, I faced the challenge of navigating a competitive culture within the team. Surpassing a colleague who had been with the company longer stirred resentment, leading to a strained work environment. The colleague's competitiveness escalated to a point where it created tension and affected the entire team's wellbeing. This situation took a toll on my ability to maintain a positive attitude at work and in my personal life.

To address the issue, my director played a pivotal role by actively engaging in conflict resolution. Meetings were arranged to facilitate open communication and my director became a mediator, ensuring she was included in our discussions and e-mail communications. Recognising the need for improved interpersonal skills, my colleague attended workshops focused on communication and, specifically, kindness in the workplace. As a last resort, my director implemented a three-strike rule, making it clear that the competitive behaviour had consequences.

Another significant challenge was the overwhelming workload that accompanied a newly established position. As the Programming Co-ordinator, I found myself grappling with numerous responsibilities, including overseeing all programming and managing adult and family events. The sheer volume of tasks was initially daunting and caused considerable stress. In response, my director proactively addressed my concerns about workload during discussions. Recognising the need for additional support, an assistant was assigned to alleviate some of the burden. This strategic move aimed to ensure that tasks could be managed more efficiently, allowing for a more balanced and sustainable work environment.

Furthermore, the lack of recognition for my efforts in the early stages of the role affected my morale and overall job satisfaction. Feeling unacknowledged can be demoralising, impacting not only personal wellbeing but professional performance. Acknowledging this concern, my director took steps to foster a culture of appreciation. Regular praise and recognition became a consistent practice, not only for me but for all team members. This shift in approach significantly improved morale, fostering a more positive and collaborative atmosphere.

In overcoming these challenges, the combined efforts of effective communication, conflict resolution, strategic delegation and a culture of recognition have contributed to a more harmonious and productive work environment. The implementation of these strategies not only addressed specific issues but laid the foundation for a healthier and more supportive workplace culture.

Heather Wheeler, Programming Co-ordinator, Mason County Public Library

Strategies for combating toxicity

This section explores practical strategies to combat toxicity, focusing on individual and systemic interventions. These strategies include enhancing emotional intelligence, addressing management issues and implementing organisational changes. By understanding and applying these approaches, leaders and staff can create a more positive, inclusive and productive work environment, aligning with principles of kindness and wellbeing.

Emotionally intelligent leadership

The role of leadership in creating and maintaining a positive work environment cannot be understated. This is even more critical in library settings due to the unique challenges faced in such environments, including systemic challenges. Emotionally intelligent leadership is pivotal in this regard. It involves understanding and managing one's emotions and those of others, fostering a supportive and inclusive atmosphere. Leaders with high emotional intelligence are better equipped to navigate complex interpersonal dynamics, recognise and address the emotional needs of their staff and create an environment where open communication and mutual respect are the norms. This approach is effective in combating forms of toxicity like exclusionary practices, inconsistent leadership, high-stress scenarios and systemic challenges such as ingrained biases or structural inequalities. Implementing theories like transformational leadership (see Chapter 15) can be game changing, encouraging teams to develop professionally and personally and fostering a culture of continuous improvement (Bass and Riggio, 2006).

Managing poor management

Dealing with ineffective or harmful management styles is a challenging aspect of combating toxicity in the workplace. Poor management can manifest itself in various forms, including lack of direction, inadequate support, favouritism or abusive behaviour. Systemic challenges such as entrenched hierarchies or outdated policies can exacerbate these issues. Addressing this requires a multifaceted approach:

- Open communication: initiating conversations with management about concerns, providing specific examples and suggesting potential solutions.
- Escalation: if direct communication does not yield results, escalating the issue to Human Resources or higher-level management may be necessary
- Professional development: encouraging the organisation to invest in leadership training that enhances emotional intelligence and management skills. This investment improves the work environment and contributes to the quality of public service, impacting community wellbeing (Goleman, 1998).
- Addressing systemic challenges: identifying and tackling systemic issues within the organisation. This might involve policy reviews, organisational restructuring or diversity and inclusion initiatives.

Beyond addressing leadership and management issues, individual and group interventions are crucial in creating a healthier work environment. These interventions can range from workshops focused on building psychological resilience to team-building activities that foster co-operation and positive relationships among staff members, all while being mindful of and addressing systemic challenges within the library system.

How these strategies specifically address types of toxicity
Emotionally intelligent leadership

- Counteracts toxic positivity: by acknowledging and managing emotions effectively, leaders can create a space where genuine feelings are expressed, countering the suppression seen in toxic positivity.
- Addresses inconsistent leadership: emotional intelligence in leadership ensures consistent and empathic communication, reducing the uncertainty and stress caused by inconsistent leadership.
- Mitigates legacy toxicity: emotionally intelligent leaders are equipped to navigate the challenges of legacy toxicity by understanding deep-rooted issues and fostering a culture of openness and change.

Managing poor management

- Combats exclusionary environments and favouritism: open communication and escalation procedures can challenge environments where favouritism and exclusion prevail.
- Reduces high-stress, low-support scenarios: by advocating better support and resources, this approach directly addresses environments where high demands are not matched with adequate support.

■ Addresses upward bullying: effective management training can help identify and mitigate upward bullying, creating a more respectful and co-operative workplace.

Addressing systemic challenges

This strategy is crucial in tackling the underlying systemic issues that may contribute to toxicity, including entrenched biases, outdated policies and structural inequalities.

Professional development and group interventions

These interventions are essential in building a resilient workforce capable of dealing with cutthroat competition and other toxic dynamics through enhanced cooperation, improved communication and shared understanding.

In essence, the strategies for combating toxicity provide a comprehensive framework for addressing the specific challenges identified in the common forms of toxicity, ensuring a holistic approach to creating a healthier, more supportive library environment.

Practical interventions

Effectively managing toxicity in the workplace requires actionable and practical interventions. This section explores strategies specifically designed for library environments, focusing on building resilience, ensuring psychological safety and promoting job crafting. These interventions aim to empower staff, foster a supportive culture and align work roles with individual strengths and preferences. By implementing these approaches, libraries can create a more dynamic, positive and productive workplace, significantly enhancing staff wellbeing and overall organisational performance.

Building resilience and psychological safety

Addressing toxicity in library environments requires practical interventions focusing on building resilience and ensuring psychological safety among staff. Implementing resilience workshops and fostering a culture that values psychological safety can promote a healthier work atmosphere.

Resilience workshops equip library staff with the skills to handle stress and adapt to change. They often combine theory-based lectures with interactive activities, helping teams develop coping mechanisms, enhance stress management skills and build resilience. Critical components of these workshops include mindfulness training, stress management techniques, scenario-based role-play and group discussions on coping mechanisms. These activities aid in personal development and contribute to a more resilient library workforce.

It is vital to create an environment where staff feel safe to voice their concerns and ideas. Psychological safety ensures employees can express themselves without fear of negative consequences. This includes open communication channels, cultivating trust among team members, facilitating feedback, encouraging risk-taking within safe boundaries and promoting inclusivity. By implementing measures to enhance psychological safety, libraries can improve problem-solving and innovation, reduce workplace conflict and enhance employee retention.

Job crafting

Job crafting is another practical approach, allowing staff to reshape their roles to better align with their strengths and interests. This strategy not only reduces stress but elevates job satisfaction and efficiency. Implementing job crafting includes conducting a needs assessment to understand staff needs, redefining tasks and roles collaboratively, implementing trial periods with regular check-ins and evaluating the impact on key performance indicators like staff turnover, job satisfaction and customer service ratings.

While these interventions are essential, understanding their implementation and tailoring them to the unique needs of each library setting is critical. By doing so, libraries can mitigate toxicity, leading to a more positive, efficient and fulfilling work environment for staff and users.

Implementing change

Transitioning from theoretical concepts to practical applications is crucial in combating workplace toxicity, especially in library settings. This section outlines a series of actionable steps that library leaders and staff can take to effectively implement change. These steps include leadership training, staff workshops, open communication channels, applying the Job Demands-Resources (JD-R) model, cultivating psychological safety, tailoring interventions to specific library contexts, continuously evaluating and adjusting strategies and celebrating progress. Each step is designed to address different aspects of workplace toxicity, from enhancing leadership skills and staff resilience to fostering a culture of open communication and psychological safety. By applying these steps, libraries can move towards creating a healthier, more inclusive and productive work environment.

From theory to practice

Successfully applying strategies to combat workplace toxicity in libraries involves a thoughtful translation of theory into practice. Here are some practical steps for library leaders and staff to implement change:

Leadership Training

Start by investing in leadership development, focusing on emotional intelligence and effective communication. Leaders should be trained to recognise and address toxic behaviours, promote inclusivity and provide consistent, supportive guidance.

Staff workshops

Conduct workshops on resilience, stress management and psychological safety. These should be interactive, allowing staff to engage with and apply the material to their specific roles and challenges.

Open communication channels

Establish regular forums for staff to voice their concerns and ideas. This could be in the form of team meetings, suggestion boxes or one-on-one sessions with management. Ensure that these channels are safe spaces where employees feel heard and respected.

Implementing the JD-R model

Use the Job Demands-Resources model to assess and balance workloads. Identify areas where demands exceed resources and take steps to address these imbalances. This might involve redistributing tasks, hiring additional staff or providing more support in high-demand areas.

Cultivating psychological safety

Work towards creating an environment where staff feel comfortable taking risks and speaking up. This involves building trust, showing empathy and encouraging collaboration and open dialogue.

Tailoring interventions

Recognise that each library is unique and customise interventions accordingly. Consider factors such as the size of the library, the community it serves and the specific challenges it faces.

Evaluating and adjusting

Continuously assess the effectiveness of the implemented changes. This can be done through staff feedback, surveys and observing changes in workplace dynamics. Be prepared to adjust strategies as needed to ensure they remain effective and relevant.

Celebrating progress

Recognise and celebrate improvements and milestones. This encourages ongoing engagement and reinforces the value of the changes made.

By following these steps, libraries can create a more positive and supportive work environment, effectively addressing and preventing toxic dynamics.

Preventive measures

To foster a healthy work environment in libraries, it's essential to implement a range of strategies that address both individual and collective needs. This section highlights these strategies, emphasising the importance of emotional intelligence, psychological safety, job crafting, regular staff training, collaboration, wellbeing programmes, effective feedback mechanisms, diversity and inclusion initiatives and continuous monitoring and evaluation. Each strategy contributes to creating a supportive, inclusive and dynamic library workplace. By integrating these approaches, library leaders and staff can work together to prevent toxicity, enhance job satisfaction and cultivate a culture that promotes personal and professional growth, benefiting both the staff and the community they serve.

Proactively building healthy work environments

Creating and maintaining a positive work culture in libraries is a proactive measure that can prevent toxicity from taking root. This involves several key strategies:

Fostering emotional intelligence

Encourage emotional intelligence in leadership and staff. This includes self-awareness, empathy and effective communication skills. Emotionally intelligent leaders can create a supportive and understanding work environment.

Promoting psychological safety

Ensure the library is a space where staff can voice their opinions, concerns and ideas. This involves establishing trust, encouraging open dialogue and appreciating diverse viewpoints.

Implementing job crafting

Allow staff to have a say in their roles. Job crafting can enable employees to shape their work to bring out their strengths, increasing job satisfaction and reducing stress.

Regular staff training and development

Offer ongoing training and professional development opportunities. This keeps staff updated with the latest library practices and shows an investment in their personal growth.

Building a collaborative culture

Encourage teamwork and collaboration. Recognise and reward collective achievements over individual successes to promote a culture of unity and shared goals.

Wellbeing programmes

Implement wellbeing programmes focusing on physical and mental health. These include mindfulness sessions, stress management workshops and health and wellness activities.

Feedback mechanisms

Establish clear and anonymous feedback mechanisms for staff to report issues or offer suggestions. Regularly review and act upon this feedback to ensure continuous improvement.

Diversity and inclusion initiatives

Actively work towards creating a diverse and inclusive environment. This includes training on unconscious bias, celebrating different cultures and ensuring equal opportunities.

Monitoring and evaluation

Regularly assess the work environment through surveys and informal check-ins to gauge the morale and wellbeing of staff. Use these insights to make necessary adjustments.

Maintaining a healthy environment is an ongoing effort that requires commitment from all levels of the library team. By taking these proactive steps, libraries can create a work culture that is not only free of toxicity but conducive to growth, innovation and a positive community impact.

Challenges of building a positive work culture

Building a positive work culture, especially consciously and deliberately, is typically more challenging than allowing a negative one to develop. This difference in effort and complexity can be understood through several psychological and organisational theories, including Fredrickson's (2001) Broaden-and-Build Theory, which posits that positive emotions broaden an individual's momentary thought-action repertoire, which in turn builds their personal resources, ranging from physical and intellectual resources to social and psychological ones. This theory suggests that experiencing positive emotions makes people feel good in the moment and leads to lasting personal growth and improved wellbeing over time. It is particularly relevant in building positive workplace cultures, as it highlights the importance of fostering positive emotions and interactions to cultivate a more supportive and resilient workforce.

Effort in building positive cultures

Creating a positive work culture requires planning, consistent effort and a commitment to fostering positive behaviours and attitudes. This involves implementing leadership training, promoting psychological safety and encouraging open communication. It requires continuous monitoring and adaptation to ensure the culture remains positive and inclusive.

Ease of negative culture development

Negative work cultures, conversely, can develop more quickly and often inadvertently. Negative behaviours and attitudes, such as gossip, exclusion and lack of communication, can spread rapidly and become normalised if not addressed promptly. Negativity can stem from systemic issues, like poor management or inadequate resources, which may grow over time without conscious effort to counteract them.

Consequences of inaction

Doing nothing or being passive in the face of emerging negativity can lead to a toxic work environment. This can result in high staff turnover, low morale, decreased productivity and a poor organisational reputation. Inaction allows negative behaviours and attitudes to take root and spread, overshadowing positive aspects of the work culture.

Link to Broaden-and-Build Theory

According to Fredrickson's (2001) Broaden-and-Build Theory, positive emotions broaden an individual's awareness and encourage novel, varied and exploratory thoughts and actions. Over time, this builds enduring personal resources, like social connections and coping mechanisms. Fostering positive emotions can lead to more creative, collaborative and resilient teams in a work setting. However, creating and maintaining such an environment requires more effort than allowing a culture of negativity to persist.

In summary, consciously building a positive work culture is more challenging than allowing a negative one to develop, primarily because it requires ongoing effort, commitment and intentional actions. This process, while demanding, is crucial for the long-term health and success of an organisation and its members.

Conclusion

As we conclude this chapter, it is vital to emphasise that creating and maintaining a healthy work environment is continuous. The strategies and insights discussed here are not one-time solutions but part of an ongoing effort to ensure that libraries remain places of positive engagement and growth. Readers are encouraged to apply these strategies in their professional contexts, continuously adapt them and commit to the ongoing work of combating workplace toxicity for the betterment of their libraries and the communities they serve.

Exercises and reflective questions

Exercise for teams

Courageous conversations workshop

Objective: to foster a culture of open communication and courage in confronting issues, inspired by Einstein's tribute to Pablo Casals, recognising the importance of not tolerating evil.

Duration: 2 hours.

Materials needed: whiteboard or flip chart; markers; note cards; scenario descriptions (based on common workplace challenges).

Process:

1 Introduction (15 mins): begin with a brief discussion of Einstein's quote, emphasising the importance of avoiding evil and actively confronting it.
2 Understanding the quote (15 mins): divide the team into small groups. Each group discusses what the quote means in the context of their work and how it applies to their day-to-day activities.
3 Role-playing scenarios (45 mins): present the groups with scenarios that reflect common challenges in the library workplace (e.g. handling difficult patrons, addressing team conflicts, dealing with unethical

behaviour). Each group role-plays their scenario, demonstrating both a passive and a courageous approach.

4 Group discussion (30 mins): reconvene and have each group share their scenarios and approaches. Discuss the outcomes of both passive and courageous responses

5 Commitment cards (15 mins): each team member writes one commitment on a note card about how they will act more courageously in their role. These cards are collected and revisited in future team meetings to assess progress.

Exercise for individuals
Kindness journalling
Objective: to cultivate a personal practice of kindness and wellbeing in the workplace, aligning with the principle of not tolerating or encouraging evil.
Duration: ongoing daily practice.
Materials needed: journal or digital document.
Process:

1 Daily reflection (10 mins daily): set aside 10 minutes for reflection at the end of each work day.

2 Journalling prompts:
   — Describe one act of kindness you observed or participated in today.
   — Reflect on a situation where you could have acted more courageously. What held you back and what could you do differently next time?
   — Identify one thing in your work environment that does not align with the ethos of kindness and wellbeing. Brainstorm ways you could address or change it.

3 Weekly review (30 mins weekly): at the end of each week, review your journal entries to identify patterns, progress and areas for improvement.

4 Monthly sharing (optional): once a month, share insights or experiences from your journal with a colleague or in a team meeting, fostering a culture of shared learning and growth in kindness.

Reflective questions
■ Reflect on a recent situation in your work environment where you noticed something that did not align with the values of kindness, wellbeing or integrity. How did you react to it and upon reflection, how could you have addressed it more effectively? Consider the balance between passive acceptance and courageous action.

- How do you believe your behaviour and actions contribute to the work culture in your library? Reflect on ways you might unintentionally support a toxic environment or, conversely, how you might be a force for positive change.
- Think about a time when a colleague displayed behaviour that seemed negative or harmful. With hindsight and considering their perspective and potential stressors, how might your understanding of their actions change? How could this insight influence your future interactions?
- Reflect on your role as a leader or influencer in your workplace, regardless of your official position. How can you embody the qualities of kindness, authenticity and courage in your daily interactions? Consider specific actions or changes you can implement to lead by example in creating a more positive and ethical work environment.
- Reflect on a scenario where you had to address a complex issue in your work environment. Did you focus on the immediate problem or did you consider the broader context – including the organisational culture, individual wellbeing and systemic factors? How might a more holistic approach have led to a different outcome?

CHAPTER 18

Managing Change with Kindness and Wellbeing in Libraries

Introduction

> Change is the law of life. And those who look only to the past or present are certain to miss the future.
>
> (John F. Kennedy, speech at Paulskirche, Frankfurt, 25 June 1963)

During my career, I have been part of many changes, including major restructures, huge building redevelopment projects and everything else in the environment of flux in modern libraries; change is not only inevitable but essential, from policy changes in government and technological advancements to shifts in user behaviours. No matter what our role in libraries, we must continually adapt to meet evolving needs. However, change can often be challenging, fraught with uncertainty and resistance from staff and the communities we serve. This chapter examines how libraries can navigate these inevitable transformations, not with trepidation but with an approach rooted in kindness and wellbeing.

The chapter's principal goal is to guide library staff at all levels in understanding how kindness and wellbeing can act as essential tools for implementing and accepting change. It is not a complete change management guide; many are out there. However, it offers practical strategies and insights derived from research and lived experience to ensure that change is managed and welcomed as a positive force for growth and service improvement.

Understanding the motivations for change and having a clear sense of reality is essential. It's important to recognise when something meets the threshold of 'good enough' and to take pride in reaching that point. Focus on measuring what truly matters. The success of any change is ultimately determined by the people it affects, as change is a profoundly personal experience, as are the emotions it generates.

The importance of kindness and wellbeing in times of change

Impact of change on library staff and users

Change in libraries, whether technological, structural or cultural, significantly impacts staff and users. Teams may face stress and anxiety due to adapting to new systems or facing uncertainty (Allen et al., 2021). Similarly, users accustomed to certain services or environments might need help with these changes.

Role of kindness and wellbeing

During these transitions, kindness and wellbeing play a pivotal role. Kindness, manifested through empathetic leadership and supportive team dynamics, facilitates smoother navigation through change for staff (Allen et al., 2021). This approach fosters an environment where concerns are heard and addressed, reducing resistance to change. Library staff's kind and understanding approach can ease users' transition to new services or environments.

Prioritising wellbeing through stress management resources and open communication builds resilience among staff (Allen et al., 2021). This resilience is crucial in ensuring staff are well-equipped to assist users and maintain high-quality service despite the changes. Kindness and wellbeing are strategic elements in effectively managing change in libraries. They benefit staff and users, underscoring the importance of these values in transitional periods.

Often, as libraries or their broader organisations and systems embark on a journey of transformation, it's common for organisations to spotlight their Employee Assistance Programme (EAP) as a bastion of support for staff. It's a step that sets a cornerstone for mental health support. However, there's a fundamental issue to this approach, suggesting a misunderstanding of true wellbeing, an anticipation of distress resulting from the change or, worse yet, a preference for throwing funds at a problem rather than fostering genuine care and connection.

True wellbeing, especially in the throes of change, is complicated. It's about ensuring staff have ample time for tasks and embracing the required transition. It involves clear, prompt communication and empowering employees to adapt and grow in skills and mindset. It's about inclusivity, valuing the voices within the community and making sure changes in roles or goals are transparent. Crucially, it means creating 'safe spaces' for open discussions about any concerns that might surface.

Supporting mental health is vital but is merely one piece of the wellbeing puzzle. A holistic approach is the only way to foster an environment where employees don't just survive but thrive through change. The concept of wellbeing, particularly within a workplace setting undergoing change, is like a complex puzzle with many interlocking pieces. Each piece is crucial for the complete picture of true employee wellbeing, beyond immediate mental health support. Here are some of the fundamental pieces of the wellbeing puzzle that are essential to consider:

- Physical health and comfort: this includes ergonomic workstations, opportunities for physical activity and consideration of the physical demands placed on employees. Regular breaks and a comfortable working environment are essential.
- Mental and emotional support: beyond EAPs, this involves creating a culture where mental health is openly discussed and destigmatised. Access to counselling, mindfulness sessions and stress management workshops can be beneficial.
- Work–life balance: Encouraging employees to maintain a healthy balance between their professional and personal lives prevents burnout. Flexible working hours and remote work options can contribute significantly here.
- Personal and professional development: opportunities for learning, upskilling and career progression are essential. Employees should feel they are growing with the library and that their personal goals are aligned with their work.
- Social connection and community: fostering a sense of belonging and community through team-building activities and social events helps build a supportive network within the workplace.
- Recognition and reward: acknowledging employees' hard work and achievements boost morale and shows that the organisation values their contribution.
- Autonomy and empowerment: allowing employees to have a say in their work and the changes happening within the organisation gives them a sense of control and investment in the outcome.

Questions to ask at the start of a change
When we are approaching any change in a library that has kindness and wellbeing at its heart, it is helpful to ask the following questions at the start and revisit them regularly:

- What is the desired outcome of this change for the wellbeing of all involved? This helps to set a positive and clear intention for the change, centring it on the wellbeing of individuals.

- How can we make this transition as smooth as possible for everyone? This question prompts consideration of the practical steps needed to minimise stress or disruption.
- Who will be affected by this change and in what ways can we support them? This encourages an empathetic perspective, ensuring support mechanisms are in place.
- What strengths do we currently possess to draw upon during this change? Recognising existing resources and resilience can be empowering and reassuring and offset the demands of the change.
- How can we maintain open and compassionate communication throughout this process? Keeping lines of communication open and empathetic is critical to managing change kindly.
- What are the potential challenges and how might we address them proactively with kindness? Anticipating challenges allows for creating kind and constructive strategies to overcome them.
- How can we incorporate feedback to ensure this change is positively received? Feedback is crucial for continuous improvement and for making people feel heard.
- How can we measure the impact of this change on wellbeing? Establishing metrics for wellbeing ensures that the change can be evaluated and adjusted as necessary.
- What learning opportunities does this change present and how can we embrace them? Framing change as a learning experience can be a positive way to foster personal and collective growth.
- Are there any risks to wellbeing that this change might pose and how can we mitigate them? Identifying and mitigating risks shows foresight and care for the wellbeing of those affected.

Considering these questions, you can navigate change with a balance of kindness and effectiveness, promoting a culture of wellbeing and support.

- Security and stability: communication about changes should be clear and transparent to provide a sense of security. Remember, being kind should be the rule with any communication. Additionally, financial wellbeing through fair pay and benefits is crucial.
- Leadership and management support: leaders should be accessible and supportive, providing guidance during times of change. Training for managers on how to support their teams' wellbeing is vital.
- Purpose and meaning: employees should feel that their work is meaningful and contribute to a greater purpose within the organisation.

This includes celebrating and thanking them for any work that is no longer going ahead because of the change.

Employees are more likely to feel valued and supported when all these pieces are in place, leading to increased engagement, productivity and a positive work environment. As changes occur, these elements of wellbeing serve as a foundation to help employees navigate the transition with resilience and optimism.

Understanding change: theoretical frameworks

The change process in libraries, whether it involves new technologies, organisational restructuring or shifts in service models, can be understood and managed more effectively by applying key theoretical frameworks. Two such frameworks are the **Bridges Transition Model** and **Cognitive Dissonance Theory.**

Bridges Transition Model

The Bridges Transition Model (Bridges and Bridges, 2009) is a framework for understanding the emotional and psychological transition during change. It is particularly relevant in organisational settings like libraries undergoing transformation. The model identifies three phases of transition:

- Letting Go: this phase involves individuals moving on from old ways, which can be challenging and emotional.
- Neutral Zone: a period of confusion and uncertainty where the old is gone, but the new isn't fully operational.
- New Beginning: people begin to embrace new ways, developing new identities and energy in the process.

This model emphasises the emotional journey of individuals. A human-centric approach involves actively engaging employees at each phase, ensuring psychological safety and offering wellbeing checks. For example, during the 'Letting Go' phase, it's crucial to acknowledge the emotional impact and provide support.

A practical application of this model was demonstrated by Butler University Libraries (Miller, 2017) during their migration to a cloud-based integrated library system. The leadership team utilised the model to develop change management strategies and track progress in employee perceptions and participation in implementing the change. This approach included a pre-

and post-migration exercise using a graphical representation of the three phases to assess staff readiness and integration into their new roles.

Cognitive Dissonance Theory

Cognitive Dissonance Theory, formulated by Festinger (1957), is another framework relevant to organisational change. It focuses on the psychological discomfort experienced when an individual holds two or more contradictory beliefs, ideas or values. This theory can help understand how individuals reconcile new information with existing beliefs in the context of organisational change, such as in educational settings. A human-centric approach would include transparent communication to address uncertainties and promote open discussions for reconciling old and new ways.

For instance, a study (Çalışkan and Gökalp, 2020) exploring how prospective teachers make sense of an impending educational change after experiencing cognitive dissonance found that individuals navigate this dissonance by considering the individual and organisational sides of change and the management of change. This study revealed that while participants found the change plan beneficial, they expressed concerns about its implementation. This research highlights the role of cognitive dissonance in shaping responses to planned change initiatives, emphasising the need for effective communication and support during transitional periods.

In practical terms, these theories can be simplified as follows:

- Bridges Transition Model: understand change as a process of emotional transition with distinct phases. Support staff through each step by acknowledging their feelings, providing clear information and celebrating milestones in the new beginning.
- Cognitive Dissonance Theory: recognise that change can create psychological discomfort due to conflicting beliefs or information. Address this by facilitating open discussions, providing clear and consistent communication and supporting staff in reconciling old and new ways.

By applying these frameworks, library leaders can better manage the human aspects of change, facilitating a smoother transition for staff and users.

Psychological safety during changes

A culture of psychological safety (Edmonson, 1999) allows staff to voice their concerns, ask questions and offer suggestions without fear of reprisal, thus facilitating smoother transitions during periods of change. It creates a supportive environment where mistakes are viewed as learning opportunities rather than failures.

Practical application in libraries

- Open forums: hold regular meetings where staff can openly discuss their thoughts and concerns about upcoming changes.
- Anonymous feedback channels: implement tools that allow for anonymous suggestions or questions, which can be especially valuable for those who may not feel comfortable speaking up in public settings.
- Leadership support: ensure that library leaders model psychological safety by admitting their vulnerabilities or uncertainties and being openly receptive to feedback.

By cultivating psychological safety, libraries can ease the stress and anxieties associated with change, leading to a more adaptable and resilient workforce. The following steps will create psychologically safe change:

- Be clear on goals: establishing clear goals is fundamental to guiding change. Knowing the end objective helps align team efforts and resources, ensuring everyone is moving in the same direction.
- Be clear on accountabilities: accountability is crucial during times of change. It ensures that individuals understand their roles and responsibilities, fostering a sense of ownership and commitment to the change process.
- Frame the work as learning: embracing change as a learning process encourages an open mindset. It prepares teams to adapt and evolve, essential when navigating new environments or procedures.
- Say when you do not know: acknowledging uncertainty or lack of knowledge can foster an environment where seeking help and collaboration becomes a norm. This is vital during change, as it often requires problem-solving and innovation.
- Ask questions: questions can stimulate critical thinking and engagement. They encourage team members to consider various aspects of the change and to contribute their unique perspectives.
- Ask for feedback: feedback mechanisms are integral to successful change management. They provide insight into how change is being received and what adjustments may be necessary.
- Allow mistakes: accepting that mistakes are part of the learning curve can create a culture of resilience. It encourages experimentation and risk-taking, which are often necessary for effective change.

- Be inclusive: inclusivity ensures that all voices are heard during change, increasing the diversity of ideas and fostering buy-in from the entire team.
- Be a collaborator: collaboration is a cornerstone of change. Working together towards common goals can ease the transition and seamlessly integrate different aspects of the organisation.
- Replace blame with curiosity: a non-punitive approach to mistakes encourages openness and continuous improvement, which are necessary for change to take hold.
- Listen: active listening ensures that feedback and concerns are acknowledged, increasing trust and co-operation during the change process. Remember, everyone is human: Recognising the personal side of change can help address the emotional impacts, reduce resistance and increase support for the change initiatives.

These principles aim to create a psychologically safe environment, which research has shown to be critical in successful change implementation. Psychological safety allows for the open expression of ideas, concerns and mistakes, which can be addressed constructively to facilitate change. By supporting psychological safety, each point indirectly supports a more adaptive and resilient organisation that can effectively manage change.

Types of change in a library setting

Different types of change occur in library settings, which will impact how the change is managed. Is it planned, unplanned, rapid, slow, internal or external change? You can have different combinations of these, e.g. planned and rapid change, that is motivated internally.

To navigate this landscape, Palmer-Trew and Jayes (2022) suggest five critical questions to ask that are useful to consider:

1 What exactly is changing? Understanding the specifics provides a foundation for action.
2 Why is it changing? Knowing the reasons gives direction and purpose.
3 What will remain unchanged? This offers stability and continuity.
4 What are the risks if we do not change? Assessing this helps in gauging the urgency and potential consequences.
5 Why now? This question anchors the change to a timely context, giving it immediacy and relevance.

It doesn't matter how many times or how many ways you tell people about the change. Many people will only engage once it affects them, so it is essential to bring everyone on board early and be prepared for people to be surprised by the change at any point. This was evident when we moved two libraries into a new building at Royal Holloway; this project was very long-term. It had a physical manifestation of a brand-new building. We did a lot of outreach, but right up to the day we packed up the office, some people seemed surprised that we asked them to clear out a cupboard or pack up their desks. This was the clearest example of this, but it is something that I have found with every change I have undertaken.

Diversity, equity and inclusion in change management

Inclusivity and cultural sensitivity in kindness and wellbeing practices

Incorporating diversity, equity and inclusion (DEI) in change management ensures that kindness and wellbeing practices are culturally sensitive and inclusive. This means recognising and respecting all library staff and users' diverse backgrounds, experiences and needs. For instance, research indicates that when DEI principles are integrated into organisational practices, they can enhance employee engagement and job satisfaction (Shore et al., 2011).

Addressing the needs of diverse library communities

Libraries serve diverse communities and change management strategies must reflect this diversity. Tailoring kindness and wellbeing initiatives to meet the varied needs of different groups within the community is essential. For example, introducing multilingual resources or programmes catering to different cultural practices can make the library more welcoming for all. Studies have shown that libraries that engage with their communities and reflect their diversity in services and collections tend to have a higher impact and relevance (Jaeger et al., 2012).

By embedding DEI principles into kindness and wellbeing practices during times of change, libraries can manage the transition more effectively and strengthen their role as inclusive community hubs. This approach ensures that the library remains a space where diversity is celebrated and everyone feels valued and included.

Practical wellbeing practices for library settings

Mindfulness techniques for stress management

In library settings, mindfulness can be a powerful tool for managing stress. As defined by the Association for Mindfulness in Education (n.d.), mindfulness is about 'paying attention here and now with kindness and curiosity' and can significantly benefit both library staff and users. In times of change in libraries, mindfulness exercises are particularly beneficial for several reasons:

- Reducing anxiety and stress: changes in library environments can induce stress and anxiety among staff and users. Mindfulness practices help in managing these emotions by fostering a sense of calm and self-awareness.
- Enhancing focus and concentration: amidst change, maintaining focus can be challenging. Exercises like 'Three senses' improve concentration and attentiveness, which is essential in adapting to new systems or practices within the library.
- Promoting adaptability: mindfulness encourages individuals to be present and open to experiences, which is crucial during transitional periods. It enables both staff and users to adapt more readily to changes in their library environment.
- Building emotional resilience: regular mindfulness practice strengthens emotional resilience, helping individuals better handle the uncertainties and pressures of change.
- Creating a supportive environment: when library staff practice mindfulness, it contributes to a more supportive and understanding atmosphere, making it easier for users to navigate library services or layout changes.

Here are two mindfulness exercises that can be integrated into the library environment:

Sound focus meditation

In the sound focus meditation, participants engage in focused listening, typically to a bell or a tone, such as one produced by a Tibetan singing bowl. The process begins with people finding a comfortable seated position and closing their eyes. As the sound of the bell or tone is played, students are encouraged to breathe quietly and concentrate on the sound, paying particular attention to the lingering notes as they gradually fade into silence. This practice aids in developing deep listening skills and a heightened sense of presence.

Three senses

This exercise focuses on three things one can feel, hear and see. This technique helps in grounding and bringing attention to the present moment, which is particularly beneficial in the unique setting of a library. The exercise is a mindfulness practice that enhances concentration and attentiveness. It can be beneficial in adapting to new systems or methods. It involves focusing on three senses one at a time, such as what you can hear, see and feel, which helps to anchor the mind in the present moment. This increased mindfulness and concentration can aid in better adapting to and managing changes in work environments like libraries.

By integrating mindfulness into their routines, libraries can create a more adaptable, focused and resilient community better equipped to handle the challenges and opportunities that come with change.

Active listening

Active listening is a cornerstone of effective communication and is vital in fostering kindness-based organisational change. It is not merely a passive activity; it's an active engagement that requires total concentration, understanding, responding and remembering what is being said. Here's why active listening is so critical in the context of organisational change centred on kindness:

- Building trust: active listening demonstrates respect and concern for the speaker's perspective. This respectful stance is foundational in building trust – essential when leading an organisation through change. When employees feel heard, they are more likely to trust the change process and the individuals leading it.
- Facilitating understanding: change can be complex and multi-faceted. Active listening helps leaders understand their team members' fears, hopes and suggestions. This understanding is crucial for leaders to address concerns effectively and to adapt their strategies to better fit the needs of their employees.
- Uncovering hidden issues: often, the most significant barriers to change are not the loudest complaints but the quiet concerns. Through active listening, leaders can uncover and address these hidden issues before they grow into more significant problems.
- Encouraging participation: a kindness-based approach to change encourages participation from all levels of the organisation. Active listening makes employees feel valued and that their contributions matter, thus fostering a collaborative environment.
- Promoting emotional intelligence: by actively listening, leaders model emotional intelligence – demonstrating awareness and consideration for others' emotions. This can set a tone that promotes empathy within the organisation, which is fundamental in any kindness-based initiative.
- Reducing resistance: when people feel heard, they are more likely to be co-operative. Active listening helps mitigate resistance to change by

addressing the root concerns of employees. It turns potential adversaries into allies by involving them in the change process.

■ Creating a culture of respect: active listening reinforces a culture of respect and caring. When everyone – from the newest employee to the highest executive – feels that their voice can be heard, it strengthens the organisation's cultural fabric, making it more resilient to the stresses of change.

■ Enhancing problem-solving: active listening is a tool that enables more effective problem-solving. By truly understanding the perspectives of others, leaders can devise solutions that are considerate, innovative and more likely to be embraced by the team.

In a kindness-based approach to organisational change, active listening is not an optional soft skill – it's an indispensable tool that enables leaders to navigate the complex emotional terrain of change management. It allows for a compassionate, empathetic and ultimately more human-centred process that aligns closely with positive psychological principles. Through active listening, an organisation doesn't just change; it evolves with its people, ensuring that the human aspect of the organisation is honoured and nurtured.

Addressing occupational stress in libraries

Research on stress among library staff highlights the need for effective stress management practices. A study exploring stress among reference library staff in academic and public libraries found that staff members are well aware of stress's impact on health and work performance. The study noted that interactions with users, particularly their complex questions and immediate demands, are significant stressors for library staff (Petek, 2018). Identifying such stressors is crucial for developing tailored strategies to cope with stress in the workplace.

In periods of change, library staff often encounter increased stress due to evolving user interactions and workplace demands. Targeted strategies are essential for managing this stress effectively:

■ Developing skills and support: tailored training prepares staff for new challenges, facilitating smoother transitions. Support programmes offer crucial stress management and counselling services.

■ Fostering resilience through mindfulness: mindfulness workshops and peer support align with the PsyCap model, bolstering resilience, optimism and adaptability amid change.

■ Adapting workplace practices for transition: flexible scheduling and feedback systems, as per the JD-R model, wellness initiatives and a

positive environment (PERMA model), help staff adjust to new demands while maintaining wellbeing.
■ Providing stress management resources: access to stress management tools is vital during change, offering immediate support and coping strategies

Integrating these strategies with wellbeing models like PsyCap, ASSET, PERMA and JD-R, which have been discussed in previous chapters, equips libraries with a comprehensive approach to manage occupational stress and foster a supportive environment, particularly during times of significant organisational change.

Implementing mindfulness, active listening and stress management practices in libraries can significantly improve the wellbeing of both staff and users. These techniques not only address the immediate challenges of occupational stress but contribute to creating a more positive and supportive library environment.

Positive psychology in action

Positive psychology emphasises the study and cultivation of positive emotions, strengths and conditions that make life most worth living and these can be especially powerful at times of change. Its practical application in libraries includes:

■ Strength-based training: use workshops and team-building exercises to help staff identify their strengths and understand how they can be leveraged during change.
■ Positive communication: frame changes and challenges as opportunities for growth and development, rather than as threats or negatives.
■ Wellbeing checkpoints: establish regular wellbeing check-ins focusing on positive psychology principles, offering staff resources or tools to foster resilience, happiness and job satisfaction.

Leadership in driving kindness and wellbeing during change

Library leaders play a pivotal role in fostering a culture of kindness and wellbeing, especially during times of change. Effective leadership in this context involves:

■ Modelling kindness: leaders should exemplify kindness in their interactions, setting a standard for the library.

- Empathetic communication: leaders must actively listen and respond empathetically to staff concerns, demonstrating understanding and compassion.
- Promoting inclusivity and support: encouraging an environment where all staff feel valued and supported, regardless of their role or experience.
- Wellbeing initiatives: implementing initiatives that promote mental, emotional and physical wellbeing, such as mindfulness sessions, wellness workshops and team-building activities.
- Recognition and appreciation: acknowledging and appreciating the efforts of staff, especially during challenging times, boosts morale and reinforces a positive culture.
- Consistent feedback and engagement: maintaining open lines of communication and providing regular feedback helps align the team with the library's goals and values.

By leveraging leadership and coaching skills, library leaders can effectively guide their teams through change, ensuring that kindness and wellbeing remain at the forefront of the library's culture. During times of change, leaders can use specific coaching questions in one-on-one meetings to foster a kind leadership style. These questions include:

- 'How are you feeling about the recent changes?' – encourages employees to express their emotions and concerns.
- 'What challenges are you currently facing with these changes?' – helps identify specific issues the employee is dealing with.
- 'What support do you need from me or the team to navigate these changes?' – shows a willingness to provide assistance and resources.
- 'How do you see these changes impacting your role?' – allows employees to reflect on the personal impact of the changes.
- 'What opportunities do you see arising from these changes?' – encourages a positive perspective and future-focused thinking.
- 'Are there any skills or training you need to adapt effectively?' – identifies areas for development and growth.
- 'How can we maintain or enhance our team's wellbeing during this period?' – focuses on collective wellbeing and team dynamics.

These questions help managers show empathy, foster open communication and support their teams through transitional periods with kindness and understanding.

Conclusion

As this chapter has explored, managing change in libraries is an intricate process that involves operational shifts and deeply affects the emotional and psychological landscape of staff and patrons. Applying frameworks like the Bridges Transition Model and Cognitive Dissonance Theory, combined with a human-centric approach, provides a comprehensive strategy for navigating these changes. Emphasising kindness and wellbeing, especially in times of transition, transforms potential challenges into opportunities for growth and community building. As library leaders, our role is pivotal in guiding this transformation, ensuring that libraries continue to be spaces of innovation, support and resilience. By prioritising the human elements of change – emotional wellbeing, clear communication and inclusive participation – we can make transitions manageable and meaningful, fostering environments where staff and patrons alike can thrive amidst change.

Exercises and reflective questions

Exercise for teams

Change journey mapping

Objective: to facilitate understanding and adaptation to change within the team.

Materials needed: sticky notes.

Procedure:

1 Gather the team: bring the team together in a comfortable setting.
2 Introduce the exercise: explain the purpose of mapping out the team's journey through the upcoming changes.
3 Create a timeline: draw an extensive timeline and mark the present moment and the anticipated end of the change process.
4 Identify key phases: using the Bridges Transition Model, identify the phases of 'Letting Go', 'Neutral Zone' and 'New Beginning'.
5 Share and map feelings: ask each team member to note their feelings, concerns and hopes at each phase on sticky notes and place them on the timeline.
6 Discuss and reflect: open the floor to discuss each stage's common feelings and concerns. Encourage team members to offer support and solutions to each other's concerns.
7 Develop action steps: based on the discussion, collectively decide on action steps to support each other through the change process.

8 Conclude with commitments: end the session with each team member committing to one way in which they will contribute positively to the team's journey through change.

Exercise for individuals
Personal reflection journalling
Objective: to help individuals process and adapt to change on a personal level.
Materials needed: journal or digital journalling tool.
Procedure:

1 Provide a journal: give each staff member a journal or encourage them to use a digital journalling tool.
2 Guided prompts: provide prompts based on Cognitive Dissonance Theory to explore their feelings about the change. Example prompts include:
   - 'What conflicting feelings do I have about the upcoming changes?'
   - 'How do these changes align with or challenge my beliefs about my role and the library?'
   - 'What are my concerns about these changes and what steps can I take to address them?'
3 Regular entries: encourage staff to make regular entries, especially during key moments of the change process.
4 Optional sharing: offer an opportunity for staff who are comfortable to share insights from their journals in team meetings or one-on-ones.

This and the previous exercise aim to support library teams and individuals in understanding and navigating the emotional aspects of change, fostering a supportive and resilient library environment.

Reflective questions
Here are a series of reflective questions for anyone experiencing change in a library setting:

- How do I feel about the changes happening in the library and what specific aspects are causing me the most concern or excitement?
- What can I learn from this change and how can it contribute to my personal and professional growth?
- How can I make this transition smoother for my colleagues and patrons?
- What strategies can I employ to adapt more effectively to these changes?

■ How can I maintain a positive and open mindset during this transition period?

CHAPTER 19

Kindness and Wellbeing in Libraries: A Vision for the Future

Introduction

As the world evolves, so must our libraries and how we support our staff. This final chapter explores the essential role of kindness and wellbeing in libraries as we move forward. By focusing on these values, we can enhance library staff's lives and positively impact the communities they serve.

As we conclude our book with this chapter, we understand that introducing kindness and wellbeing into libraries isn't just about changing routines but a more profound shift in mindset and culture. It challenges traditional methods and asks us to rethink how library staff work and interact. Though this journey has challenges, it leads to a more empathetic and supportive workplace, with benefits beyond the library's walls.

Looking to the future, this chapter not only reflects on what has been discussed throughout the book but sets a vision for the evolution of libraries. It's a call to action for libraries to pioneer a work culture where kindness and wellbeing are at the forefront, paving the way for a more inclusive and vibrant future for all who step through their doors. It guides library leaders and staff through the complexities and nuances of this transformation. It explores the shifting needs and expectations of a diverse, multi-generational workforce, the role of transformational leadership and the practicalities of implementing kindness initiatives in a dynamic environment. From understanding the unique perspectives of different generational cohorts to navigating the challenges of cultural change, we will provide insights and strategies to foster a culture where kindness and wellbeing are deeply ingrained values.

As libraries evolve, the focus on creating a supportive and nurturing work environment for staff becomes increasingly important. This chapter will highlight the long-term benefits of such an approach, not just for staff wellbeing but in enhancing the overall library experience for patrons. Through this journey, we envision libraries as centres of learning and information and beacons of kindness, empathy and community wellbeing.

Join us as we explore the transformative power of kindness and wellbeing in library cultures and how embracing these values can lead to a more cohesive, satisfied and effective library workforce ready to meet the challenges and opportunities of the future.

Reflective questions

- Evaluating the current library environment: reflect on how your library is adapting to the rapid social and technological changes. Are there areas where the library could better embrace these changes?
- Understanding the role of staff in transformation: consider how each staff member, including yourself, contributes to the library's culture. How can you personally contribute to making the library a more kind and supportive environment?
- Embracing change as opportunity: think about the concept of change within your library. How do you perceive change – as a challenge or an opportunity? What steps can you take to view change more positively?

The vision of kindness

The vision of kindness in this book recognises that the heart and soul of any library are its people: the library staff, volunteers and all those who work tirelessly behind the scenes. Through their actions, attitudes and interactions, a library can embody and spread the ethos of kindness.

Case Study 19.1: Introducing a new vision

Lancaster University Library developed a new vision in 2021. While not explicitly referencing kindness, the vision has a focus on inclusivity and engagement and co-creation with our communities.

Our vision has drawn upon the University's institutional values:

- We respect each other by being open and fair and promoting diversity.
- We build strong communities by working effectively together in a supportive way.
- We create positive change by being ambitious in our learning, expertise and action.

In response the Library has made a firm commitment to 'value the diverse backgrounds and talents of our staff and communities' and 'lead and champion activities that promote and celebrate openness and inclusivity'.

This has led to celebration and recognition events that have included displays and online resource collections, talks and seminars, film screenings, reading groups and open days. It has informed the development of our Community Card initiative, to open the University Library up to the wider local community and the development of Community Collections, with organisations such as Lancaster Black History Society. The strategic focus on positive change has led to the adoption of inclusive recruitment practices and work with refugee and asylum-seeker communities. The vision has empowered staff to make positive changes and engage with diverse communities across a broad range of the Library's work.

For more on Lancaster University Library's Towards 2025 Vision see www.lancaster.ac.uk/library/towards-2025.

Tim Leonard, Lancaster University

Central to this vision is nurturing a culture of kindness within the library workforce. This involves creating a work environment where staff members feel valued, supported and empowered. It means investing in their wellbeing, offering opportunities for professional development focused on empathy and compassionate service and fostering a team spirit that celebrates diversity and inclusivity.

Staff training plays a crucial role in this vision. Training programmes can be designed to enhance technical skills and cultivate emotional intelligence, active listening and conflict-resolution abilities. This equips library staff with the tools to engage with users empathetically, handle challenging situations gracefully and create a welcoming atmosphere for all.

The impact of a kindness-focused approach extends beyond the internal workings of the library. Staff who feel appreciated and supported are likelier to extend that sense of goodwill to library users. They become ambassadors of kindness, setting the tone for user interactions and influencing the library experience. These acts of kindness can significantly enhance user satisfaction and foster a strong sense of community through a warm greeting, patient help with a library resource or an understanding ear.

Incorporating kindness into performance metrics and recognition systems is another important aspect. Recognising and rewarding acts of kindness and exemplary service can motivate staff and reinforce the importance of these values. Celebrating stories of kindness within the library can inspire others and cultivate an environment where kindness is the norm.

Leadership in libraries plays a crucial role in championing this vision. Library leaders can model kindness through their actions and decisions, creating a ripple effect throughout the organisation. They can advocate policies and practices that prioritise staff wellbeing and foster a culture of kindness, from flexible work arrangements to support for mental health.

In essence, the vision of kindness in libraries, focusing on the people working in them, is about transforming libraries into spaces where kindness is as fundamental as the books on the shelves. It's about recognising that the true power of a library lies in its people and the connections they forge. By nurturing a culture of kindness among library staff, libraries can become beacons of warmth, compassion and community wellbeing.

Reflective questions
- Recognising the role of every individual: reflect on how your role, no matter what it is, contributes to your library's overall atmosphere of kindness. How do your actions, attitudes and interactions promote kindness?
- Assessing the work environment: think about your current work environment. Does it foster a sense of value, support and empowerment among the staff? What changes could be made to enhance this environment?

Understanding and buy-in: overcoming challenges in kindness initiatives for library staff

One of the foremost challenges in implementing kindness initiatives in libraries is securing deep understanding and buy-in from staff. Often, such initiatives might be perceived as secondary to the core responsibilities of library work, leading to scepticism about their relevance and effectiveness. To overcome this, it's essential to communicate clearly the multifaceted benefits of these initiatives. It's crucial to illustrate how users stand to benefit and how the staff themselves can experience positive impacts, such as improved workplace atmosphere and personal wellbeing.

Another significant challenge is effective training, particularly when resources are stretched thin. Developing and delivering training programmes that are both engaging and practical and that resonate with the daily experiences of library staff demands financial resources and specialised expertise. The aim is to equip staff with the skills and understanding necessary to integrate kindness into everyday interactions and duties.

Introducing new values like kindness and wellbeing into an established library culture often encounters resistance, especially as most people think they are kind. This resistance can stem from comfort with the status quo, apprehension about change or uncertainty about how these new values align with the library's mission. Addressing this resistance requires a sensitive and inclusive approach that respects existing cultures while gradually introducing new perspectives. Library staff typically operate under considerable workload and time pressures. Implementing new initiatives centred on kindness can be viewed as an added task rather than an integral part of their job. Integrating these initiatives into existing workflows and responsibilities is critical to avoiding additional strain on staff.

The diversity of library staff, in terms of roles, backgrounds and experiences, presents another challenge in developing universally relevant and effective kindness initiatives. Designing these programmes to be adaptable and sensitive to this wide range of needs and perspectives is essential.

The impact of kindness initiatives can be challenging to measure, especially when compared to more tangible library metrics like circulation numbers. The effects of kindness and wellbeing practices are often qualitative and manifest themselves over a longer term. Developing innovative metrics and recognition systems to gauge and acknowledge this impact is essential.

A further challenge is keeping the staff continuously engaged with kindness initiatives. There is a risk of such initiatives losing momentum and being perceived as temporary or non-essential. Maintaining enthusiasm and engagement requires ongoing efforts and regular updates to these initiatives. The effectiveness and adoption of kindness initiatives are significantly influenced by the support and example set by library leadership. Consistent and enthusiastic endorsement from leaders is crucial in embedding these values into the library culture.

Lastly, it is vital to balance fostering a culture of kindness and maintaining professional boundaries. Staff need guidance on effectively integrating kindness into their roles without overstepping boundaries or compromising professional standards.

By thoughtfully addressing these challenges and committing to strategic implementation, libraries can embed kindness and wellbeing into their organisational culture, positively impacting staff and the community they serve.

Balancing idealism with practical realities in library staff kindness initiatives

In the pursuit of integrating kindness and wellbeing practices in libraries, there's often a delicate balance to be struck between aspirational goals and practical realities, especially when it comes to library staff. This balance involves navigating the tension between the lofty vision of widespread kindness and the day-to-day practicalities of implementing such initiatives in a library setting.

Realistic goal setting for staff

While the aim to create a universally kind and empathetic library environment is noble, setting realistic goals is essential. Library staff operate in a dynamic environment with diverse user needs, limited resources and varying personal capacities. Initiatives should be designed with an understanding of these constraints, setting achievable targets that don't overburden staff.

Managing staff expectations

Staff expectations regarding kindness initiatives need to be managed effectively. There can be a risk of disillusionment if the initiatives are perceived as too ambitious or disconnected from the daily realities of library work. It's crucial to clearly communicate the objectives, potential impacts and limitations of these initiatives to the staff, ensuring everyone is on the same page.

Practical challenges in day-to-day operations

Library staff face numerous practical challenges in daily operations, from managing user inquiries to administrative tasks. Integrating kindness initiatives into this busy workflow requires thoughtful planning and flexibility. The initiatives should complement, rather than complicate, the staff's regular duties.

Resource allocation and prioritisation

Allocating resources for kindness initiatives, such as time for training or funds for programme development, must be balanced against other critical library functions. This requires strategic prioritisation, ensuring that resources are used efficiently and effectively to benefit staff and users.

Adapting initiatives to fit library culture

Every library has its unique culture and working environment. Kindness initiatives should be tailored to fit these specific contexts, considering the staff's existing values, practices and interactions. A one-size-fits-all approach is less likely to be successful.

Feedback loops and continuous improvement

It is vital to establish feedback mechanisms where staff can voice their experiences and suggestions regarding kindness initiatives. This feedback can help continuously refine and adapt the initiatives, ensuring they remain relevant and practical for the staff.

Community expectations and engagement

Managing community expectations is crucial. The library users should be aware of the kindness initiatives and their intended impact and limitations. Engaging the community in these initiatives can help align their expectations with what the library staff can realistically provide.

Sustaining long-term commitment

Finally, sustaining a long-term commitment to kindness and wellbeing in libraries requires patience and persistence. Staff should be encouraged and supported in their efforts, recognising that the journey towards a kinder library environment is ongoing and evolves.

By addressing these aspects, libraries can successfully navigate the gap between idealistic aspirations and the practical realities of their environments. This balanced approach ensures that kindness initiatives are inspiring and achievable, leading to sustainable and meaningful improvements in the library's culture and service.

Navigating cultural and institutional barriers in library staff kindness initiatives

Introducing kindness and wellbeing initiatives for library staff often involves navigating and transforming deeply ingrained institutional cultures and norms. These entrenched practices and beliefs can present significant barriers to change. With strategic approaches, it's possible to gradually shift these norms to embrace kindness and wellbeing.

Understanding existing cultural dynamics

The first step is to thoroughly understand the existing culture within the library. This includes recognising how current norms, values and behaviours among staff may support or hinder the adoption of kindness initiatives. It's important to identify aspects of the culture that are resistant to change and to understand the reasons behind this resistance, whether they be tradition, fear of change or lack of awareness.

Building a case for kindness initiatives

To overcome scepticism and resistance, it's crucial to clearly articulate the benefits of kindness initiatives for library staff. This might involve presenting research on the positive impacts of kindness on workplace morale, efficiency and staff retention. Demonstrating how these initiatives align with the library's overall mission and goals can help gain buy-in.

Engaging staff in the change process

Involving library staff in developing and implementing kindness initiatives can be a powerful strategy for overcoming cultural barriers. This participatory approach ensures that staff feel ownership over the changes and are more likely to support and engage with the initiatives. It allows for incorporating their insights and experiences, making the initiatives more relevant and effective.

Role modelling by library leadership

Leadership plays a crucial role in driving cultural change. When leaders actively model kindness and wellbeing behaviours, it sets a tone for the rest of the staff. Leadership should consistently demonstrate empathy, respect and concern for staff wellbeing, encouraging a trickle-down effect throughout the organisation.

Small steps leading to big changes

Cultural change is often most effective when it occurs gradually. Starting with small, manageable initiatives can help staff adjust to new ways of thinking and acting. Over time, these small changes can lead to significant shifts in the overall culture.

Creating safe spaces for discussion and feedback

Open communication is critical to navigating cultural barriers. Creating safe spaces where staff can express their concerns, share their ideas and provide feedback on kindness initiatives encourages a culture of openness and trust. Regular meetings, suggestion boxes or informal discussions can facilitate this dialogue.

Celebrating successes and learning from challenges

Acknowledging and celebrating the successes of kindness initiatives, even small ones, can help build momentum and enthusiasm. Equally important is openly addressing and learning from challenges or setbacks, showing a commitment to continuous improvement.

Continuous training and education

Offering ongoing training and education to library staff on kindness, emotional intelligence and wellbeing can help gradually shift cultural norms. This education should focus on the 'why' and the 'how' of incorporating these values into daily work.

By addressing these elements, libraries can effectively navigate and transform cultural and institutional barriers, creating a more conducive environment for adopting kindness and wellbeing initiatives among staff. This transformation benefits the team and positively impacts the service quality and the community's perception of the library.

The role of leadership in overcoming challenges in library kindness initiatives

Leadership plays a pivotal role in successfully implementing kindness initiatives in libraries. Several key strategies and insights can effectively guide these efforts.

Setting the tone for a culture of kindness

As a leader, one of the most impactful actions is to set the tone for the organisational culture. This involves explicitly prioritising kindness and wellbeing in both word and deed. Leaders can articulate the vision for these initiatives, making clear how they align with the library's broader goals and values. By openly discussing the importance of kindness, leaders can create an environment where such values are encouraged and expected.

Leading by example

The adage 'actions speak louder than words' holds particularly true in leadership. Demonstrating kindness and wellbeing behaviours in daily interactions sets a powerful example for staff. This could involve showing empathy and understanding in staff communications, actively participating in kindness initiatives or demonstrating work–life balance. Systemic team approaches can be invaluable here, providing a framework for understanding how individual behaviours can influence team dynamics.

Providing support and resources

Effective leadership involves providing staff with the necessary support and resources to engage with kindness initiatives. This might mean allocating time for staff to participate in relevant training, providing access to wellbeing resources or ensuring that staff have the tools to implement kindness in their work.

Fostering an environment of open communication

Encouraging open and honest communication is essential for any cultural change. Leaders can create platforms for staff to share their thoughts, concerns and ideas about kindness initiatives. This can help identify potential challenges, gather feedback and make staff feel valued and heard.

Recognising and celebrating acts of kindness

Acknowledging and celebrating acts of kindness within the library can reinforce the importance of these behaviours. Leaders can recognise individual or team contributions to kindness initiatives through formal recognition programmes or simple, everyday acknowledgements. This motivates staff and helps embed kindness as a valued part of the library culture.

Building and sustaining momentum

Maintaining enthusiasm and commitment to kindness initiatives over time can be challenging. Leaders can sustain momentum by regularly revisiting and reinforcing the importance of these initiatives, integrating them into regular meetings and setting ongoing goals.

Modelling resilience and adaptability

Finally, leading kindness initiatives often requires resilience and adaptability, especially when facing resistance or challenges. Challenging these difficulties with grace and a positive attitude can inspire staff to embrace change and overcome obstacles.

By applying these strategies, leaders can effectively navigate the challenges of implementing kindness initiatives in libraries, leveraging their experiences and skills to foster a culture that values and practises kindness and wellbeing. This leadership approach not only enhances the work environment for staff but positively impacts the services provided to the community.

Long-term engagement with kindness and wellbeing practices among library staff addressing challenges for a sustainable culture

Embedding kindness as a core value among library staff is a journey beyond mere actions; it requires a deep commitment to the principles of care and support. This means understanding that the role of library staff extends far beyond providing information; it involves fostering a nurturing and compassionate environment. To fully realise this vision, it's crucial to recognise and address underlying issues that impede the development of a kindness culture. Tackling challenges like workplace conflicts, communication breakdowns and any form of bias or exclusion is essential. Creating a genuinely kind culture demands facing these difficulties head-on through open dialogue, targeted training and thoughtful policy changes.

Engaging staff in kindness initiatives is vital for maintaining their enthusiasm and commitment. Regular discussions, emotional intelligence training and opportunities to share experiences of kindness help keep these values alive and relevant. Furthermore, celebrating kindness through recognition programmes reinforces these ideals and sustains motivation.

Integrating kindness into the daily routines of library staff is another key aspect. Simple practices like starting meetings with positive affirmations, fostering a culture of mutual support and dedicating time to reflect on and discuss acts of kindness can make a significant difference. These small but consistent actions help normalise kindness as part of the working day.

A supportive work environment is the bedrock of fostering kindness. Policies that promote work–life balance, mental health and an inclusive and respectful workplace are fundamental. It's essential that staff feel valued, heard and respected, creating an atmosphere where kindness can thrive.

Continuous learning and development in areas related to kindness and wellbeing are crucial to keep these concepts front and centre for staff. Providing access to workshops, seminars and resources on empathy, effective communication and self-care ensures that staff have the tools and knowledge to continue growing in these areas.

Regular feedback from staff regarding the impact and relevance of kindness initiatives is invaluable. This feedback should be used to adapt and evolve these programmes, enabling staff to actively shape their work environment and library culture.

Leadership plays a pivotal role in modelling and promoting kindness. Leaders who consistently demonstrate empathy and appreciation set a powerful example, fostering a kindness culture throughout the library.

While nurturing a kind environment, it's important to balance kindness with professional responsibilities. Staff should be encouraged to integrate kindness into their roles to enhance their primary job functions, ensuring that the ethos of kindness complements and enriches their professional duties.

By focusing on these critical areas and especially by addressing challenging issues, libraries can cultivate a sustainable, authentic culture of kindness and wellbeing. This approach benefits the staff and users, creating a more welcoming, empathetic and nurturing library environment.

Innovations in positive psychology for future library cultures
Evidence-based processes of change in positive psychology interventions

Innovative research in positive psychology emphasises a shift towards specific, evidence-based processes of change (Ciarrochi et al., 2021). In library settings, this approach can be transformative. By focusing on interventions that boost autonomous motivation, librarians can experience greater job satisfaction and personal fulfilment. Cognitive flexibility, another key component, enables librarians to adapt to changing work environments and challenges, fostering resilience and creativity. These interventions, when tailored to the unique demands and context of library work, not only enhance individual wellbeing but also contribute to a more supportive and dynamic library culture. Such tailored interventions could include workshops on emotional intelligence, mindfulness sessions to improve focus and mental agility or team-building exercises that strengthen interpersonal connections and collaboration skills. By integrating these evidence-based practices, libraries can create a workplace where wellbeing is not just an aspiration but a tangible outcome.

The third wave of positive psychology

The third wave of positive psychology integrates both the positive and negative aspects of life, considering the importance of context and cultural diversity (Lomas et al., 2020). Libraries can employ this holistic approach to balance professional challenges with positive experiences. This perspective highlights the need for strategies that appreciate the full spectrum of human experiences in the library profession.

Personalised interventions and contextual sensitivity

There is an increasing focus on creating personalised interventions in positive psychology, taking into account individual contexts and backgrounds (Hayes and Hofmann, 2018). In library environments, this means crafting interventions that are specifically suited to the needs and circumstances of library staff, effectively addressing unique workplace stressors and enhancing wellbeing.

As we explore positive psychology in libraries, it's clear that there's more to it than just the latest methods or looking at both the good and tough parts of life. This leads us to think about wellbeing in a bigger way. We move from just looking at mental wellbeing to considering all parts of a person's wellbeing, including their physical health, how they think, their workplace and their financial security. This is where the PERMA+4 model comes in. It takes the good parts of positive psychology and adds important areas like health, mindset and work conditions. This model helps us to see wellbeing in libraries as about the whole person, not just their mental health.

Evolving approaches to wellbeing

Wellbeing isn't static; the theories and models contributing to our under-standing constantly evolve. Part of our role as people practising kindness and wellbeing is to continue exploring them as concepts. For example, in our earlier discussions, we explored the PERMA model. This model emphasises five critical elements for achieving wellbeing: Positive emotion, Engagement, Relationships, Meaning and Accomplishment. Each component plays a crucial role in fostering an individual's sense of fulfilment and happiness, making it a valuable tool in understanding and enhancing wellbeing in various settings, including the workplace.

However, as research in psychology evolves, so too do our models for understanding wellbeing. The PERMA+4 model (Donaldson, van Zyl and Donaldson, 2021) adapts the original framework, taking into account new insights and societal shifts in our understanding of what constitutes wellbeing. This evolution is crucial in addressing the changing needs and perspectives of modern work environments.

The PERMA+4 framework, an evolution of Seligman's original PERMA model, integrates new elements into organisational contexts. While PERMA focuses on Positive emotions, Engagement, Relationships, Meaning and Accomplishments, PERMA+4 adds Physical Health, Mindset, Work Environment and Economic Security. These additional components acknowledge the integral role of physical health and a positive mindset in overall wellbeing. The framework underscores the interconnectedness of psychological wellbeing with physical health and proactive, optimistic mindsets, presenting a holistic approach to wellbeing in dynamic work environments like libraries. To apply the PERMA+4 framework in libraries, you can take several steps:

- Positive emotions: create an environment that promotes positivity through activities like team-building exercises or appreciation events.
- Engagement: encourage staff to engage in meaningful tasks that align with their skills and interests. This can be done through job crafting or providing opportunities for professional development.
- Relationships: foster strong interpersonal relationships among staff through team projects, social events and effective communication practices.
- Meaning: align work with purpose, like serving the community or contributing to educational goals.
- Accomplishments: recognise and celebrate staff achievements, both big and small.
- Physical Health: promote physical wellness with initiatives like ergonomic workspaces, regular health screenings or fitness programmes.
- Mindset: cultivate a growth mindset by encouraging learning, resilience and adaptability.

- Work environment: ensure a safe, comfortable, inviting library space that enhances productivity and wellbeing.
- Economic security: provide fair wages, benefits and financial planning and support resources.

Implementing these strategies can lead to a more engaged, healthy and productive library workforce.

In conclusion, the evolving approaches to wellbeing, particularly through the PERMA+4 model, represent a significant shift in understanding and fostering wellbeing in the workplace. This comprehensive framework emphasises the established psychological aspects of wellbeing and integrates crucial elements of physical health, mindset, work environment and economic security. By applying PERMA+4 in library settings, we can create a more holistic, supportive and dynamic culture that benefits the staff and enhances the overall library environment. This forward-thinking approach ensures that our practices remain relevant and effective in meeting the diverse needs of modern workplaces.

Ensuring positive departures: the importance of treating people well when they leave the library

The way staff members are treated when they leave their roles at a library profoundly impacts both the individual and the organisation's culture. Positive and respectful farewells are not just about kindness; they're strategic and impactful actions that reinforce a culture of respect and appreciation.

Positive farewells

Here's how libraries can ensure that departures are handled with grace and positivity, turning former staff into lasting champions of the library.

Celebrating departures as happy goodbyes

When someone leaves the library, it's essential to make their departure a happy and memorable occasion. Celebrating their achievements and expressing gratitude for their contributions reinforces their sense of value. Organising a farewell party or a small gathering allows colleagues to share good memories and offer best wishes, creating a positive final impression.

Conducting exit interviews with empathy

Exit interviews are crucial for understanding why staff members choose to move on. These discussions should be approached with care and empathy, allowing the departing individual to share their experiences and feedback honestly. This shows respect for their perspective and provides valuable information to improve the library's work environment.

Maintaining connections post-departure

Encouraging ongoing relationships with former staff members helps sustain a supportive community around the library. Inviting them to remain part of the library's extended network through social media or alumni events keeps these connections alive and fosters a sense of ongoing inclusion.

Celebrating former staff's future successes

Acknowledging and celebrating the future achievements of former staff reflects well on the library. Sharing their success stories can inspire current staff and highlight the library's role in their professional growth, enhancing its reputation as a nurturing and supportive workplace.

Providing ongoing support and mentoring

Even after their departure, offering guidance or mentorship to former staff demonstrates a genuine, ongoing commitment to their professional development. This can include career advice, professional references or just staying available for consultations.

Encouraging recommendations and referrals

Former staff who speak highly of their experience at the library are invaluable advocates. Encouraging them to refer potential candidates or spread positive word-of-mouth can significantly enhance the library's image and attract talented professionals.

Continuing to show care

Small gestures like sending birthday cards or acknowledging significant milestones of former staff show that the library values and remembers its shared history with them. These acts of kindness reinforce a lasting bond and show that the library cares about people, not just as employees but as individuals.

By implementing these practices, libraries can ensure that staff departures are handled with dignity and kindness, leaving a lasting positive impression. This approach turns departing staff into ambassadors of goodwill, spreading a positive image of the library and reinforcing its reputation as a caring, respectful and supportive workplace.

Digital transformation and wellbeing in libraries

The digital transformation in libraries, while streamlining services, can impact staff wellbeing in many ways. This transformation directly connects with the PERMA model (as introduced in Chapter 2), where Positive emotions can be fostered through a sense of accomplishment in mastering new digital tools. Engagement is enhanced when staff find meaningful connections between their traditional roles and new digital responsibilities.

Under the ASSET model, it's essential to consider how digital changes affect the psychosocial environment of the workplace. Open communication channels and a supportive community can mitigate the stress associated with learning and adapting to new technologies.

The Job Demands-Resources (JD-R) model is crucial in this context. The increased demands of digital literacy need to be balanced with resources like ongoing training, mentorship programmes and access to technical support. This balance is key to preventing burnout and enhancing job satisfaction. When staff are provided with the right tools and support, their ability to adapt to digital changes becomes a pathway to personal and professional growth, aligning with the Accomplishment aspect of the PERMA model.

By thoughtfully integrating these models, libraries can ensure that the digital transformation positively impacts staff wellbeing, reinforcing a culture of kindness and resilience. This approach not only enhances operational efficiency but also aligns with the core values of library services – fostering learning, growth and community engagement.

Evolving staff needs and expectations in the modern workforce: implications for library cultures

The landscape of the modern workforce is undergoing a significant transformation, influenced heavily by the influx of younger generations and evolving societal norms. This shift is characterised by changing employee needs and expectations. This trend holds specific implications for library staff and management.

Today's workforce, especially younger professionals, places a high premium on authentic, transformational leadership. This approach emphasises a leader's ability to inspire and motivate, fostering an environment where team members can reach their full potential. In the context of libraries, leaders must be equipped with a strong operational understanding and the ability to connect with staff on a personal and motivational level.

As Darby and Morrell's study (2019) highlighted, the modern workplace, including libraries, is now more likely than ever to comprise up to five different generations. Each generational group, from Baby Boomers to Generation Z, brings unique perspectives and expectations. Understanding these differences is crucial for library management, as it informs strategies for job satisfaction, decision-making and motivation tailored to diverse staff needs

Although a smaller segment of the workforce, Generation Z is asserting a strong preference for work–life integration and flexibility. This expectation is particularly relevant for libraries. They may need to reconsider their operational strategies to accommodate shorter working weeks or more flexible scheduling. Furthermore, Generation Z's expectation for employers to engage in corporate social responsibility aligns with the role of libraries as community-oriented institutions.

The trends identified by PwC (n.d.), including technological advancements and demographic shifts, suggest a future workforce that ranges from collective cultures prioritising social responsibility to more individualistic, demand-driven cultures. For libraries, this could mean adapting to a more digitally integrated service delivery or addressing the individualistic needs of both staff and patrons.

A more people-centric approach is becoming predominant in workforce management. This approach strongly emphasises holistic wellbeing, recognising its impact on staff engagement, motivation and productivity. In library settings, this translates to a greater focus on the health and overall wellbeing of the staff, balancing profitability and operational efficiency with the welfare of the individuals.

Libraries, characterised by their multi-generational staff and the evolving expectations around work–life balance and social responsibility, must be particularly sensitive to these workforce trends. Library leadership should strive to create an environment that respects and responds to these evolving needs, fostering a workplace culture that supports diverse generational requirements and aspirations.

In conclusion, libraries, like many other sectors, must navigate these changing workforce dynamics. Adapting to these shifts is not only critical for maintaining a cohesive, multi-generational workforce. Still, it is essential for aligning with broader societal and economic changes shaping the future of work. This adaptation will enable libraries to continue serving their communities effectively while ensuring a supportive and fulfilling work environment for their staff.

Concluding thoughts on the journey ahead: embedding kindness and wellbeing in library cultures for staff

As we reflect on the path towards embedding kindness and wellbeing into the heart of library cultures, particularly focusing on staff, it's important to recognise both the challenges and the profound rewards of this journey. Integrating kindness into libraries is not a simple or quick process; it requires a thoughtful, deliberate approach and a commitment to cultural change that can sometimes test our resolve.

While daunting at times, this journey holds the promise of transformation – not just for the staff but the entire library ecosystem. By fostering an environment of kindness and wellbeing, we create a space where staff feel valued, supported and empowered. This, in turn, enhances their ability to serve users with the same level of care and empathy, creating a ripple effect that extends into the broader community.

Patience and persistence are key virtues on this journey. Change, especially cultural change, takes time and consistent effort. It's important to celebrate small victories and learn from the challenges that inevitably arise. Each step forward, no matter how small, is a part of the larger transformation towards a more compassionate and supportive library environment.

Library leaders are now called upon to exhibit transformational leadership, going beyond traditional management to inspire and motivate a diverse workforce. This leadership style is essential in building a motivated, committed library staff. The presence of multiple generations in the workplace further adds complexity, necessitating tailored strategies to meet varied needs and expectations from Baby Boomers to Generation Z.

The aspirations of Generation Z, notably for work–life integration and social responsibility, align well with the evolving role of libraries as community-centric institutions. Libraries must adapt to these new expectations through flexible work arrangements and active community engagement. Simultaneously, future workforce trends such as digital transformation and demographic shifts will shape the library environment, requiring libraries to be agile and forward-thinking in their approach.

The long-term benefits of creating kinder library environments are immense. For staff, working in a culture that values their wellbeing and encourages kindness can lead to greater job satisfaction, lower stress levels and a stronger sense of community and belonging. A kind and empathetic library staff enhances users' experience, making the library a welcoming and nurturing space for all.

In conclusion, the journey towards embedding kindness and wellbeing in library cultures requires vision, dedication and a deep understanding of the transformative power of kindness. It's a journey well worth undertaking, promising a future where libraries are not just places of learning and information but beacons of kindness and wellbeing for the people who work in them and their communities. Welcome to the kindness revolution.

Exercises and reflective questions

Exercise for teams

Kindness and wellbeing reflection and action plan

Objective: to offer a comprehensive, reflective exercise for library staff to encapsulate the learnings from the entire book and to create a personalised action plan for continuing the journey of kindness and wellbeing in their professional and personal lives.

Overview: this exercise serves as a capstone for the book, allowing participants to reflect on the entire journey, identify key takeaways and plan specific actions to embed these concepts into their everyday practices.

Steps:

1 Reflective writing: each participant writes a brief reflection on their key takeaways from the book. Prompts could include:
   - 'What are the most impactful lessons you've learned about kindness and wellbeing?'
   - 'How have your views on kindness in the workplace changed?'
   - 'Describe a moment during this journey that was particularly enlightening or transformative for you.'
2 Group discussion:
   - Organise a group session where participants share their reflections. This can be done in person or virtually.
   - Encourage open and respectful listening and discuss emerging common themes or surprising insights.
3 Personal action plan: each participant creates a personal action plan. This plan should include:
   - specific kindness and wellbeing goals they want to achieve in their role
   - practical steps to implement these goals
   - how do they intend to measure or reflect on their progress?
4 Peer review: pair up participants to review each other's action plans. This peer review process provides an opportunity for constructive feedback and mutual support.
5 Commitment pledge: conclude the exercise with a commitment pledge, where each staff member commits to their action plan and shares one key aspect with the group.

6 Regular check-ins: schedule periodic check-ins as a group or with a peer
   partner to discuss progress and challenges and recalibrate the action
   plans as necessary.
   Benefits:
   ■ Promotes deep integration of the book's concepts into daily practice.
   ■ Fosters a community of support and accountability among library
     staff.
   ■ Encourages continuous personal and professional development in the
     realms of kindness and wellbeing.
   ■ Strengthens the library's culture by embedding these values at an
     individual level.

Exercise for individuals
Personal kindness and wellbeing roadmap
Objective: to enable individuals to internalise and apply the principles of
   kindness and wellbeing from the book in their personal and professional
   lives.
Overview: this self-guided exercise is designed for individual library staff
   members to reflect on their journey through the book, identify personal
   insights and lessons learned and create a tailored roadmap for
   integrating kindness and wellbeing into their daily routines.
Steps:

1 Personal reflection:
   ■ Allocate quiet time for personal reflection.
   ■ Use prompts such as:
   — 'What key lessons about kindness and wellbeing resonated with me?'
   — 'How have these concepts influenced my perspective on work and
     personal life?'
   — 'Recall a moment where practising kindness or wellbeing made a
     difference in your day'.
2 Writing a personal vision statement: craft a personal vision statement
   focusing on how you envision integrating kindness and wellbeing into
   your life. This should be inspiring, clear and achievable.
3 Setting specific goals: identify specific, measurable goals related to
   kindness and wellbeing. These could be daily, weekly or monthly goals,
   like performing a kind act each day or dedicating time weekly for self-
   care.
4 Developing an action plan:
   ■ For each goal, outline concrete steps or actions to achieve it. Include
     timelines or regular checkpoints to assess progress.

- Consider potential obstacles and think about strategies to overcome them.
5 Journalling:
    - Keep a regular journal to document your experiences, challenges, successes and reflections as you implement your roadmap.
    - This can serve as a tool for self-reflection and tracking progress.
6 Seeking feedback: share your goals and progress with a trusted colleague, friend or mentor. Their insights can provide additional perspectives and encouragement.
7 Periodic review and adaptation: set a regular interval (e.g., monthly or quarterly) to review your roadmap. Reflect on what's working and what's not and make adjustments as needed.
    Benefits:
    - Encourages a deep, personal engagement with the concepts of kindness and wellbeing.
    - Fosters self-awareness and personal growth.
    - Helps in translating abstract concepts into tangible actions and habits.
    - Creates a sense of personal accountability and progress in cultivating a kinder, more mindful approach to life and work.

Reflective questions

- Evaluating the importance of kindness and wellbeing in library culture: reflect on your personal experiences in the library. How have acts of kindness and wellbeing initiatives impacted the atmosphere and efficiency of the library?
- Personal contribution to cultural transformation: in what ways do you think your behaviour and attitude contribute to the culture of kindness and wellbeing in your library? Can you identify any areas for personal growth in this regard?
- Adapting to generational shifts: consider the diverse generational mix within your library staff. How can you adapt your approach to kindness and wellbeing to be inclusive and effective across different age groups?
- Leadership's role in fostering kindness: how do you perceive the role of library leadership in promoting and embedding a culture of kindness and wellbeing? Are there any actions or policies you believe could enhance their effectiveness?
- Vision for the future: imagine your library in five years, thriving in an environment where kindness and wellbeing are deeply embedded. What changes do you see and how do you see yourself contributing to this vision?

References and Further Reading

4 Day Week Global (n.d.) *The 4 Day Week UK Pilot Programme Results*, www.4dayweek.com/uk-pilot-results.

Abraham, M., Kaliannan, M., Avvari, M. V. and Thomas, S. (2023) Reframing Talent Acquisition, Retention Practices for Organisational Commitment in Malaysian SMEs: A Managerial Perspective, *Journal of General Management*, June, https://doi.org/10.1177/03063070231184336.

Aguilera-Hermida, A. P. (2020) College Students' Use and Acceptance of Emergency Online Learning due to COVID-19, *International Journal of Educational Research Open*, **1**, 100011.

Ahmad, G. and Klotz, A. C. (2020) Can Good Followers Create Unethical Leaders? How Follower Citizenship Leads to Leader Moral Licensing and Unethical Behavior, *Journal of Applied Psychology*, **106** (9), https://doi.org/10.1037/apl0000839.

Algoe, S. B., Fredrickson, B. L. and Gable, S. L. (2013) The Social Functions of the Emotion of Gratitude via Expression, *Emotion*, **13** (4), 605–9, https://doi.org/10.1037/a0032701.

Allen, K.-A., Svendsen, G. T., Marwan, S. and Arslan, G. (2021) Trust and Belonging in Individual and Organizational Relationships. In Camilleri, M. A. (ed.) *Strategic Corporate Communication in the Digital Age*, 19–31, Emerald Publishing, https://doi.org/10.1108/978-1-80071-264-520211002.

Association for Mindfulness in Education (n.d.) *What Is Mindfulness?*, www.mindfuleducation.org/what-is-mindfulness.

Bakker, A. B. and Demerouti, E. (2007) The Job Demands-Resources Model: State of the Art, *Journal of Managerial Psychology*, **22** (3), 309–28, https://doi.org/10.1108/02683940710733115.

Bass, B. M. (1999) Two Decades of Research and Development in Transformational Leadership, *European Journal of Work and Organizational Psychology*, **8** (1), 9–32, https://doi.org/10.1080/135943299398410.

Bass, B. M. and Avolio, B. J. (eds) (1994) *Improving Organizational Effectiveness Through Transformational Leadership*, SAGE.

Bass, B. M. and Riggio, R. E. (2006) *Transformational Leadership*, 2nd edn, Psychology Press.

Batson, C. D. (2006) Folly Bridges. In Van Lange, P. A. M. (ed.) *Bridging Social Psychology: Benefits of Transdisciplinary Approaches*, 59–64, Lawrence Erlbaum.

Bolino, M. C., Klotz, A. C. and Turnley, W. H. (2018) The Unintended Consequences of Organizational Citizenship Behaviors for Employees, Teams and Organizations. In Podsakoff, P. M., Mackenzie, S. B. and Podsakoff, N. P. (eds) *The Oxford Handbook of Organizational Citizenship Behavior*, 185–202, Oxford University Press.

Booth, D. and Masayuki, H. (eds) (2004) *The Arts Go to School: Classroom-Based Activities that Focus on Music, Painting, Drama, Movement, Media and More*, Pembroke Publishers.

Borntrager, C., Caringi, J. C., van den Pol, R., Crosby, L., O'Connell, K., Trautman, A. and McDonald, M. (2012) Secondary Traumatic Stress in School Personnel, *Advances in School Mental Health Promotion*, **5** (1), 38–50, https://doi.org/10.1080/1754730X.2012.664862.

Bridges, W. and Bridges, S. (2009) *Managing Transitions: Making the Most of Change*, 3rd edn, Da Capo Press/Perseus.

Brown, M. E. and Treviño, L. K. (2006) Ethical Leadership: A Review and Future Directions, *The Leadership Quarterly*, **17** (6), 595–616.

Buffer (2021) *State of Remote Work 2021*, https://buffer.com/state-of-remote-work/2021.

Business in the Community (2019) The Business in the Community Workwell Model, www.bitc.org.uk/the-wellbeing-workwell-model.

Calder, L. (n.d.) *The Essential Pema: Study Guide to the Writings of Pema Chödrön*, https://pemachodronfoundation.org/articles/the-essential-pema-study-guide.

Çalışkan, Ö. and Gökalp, G. (2020) A Micro-Level Perspective in Organizational Change: Cognitive Dissonance, Sense-Making and Attitude Change, *Educational Administration: Theory and Practice*, **26** (4), 719–41.

Cameron, K. (2011) Responsible Leadership as Virtuous Leadership, *Journal of Business Ethics*, **98** (S1), 25–35.

Cameron, K. S. and Caza, A. (2004) Contributions to the Discipline of Positive Organizational Scholarship, *American Behavioral Scientist*, **47** (6), 731–9.

Cameron, K. S. and Quinn, R. E. (2011) *Diagnosing and Changing Organizational Culture: Based on the Competing Values Framework*, Jossey-Bass.

Cameron, K. S. and Spreitzer, G. M. (eds) (2012) *The Oxford Handbook of Positive Organizational Scholarship*, Oxford University Press.

Canterbury Christ Church University (2023) *We Have Said, Goodbye to Library Fines, Now We Say 'Adieu To Administration Fees Too'*, https://blogs.canterbury.ac.uk/library/we-have-said-goodbye-to-library-fines-now-we-say-adieu-to-administration-fees-too.

Carlson, N. R. (1998) *Physiology of Behavior*, Allyn & Bacon.

Ciarrochi, J., Hayes, S. C., Oades, L. G. and Hofmann, S. G. (2021) Toward a Unified Framework for Positive Psychology Interventions: Evidence-Based Processes of Change in Coaching, Prevention and Training, *Frontiers in Psychology*, **12**, 809362, https://doi.org/10.3389/fpsyg.2021.809362.

CIPD (2022) *Bullying and Incivility at Work: An Evidence Review*, www.cipd.org./uk/knowledge/evidence-reviews/evidence-bullying-and - incivility-at-work.

Coghlan, D. and Brydon-Miller, M. (2014) *The SAGE Encyclopedia of Action Research*, vol. 2, SAGE, http://dx.doi.org/10.4135/9781446294406.

Condon, P., Desbordes, G., Miller, W. B. and DeSteno, D. (2013) Meditation Increases Compassionate Responses to Suffering, *Psychological Science*, **24** (10), 2125–7, https://doi.org/10.1177/0956797613485603.

Corredor, J. M. (1957) *Conversations with Casals*, 1st edn, E. P. Dutton & Co.

Curry, O. S., Rowland, L. A., Van Lissa, C. J., Zlotowitz, S., McAlaney, J. and Whitehouse, H. (2018) Happy to Help? A Systematic Review and Meta-Analysis of the Effects of Performing Acts of Kindness on the Wellbeing of the Actor, *Journal of Experimental Social Psychology* **76** (May), 320–9, https://doi.org/10.1016/j.jesp.2018.02.014.

Dal Cason, D., Casini, A. and Hellemans, C. (2020) Moral Courage Fostering Bystander Intervention Against Workplace Bullying: Findings from an Exploratory Study with a Video-Vignette Procedure, *International Journal of Bullying Prevention*, **2** (1), 53–64, https://doi.org/10.1007/s42380-020-00062-7.

Darby, V. and Morrell, D. L. (2019) Generations at Work: A Review of Generational Traits and Motivational Practices Impacting Millennial Employees, *Drake Management Review*, **8** (1&2), https://escholarshare.drake.edu/server/api/core/bitstreams/a1bcab73-5678-40e9-ab8d-0576d2e7717e/content.

Davis, M. H., Luce, C. and Kraus, S. J. (1994) The Heritability of Characteristics Associated with Dispositional Empathy, *Journal of Personality*, **62**, 369–91.

Deci, E. L. and Ryan, R. M. (2000) The 'What' and 'Why' of Goal Pursuits: Human Needs and the Self-Determination of Behavior, *Psychological Inquiry*, **11** (4), 227–68.

Deery, S., Iverson, R. and Walsh, J. (2002) Work Relationships in Telephone Call Centres: Understanding Emotional Exhaustion and Employee Withdrawal, *Journal of Management Studies*, **39** (40), 471–96.

Demerouti, E., Bakker, A. B., Nachreiner, F. and Schaufeli, W. B. (2001) The Job Demands-Resources Model of Burnout, *Journal of Applied Psychology*, **86** (3), 499–512.

Diener, E. (2000) Subjective Wellbeing: The Science of Happiness and a Proposal for a National Index, *American Psychologist*, **55** (1), 34–43.

Donaldson, S. I., van Zyl, L. E. and Donaldson, S. I. (2021) PERMA+4: A Framework for Work-Related Wellbeing: Performance and Positive Organizational Psychology 2.0, *Frontiers in Psychology*, **12**, 817244, https://doi.org/10.3389/fpsyg.2021.817244.

Dovidio, J. F. and Penner, L. A. (2003) Helping and Altruism. In Fletcher, G. J. O. and Clark, M. S. (eds) *Blackwell Handbook of Social Psychology: Interpersonal Processes*, 162–95, Wiley, https://doi.org/10.1002/9780470998557.ch7.

Downton, J. V. (1973) *Rebel Leadership: Commitment and Charisma in a Revolutionary Process*, Free Press.

Drummond, A. (2010) 'Jack of All Trades and Master of None': The Future of Occupational Therapy?, The Elizabeth Casson Memorial Lecture 2010, *British Journal of Occupational Therapy*, **73** (7), 292–9, https://doi.org/10.4276/030802210X12759925544263.

Edmondson, A. C. (1999) Psychological Safety and Learning Behavior in Work Teams, *Administrative Science Quarterly*, **44** (2), 350–83.

Edmondson, A. C. (2004) Learning from Mistakes is Easier Said than Done: Group and Organizational Influences on the Detection and Correction of Human Error, *The Journal of Applied Behavioral Science*, **40** (1), 66–90, https://doi.org/10.1177/0021886304263849.

Einarsen, K., Nielsen, M. B., Hetland, J., Olsen, O. K., Zahlquist, L., Mikkelsen, E. G., Koløen, J. and Einarsen, S. V. (2020) Outcomes of a Proximal Workplace Intervention Against Workplace Bullying and Harassment: A Protocol for a Cluster Randomized Controlled Trial Among Norwegian Industrial Workers, *Frontiers in Psychology*, **11**, 2013, https://doi.org/10.3389/fpsyg.2020.02013.

Engert, V., Plessow, F., Miller, R., Kirschbaum, C. and Singer, T. (2014) Cortisol Increase in Empathic Stress is Modulated by Emotional Closeness and Observation Modality, *Psychoneuroendocrinology*, **45** (July), 192–201, https://doi.org/10.1016/j.psyneuen.2014.04.005.

Ettarh, F. (2018) Vocational Awe and Librarianship: The Lies We Tell Ourselves, *In the Library with the Lead Pipe*, www.inthelibrarywiththeleadpipe.org/2018/vocational-awe.

Fair Library Jobs – Manifesto (2024) https://sites.google.com/view/fairlibraryjobs/manifesto.

Festinger, L. (1957) *A Theory of Cognitive Dissonance*, Stanford University Press.

Figley, C. R. (ed.) (2002) *Treating Compassion Fatigue*, Brunner-Routledge, https://doi.org/10.4324/9780203890318.

Frankl, V. E. (1946) *Man's Search for Meaning*, Beacon Press.

Frankl, V. E. (1985 [1963]) *Man's Search for Meaning*, Pocket Books.

Fredrickson, B. L. (2001) The Role of Positive Emotions in Positive Psychology: The Broaden-and-Build Theory of Positive Emotions, *American Psychologist*, **56** (3), 218–26.

Fredrickson, B. L. (2013) Positive Emotions Broaden and Build. In Devine, P. and Plant, A. (eds) *Advances in Experimental Social Psychology*, Vol. 47, 1–53, Academic Press, https://doi.org/10.1016/B978-0-12-407236-7.00001-2.

Frei, F. X. and Morriss, A. (2020) Begin with Trust, *Harvard Business Review*, **98** (3), 112–21.

Freire, P. (1996) *Pedagogy of the Oppressed*, 2nd edn, Penguin.

Friedman, H. S. and Riggio, R. E. (1981) Effect of Individual Differences in Nonverbal Expressiveness on Transmission of Emotion, *Journal of Nonverbal Behavior*, **6** (2), 96–104, https://doi.org/10.1007/BF00987285.

Gautrey, B. (ed.) (2022) *UK's Best Workplaces 2022*, Redactive Media Group.

Goetz, J. L., Keltner, D. and Simon-Thomas, E. (2010) Compassion: An Evolutionary Analysis and Empirical Review, *Psychological Bulletin*, **136** (3), 351–74, https://doi.org/10.1037/a0018807.

Goleman, D. (1998) *Working with Emotional Intelligence*, Bantam Books.

Goleman, D. (2017) Leadership That Gets Results. In Hooper, A. (ed.) *Leadership Perspectives*, Routledge, 85–96, https://doi.org/10.4324/9781315250601-9.

GoodHire (2021) *The State of Remote Work in 2021 Survey*, www.goodhire.com/resources/articles/state-of-remote-work-survey.

Gouldner, A. W. (1960) The Norm of Reciprocity: A Preliminary Statement, *American Sociological Review*, **25** (2), 161–78.

Graen, G. B. and Scandura, T. A. (1987) Toward a Psychology of Dyadic Organizing, *Research in Organizational Behavior*, **9**, 175–208.

Graen, G. B. and Uhl-Bien, M. (1995) Relationship-Based Approach to Leadership: Development of Leader-Member Exchange (LMX) Theory of Leadership Over 25 Years: Applying a Multi-Level Multi-Domain Perspective, *Leadership Quarterly*, **6** (2), 219–47, https://doi.org/10.1016/1048-9843(95)90036-5.

Greenhaus, J. H. and Allen, T. D. (2011) Work–Family Balance: A Review and Extension of the Literature. In *Handbook of Occupational Health Psychology*, 2nd edn, 165–83, American Psychological Association.

Greenhaus, J. H., Collins, K. M., Singh, R. and Parasuraman, S. (1997) Work and Family Influences on Departure from Public Accounting, *Journal of Vocational Behavior*, **50** (2), 249–70.

Greenleaf, R. (2007) The Servant as Leader. In *Corporate Ethics and Corporate Governance*, 79–85, Springer, https://doi.org/10.1007/978-3-540-70818-6_6.

Gross, C. (2023) A Better Approach to Mentorship, *Harvard Business Review*, https://hbr.org/2023/06/a-better-approach-to-mentorship.

Haimé, S. (2023) Navigating Whiteness and Reflecting on Identity, Vocational Awe and Allyship in Hegemonic Library Cultures, *UKSG Newsletter*, www.uksg.org/newsletter/uksg-enews-534/navigating-whiteness-and-reflecting-identity-vocational-awe-and-allyship.

Hart, R. (2021) *Positive Psychology: The Basics*, Routledge.

Hayes, S. C. and Hofmann, S. G. (2018) *Process-Based CBT: The Science and Core Clinical Competencies of Cognitive Behavioral Therapy*, New Harbinger Publications.

Heine, S. J., Proulx, T. and Vohs, K. D. (2006) The Meaning Maintenance Model: On the Coherence of Social Motivations, *Personality and Social Psychology Review*, **10** (2), 88–110, https://doi.org/10.1207/s15327957pspr1002_1.

Himmelstein, D. (2020) As Compassion Fatigue Takes its Toll, Schools and Public Libraries Take Steps to Support Librarians, *School Library Journal*, 19 February, www.slj.com/story/as-compassion-fatigue-takes-its-toll-schools-public-libraries-take-steps-to-support-librarians.

Hobfoll, S. E. (1989) Conservation of Resources: A New Attempt at Conceptualizing Stress, *American Psychologist*, **44** (3), 513–24, https://doi.org/10.1037/0003-066X.44.3.513.

Hochschild, A. (1983) *The Managed Heart: Commercialization of Human Feeling*, University of California Press.

Howard, K. L. (1989) *Rusting Out, Burning Out, Bowing Out: Stress and Survival on the Job*, Gage Distribution Co.

Howington, J. (n.d.) *Remote Work Statistics and Trends: The Latest in Remote Work*, Flexjobs, www.flexjobs.com/blog/post/remote-work-statistics.

Huhtala, M., Kaptein, M., Muotka, J. and Feldt, T. (2022) Longitudinal Patterns of Ethical Organisational Culture as a Context for Leaders' Wellbeing: Cumulative Effects Over 6 Years, *Journal of Business Ethics*, **177** (2), 421–42.

Hydon, S., Wong, M., Langley, A. K., Stein, B. D. and Kataoka, S. H. (2015) Preventing Secondary Traumatic Stress in Educators, *Child and Adolescent Psychiatric Clinics of North America*, **24** (2), 319–33, https://doi.org/10.1016/J.CHC.2014.11.003.

Innovative Workplace Institute (n.d.) Workplace Wellbeing Assessment: PROWELL, www.innovativeworkplaceinstitute.org/workplace-wellbeing-prowell.php.

Ishaq, M. and Hussain, A. M. (2022) Do Black Employees' Rights Matter? The Lived Experience of BAME Staff in UK Academic Libraries. In Crilly, J. and Everitt, R. (eds) *Narrative Expansions: Interpreting Decolonisation in Academic Libraries*, 39–55, Facet Publishing.

Ivanov, A., Sharman, R. and Rao, H. R. (2015) Exploring Factors Impacting Sharing Health-Tracking Records, *Health Policy and Technology*, **4** (3), 263–76, https://doi.org/10.1016/j.hlpt.2015.04.008.

Jaeger, P. T., Bertot, J. C., Thompson, K. M., Katz, S. M. and DeCoster, E. J. (2012) The Intersection of Public Policy and Public Access: Digital Divides, Digital Literacy, Digital Inclusion and Public Libraries, *Public Library Quarterly*, **31** (1), 1–20, https://doi.org/10.1080/01616846.2012.654728.

Janaway, C. (1999) Schopenhauer's Pessimism, *Royal Institute of Philosophy Supplement*, **44** (March), 47–63, https://doi.org/10.1017/S1358246100006664.

Jensen, J. M. and Raver, J. L. (2021) A Policy Capturing Investigation of Bystander Decisions to Intervene against Workplace Incivility, *Journal of Business and Psychology*, **36** (5), 883–901, https://doi.org/10.1007/s10869-020-09712-5.

Jung, C. G. (1933) *Modern Man in Search of a Soul*, trans. Dell, W. S. and Baynes, C. F., Harcourt Brace Jovanovich

Kahn, W. A. (1990) Psychological Conditions of Personal Engagement and Disengagement at Work, *Academy of Management Journal*, **33** (4), 692–724.

Keltner, D. and Haidt, J. (1999) Social Functions of Emotions at Four Levels of Analysis, *Cognition and Emotion*, **13** (5), 505–21.

Keltner, D., Kogan, A., Piff, P. K. and Saturn, S. R. (2014) The Sociocultural Appraisals, Values, and Emotions (SAVE) Framework of Prosociality: Core Processes from Gene to Meme, *Annual Review of Psychology*, **65**, 425–60.

Keyes, C. L. M. (1998) Social Wellbeing, *Social Psychology Quarterly*, **61**, 121–40, http://dx.doi.org/10.2307/2787065.

Kinetiq (2023) *Workforce Mapping 2023*, CILIP, 14 June, www.cilip.org.uk/page/workforcemapping.

Klimecki, O. M. (2019) The Role of Empathy and Compassion in Conflict Resolution, *Emotion Review*, **11** (4), 310–25, https://doi.org/10.1177/1754073919838609.

Kogan, A., Oveis, C., Carr, E. W., Gruber, J., Mauss, I. B., Shallcross, A., Impett, E. A., van der Lowe, I., Hui, B. and Keltner, D. (2014) Vagal Activity is Quadratically Related to Prosocial Traits, Prosocial Emotions, and Observer Perceptions of Prosociality, *Journal of Personality and Social Psychology*, **107** (6), 1051.

Kooij, D. T., De Lange, A. H., Jansen, P. G., Kanfe, R. and Dikkers, J. S. (2011) Age and Work-Related Motives: Results of a Meta-Analysis, *Journal of Organizational Behavior*, **32** (2), 197–225.

Kotter, J. P. (1996) *Leading Change*, Harvard Business School Press.

Latané, B. and Rodin, J. (1969) A Lady in Distress: Inhibiting Effects of Friends and Strangers on Bystander Intervention, *Journal of Experimental Social Psychology*, **5** (2), 189–202.

Leary-Joyce, J. and Lines, H. (2018) *Systemic Team Coaching*, Aoec Press.

Leung, S. Y. and Lopez-McKnight, J. R. (2021) *Knowledge Justice*, MIT Press.

Lewin, K., Lippitt, R. and White, R. (1939) Patterns of Aggressive Behavior in Experimentally Created Social Climates, *Journal of Social Psychology*, **10** (2), 269–99.

Lewis, J., Hopkins, R., Drabwell, L. and Standfield, L. (2022) *The Future of Wellbeing 2022: Insights from C-Suite and Risk Managers on the Front Line*, Deloitte.

Lomas, T., Waters, L., Williams, P., Oades, L. G. and Kern, M. L. (2020) Third Wave Positive Psychology: Broadening Towards Complexity, *Journal of Positive Psychology*, August, 1–15, https://doi.org/10.1080/17439760.2020.1805501.

London, M. (2003) *Job Feedback: Giving, Seeking and Using Feedback for Performance Improvement*, Lawrence Erlbaum Associates.

Luthans, F. (2002) The Need for and Meaning of Positive Organizational Behavior, *Journal of Organizational Behavior*, **23** (6), 695–706, https://doi.org/10.1002/job.165.

Luthans, F. and Church, A. (2002) Positive Organizational Behavior: Developing and Managing Psychological Strengths, *Academy of Management Executive*, **16** (1), 57–72, https://doi.org/10.5465/AME.2002.6640181.

Luthans, F., Youssef, C. M. and Avolio, B. J. (2007) Psychological Capital: Investing and Developing Positive Organizational Behavior, *Positive Organizational Behavior*, **1** (2), 9–24.

Lyubomirsky, S., King, L. and Diener, E. (2005) The Benefits of Frequent Positive Affect: Does Happiness Lead to Success? *Psychological Bulletin*, **131** (6), 803–55.

Lyubomirsky, S., Sheldon, K. M. and Schkade, D. (2005) Pursuing Happiness: The Architecture of Sustainable Change, *Review of General Psychology*, **9** (2), 111–31, https://doi.org/10.1037/1089-2680.9.2.111.

Malti, T. (2020) Kindness: A Perspective from Developmental Psychology, *European Journal of Developmental Psychology*, **18** (5), 629–57, https://doi.org/10.1080/17405629.2020.1837617.

Marcum, T. and Young, J. (2019) Blowing the Whistle in the Digital Age: Are You Really Anonymous? The Perils and Pitfalls of Anonymity in Whistleblowing Law, *De Paul Business and Commercial Law Journal*, **17** (1), 1–38.

Martela, F. and Steger, M. F. (2016) The Three Meanings of Meaning in Life: Distinguishing Coherence, Purpose and Significance, *Journal of Positive Psychology*, **11** (5), 531–45.

Maslow, A. H. (1943) A Theory of Human Motivation, *Psychological Review*, **50** (4), 370–96.

Metz, T. (2021) The Meanings of God: Reply to Four Critics, *International Journal of Philosophy and Theology*, **82** (4–5), 366–74, https://doi.org/10.1080/21692327.2021.2020151.

Meyer, P. (1960) The Wheel of Life, www.pauljmeyer.com.

Miller, J. L. (2017) Managing Transitions: Using William Bridges' Transition Model and a Change Style Assessment Instrument to Inform Strategies and Measure Progress in Organizational Change Management, *Scholarship and Professional Work*, **74**, https://digitalcommons.butler.edu/librarian_papers/74.

Monroe, C., Loresto, F., Horton-Deutsch, S., Kleiner, C., Eron, K., Varney, R. and Grimm, S. (2021) The Value of Intentional Self-Care Practices: The Effects of Mindfulness on Improving Job Satisfaction, Teamwork and Workplace Environments, *Archives of Psychiatric Nursing*, **35** (2), 189–94, https://doi.org/10.1016/j.apnu.2020.10.003.

Mor Barak, M. E. (2014) *Managing Diversity: Toward a Globally Inclusive Workplace*, SAGE.

Neeley. T. (2021) *Back to the Office? The Future of Remote and Hybrid Work, with Tsedal Neeley, PhD*, www.apa.org/news/podcasts/speaking-of-psychology/remote-hybrid-work.

Neff, K. D. (2003a) The Development and Validation of a Scale to Measure Self-Compassion, *Self and Identity*, **2**, 223 50.

Neff, K. D. (2003b) Self-Compassion: An Alternative Conceptualization of a Healthy Attitude Toward Oneself, *Self and Identity*, **2**, 85–101.

NHS (n.d.) *Reframing Unhelpful Thoughts – Self-Help CBT Techniques – Every Mind Matters*, www.nhs.uk/every-mind-matters/mental-wellbeing-tips/self-help-cbt-techniques/reframing-unhelpful-thoughts.

Paakkanen, M., Martela, F., Hakanen, J., Uusitalo, L. and Pessi, A. (2021) Awakening Compassion in Managers – a New Emotional Skills Intervention to Improve Managerial Compassion, *Journal of Business and Psychology*, **36** (6), 1095–108.

Palmer-Trew, S. and Jayes, J. (2022) *The Everyday Change Play Book: Because Change Doesn't Need to be Shit*, independently published.

Pearson, C. M. and Porath, C. L. (2005) On the Nature, Consequences and Remedies of Workplace Incivility: No Time for 'Nice'? Think Again, *Academy of Management Perspectives*, **19** (1), 7–18, https://doi.org/10.5465/ame.2005.15841946.

Penner, L. A., Dovidio, J. F., Piliavin, J. A. and Schroeder, D. A. (2005) Prosocial Behavior: Multilevel Perspectives, *Annual Review of Psychology*, **56**, 365–92.

Penner, L. A. and Orom, H. (2010) Enduring Goodness: A Person X Situation Perspective on Prosocial Behavior. In Mikulincer, M. and Shaver, P. R. (eds) *Prosocial Motives, Emotions and Behavior: The Better Angels of Our Nature*, American Psychological Association, 55–72.

Perkins, D. N. (2009) *Making Learning Whole: How Seven Principles of Teaching Can Transform Education*, Jossey-Bass.

Petek, M. (2018) Stress Among Reference Library Staff in Academic and Public Libraries, *Reference Services Review*, **46** (1), 128–45, https://doi.org/10.1108/RSR-01-2017-0002.

Peters, P. S. (2012) *The Chimp Paradox*, Vermilion.

Peterson, C. and Seligman, M. E. P. (2004) *Character Strengths and Virtues: A Handbook and Classification*, APA Press and Oxford University Press.

Pitts, M. J. and Socha, T. J. (eds) (2013) *Positive Communication in Health and Wellness*, Peter Lang.

Porath, C. and Pearson, C. (2013) The Price of Incivility, *Harvard Business Review*, **91** (2), 114–21, https://hbr.org/2013/01/the-price-of-incivility.

Putnam, R. D. (2000) *Bowling Alone: The Collapse and Revival of American Community*, Simon & Schuster.

PwC (n.d.) *Workforce of the Future – The Competing Forces Shaping 2030*, www.pwc.com/gx/en/services/workforce/publications/workforce-of-the-future.html.

Quezada, R. L., Talbot, C. and Quezada-Parker, K. B. (2020) From Bricks and Mortar to Remote Teaching: A Teacher Education Program's Response to COVID-19, *Journal of Education for Teaching*, **46** (4), 472– 83.

Reizer, A., Galperin, B. L. and Koslowsky, M. (2020) Editorial: Is Prosocial Behavior Always Good for the Workplace? On the Direction and Strength of the Relationship Between Prosocial Behaviors and Workplace Outcomes, *Frontiers in Psychology*, **11**, article 1886, https://doi.org/10.3389/fpsyg.2020.01886.

Robertson, I. and Cooper, C. (2011) *Wellbeing, Productivity and Happiness at Work*, Palgrave Macmillan.

Rosen, C. C., Harris, K. J. and Kacmar, K. M. (2011) LMX, Context Perceptions and Performance: An Uncertainty Management Perspective, *Journal of Management*, **37** (3), 819–38, https://doi.org/10.1177/0149206310365727.

Rosen, M. A., DiazGranados, D., Dietz, A. S., Benishek, L. E., Thompson, D., Pronovost, P. J. and Weaver, S. J. (2018) Teamwork in Healthcare: Key Discoveries Enabling Safer, High-Quality Care, *American Psychologist*, **73** (4), 433–50, https://doi.org/10.1037/amp0000298.

Rosenberg, M. B. (2015) *Nonviolent Communication: A Language of Life*, 3rd edn, PuddleDancer Press.

Ryan, R. M. and Deci, E. L. (2000) Self-Determination Theory and the Facilitation of Intrinsic Motivation, Social Development and Wellbeing, *American Psychologist*, **55** (1), 68–78.

Ryff, C. D. (1989) Happiness is Everything or is it? Explorations on the Meaning of Psychological Wellbeing, *Journal of Personality and Social Psychology*, **57** (6), 1069–81.

Salovey, P. and Mayer, J. D. (1990) Emotional Intelligence, *Imagination, Cognition and Personality*, **9** (3), 185–211, https://doi.org/10.2190/DUGG-P24E-52WK-6CDG.

Sandstrom, G. M., Boothby, E. J. and Cooney, G. (2022) *Talking to Strangers: A Week-Long Intervention Reduces Psychological Barriers to Social Connection*, University of Sussex, https://hdl.handle.net/10779/uos.23490227.v1.

Sandstrom, G. M. and Dunn, E. W. (2014) Social Interactions and Wellbeing: The Surprising Power of Weak Ties, *Personality and Social Psychology Bulletin*, **40** (7), 910–22, https://doi.org/10.1177/0146167214529799.

Schaufeli, W. B. and Bakker, A. B. (2004) Job Demands, Job Resources and Their Relationship with Burnout and Engagement: A Multi-Sample Study, *Journal of Organizational Behavior*, **25** (3), 293–315.

Schein, E. H. (2010) *Organizational Culture and Leadership*, 4th edn, Jossey-Bass.

Schilpzand, P., De Pater, I. E. and Erez, A. (2016) Workplace Incivility: A Review of the Literature and Agenda for Future Research, *Journal of Organizational Behavior*, **37** (4), https://doi.org/10.1002/job.1976.

Seligman, M. E. P. (2011) *Flourish: A New Understanding of Happiness, Wellbeing – and How to Achieve Them*, Nicholas Brealey Publishing.

Seppälä, E. (2014) The Hard Data on Being a Nice Boss, *Harvard Business Review*, 24 November, https://hbr.org/2014/11/the-hard-data-on-being-a-nice-boss.

Shore, L. M., Randel, A. E., Chung, B. G., Dean, M. A., Holcombe Ehrhart, K. and Singh, G. (2011) Inclusion and Diversity in Work Groups: A Review and Model for Future Research, *Journal of Management*, **37** (4), 1262–89, https://doi.org/10.1177/0149206310385943.

Singer, T. and Lamm, C. (2009) The Social Neuroscience of Empathy, *Annals of the New York Academy of Sciences*, 1156, 81–96.

De Smet, A., Gast A., Lavoie, J. and Lurie, M. (2023) New Leadership for an Era of Thriving Organizations, *McKinsey Quarterly*, 4 May, www.mckinsey.com/capabilities/people-and-organizational-performance/our-insights/new-leadership-for-a-new-era-of-thriving-organizations.

Snepvangers, P. (2023) Ranked: The Biggest Individual Library Fines Given to Students at Russell Group Universities, *The Tab*, https://thetab.com/uk/2023/02/27/ranked-the-biggest-individual-library-fines-given-to-students-at-russell-group-universities-296100.

Stewart, H. (2013) *The Happy Manifesto: Make Your Organization a Great Workplace*, Kogan Page.

Stone, R. S. B. (2018) Code Lavender: A Tool for Staff Support, *Nursing*, **48** (4), 15–17, https://doi.org/10.1097/01.NURSE.0000531022.93707.08.

Stubbing, A. (2022) *Data-Driven Decisions: A Practical Toolkit for Librarians and Information Professionals*, Facet Publishing.

TUC (2019) British Workers Putting in Longest Hours in the EU, TUC Analysis Finds, www.tuc.org.uk/news/british-workers-putting-longest-hours-eu-tuc-analysis-finds.

Tugade, M. M. and Fredrickson, B. L. (2004) Resilient Individuals Use Positive Emotions to Bounce Back from Negative Emotional Experiences, *Journal of Personality and Social Psychology*, **86** (2), 320.

Universities UK (2020) *Tackling Racial Harassment in Higher Education*, www.universitiesuk.ac.uk/sites/default/files/field/downloads/2021-08/tackling-racial-harassment-in-higher-education.pdf.

van Kleef, G. A., Oveis, C., van der Löwe, I., LuoKogan, A., Goetz, J. and Keltner, D. (2008) Power, Distress and Compassion Turning a Blind Eye to the Suffering of Others, *Psychological Science*, **19** (12), 1315–22.

Whitworth, L., Kimsey-House, H. and Sandahl, P. (2007) *Co-Active Coaching*, Davis-Black Publishing.

Wright, T. A. and Cropanzano, R. (2004) The Role of Psychological Wellbeing in Job Performance: A Fresh Look at an Age-Old Quest, *Organizational Dynamics*, **33** (4), 338–51.

Wrzesniewski, A. and Dutton, J. E. (2001) Crafting a Job: Revisioning Employees as Active Crafters of Their Work, *Academy of Management Review*, **26** (2), 179–201, https://doi.org/10.5465/amr.2001.4378011.

Yalom, I. D. (1980) *Existential Psychotherapy*, Basic Books.

Index